W9-AED-441

LIMA BARRETO

LIMA BARRETO

bibliography and translations

The
Yale
Series
of
Afro-American
Reference
Publications

Charles T. Davis
Editor

LIMA BARRETO

bibliography and translations

MARIA LUISA NUNES

G.K. HALL &CO.

70 LINCOLN STREET, BOSTON, MASS.

PQ9697
L544
L538X

Copyright © 1979 by Maria Luisa Nunes

Library of Congress Cataloging in Publication Data
Lima Barreto, Afonso Henrique de, 1881-1922.
  Lima Barreto, bibliography and translations.

  (The Yale series of Afro-American reference publictions)
  Translation of Vida e morte de M. J. Gonzaga de Sa and of
Clara dos Anjos.
  I. Lima Barreto, Afonso Henrique de, 1881-1922. Clara dos Anjos.
1979.   II. Nunes, Maria Luisa.   III. Title.   IV. Series.
PZ3.L63355Li   [PQ9697.L544]   869'.3   78-27808
ISBN 0-8161-8212-4

This publication is printed on permanent/durable acid-free paper
MANUFACTURED IN THE UNITED STATES OF AMERICA

Contents

69980

Preface

The consciousness-raising movements of the decade of the sixties had wide appeal for blacks throughout many different cultural areas of the world. They wanted to know what was common to the black experience in North America, South America, the Caribbean, Africa, and wherever else they were found. Most of them shared a similar heritage of slavery and colonization, but each cultural expression of the black experience in the world had its own distinctive traits.

The experience of blacks in Brazil differed from that of blacks in the United States. One reflection of that difference appears in Brazilian literature. In the nineteenth century and early decades of the twentieth, black writers in Brazil were never limited to writing about the problems of the color line as they generally were in the United States. But their silence about their experience as blacks or mulattoes in a multiracial society was in itself revealing. The only black writer to break this silence was Afonso Henriques de Lima Barreto. Unfortunately, none of Barreto's voluminous works were available in English translations in the 1970's. Consequently, when I decided to develop a course on ''Black Brazilian Writers'' for Yale University's Afro-American Studies Program, I had to have Barreto's novels translated. Yale University's Moore Fund for Curriculum Improvement provided the means for translating two works by Lima Barreto for use in this course.

The present volume is the result of those translations, *The Life and Death of M.J. Gonzaga de Sa,* first translated by Rosa and John Dwyer, and *Clara dos Anjos,* first translated by Earl Fitz. Working from their English texts, I have checked the original works and completed the translations here presented. It is important that we have access to these works to which I have added a biographical sketch of Lima Barreto, critical introductions to the translations, plus annotated bibliographies of the works of Lima Barreto and works about him, because they give us insights into the way in which Brazilian culture structures its race relations.

Once we are aware of the prestige of the ''white esthetic,'' ''whitening,'' the lack of opportunities for dark-skinned mulattoes and blacks, and of the sexual exploitation of the nonwhite woman, we have a notion of what constitutes Brazilian racism. Lima Barreto's works give us all these insights, in addition to their artistic merit. This new awareness of racism on the part of outsiders may be important to the black Brazilian's quest for true equality rather than accommodation to Brazil's ''racial democracy.''

Lima Barreto himself was fully aware not only of his country's racial climate, but of other important issues, which he satirized in his militant literary output. In this respect, he followed in the footsteps of the greatest nineteenth-century Portuguese writer, Eça de Queiroz. Using ridicule and caricature, Barreto hoped to point out to his society its foibles. His primary targets were the Brazilian bureaucracy, the world of journalism, Brazilian race relations, United States imperialism in Latin America and its oppression of blacks at home, the Republican oligarchy, São Paulo coffee policy, among others. He seemed to have particularly strong feelings on the subject of soccer, which he referred to as ''football.'' He felt that its effects on Brazilian youth would be deleterious, and its organization involved certain racist attitudes, such as the selection of an all-white team to represent Brazil in Argentina. In *Clara dos Anjos,* one of the characters' cohorts in petty crime and general vagabondage is the owner of several ''football'' uniforms.

Antifeminism is an issue on which Lima Barreto would be challenged today. This is a curious paradox. Barreto was against the entrance of women into the bureaucracy and often satirized the Brazilian feminist movements as mere imitations of the British and American ones. On the other hand, in a country where men could murder adulterous wives and be absolved by a jury, he was against uxoricide. In his novels, such as *Clara dos Anjos,* Barreto offers advice to Brazilian women about how to realize themselves and in other works such as *Triste Fim de Policarpo Quaresma* and *Numa e Ninfa,* women characters are markedly superior to their mates. On the issue of women, Barreto was a curious mixture of attitudes, maintaining that women writers were incapable of great human idealism and women musicians could only reproduce but not create. He never married and from his own writings, we know that he was very shy with women and had limited relations with prostitutes whom he spiritualizes in his works.

In the present volume, the translations of two of Lima Barreto's works do not fully convey the Brazilian author's role as an innovator in the Portuguese language. Temporally situated at the end of one century and the beginning of another, Lima Barreto is the most important and talented transitional figure in Brazilian premodernism. He died the year of the Modern Art Week of São Paulo in 1922. He rebelled against the sterile classicism of the pedantic, purist grammarians and, like Eça de Queiroz whom he greatly admired, he created new periods for the Portuguese language thus prefiguring the modernists of 1922. In many ways, Lima Barreto represents a paradoxical stage between the past and the future, not least in his condition as a man of color in the New World, caught between the history of slavery and the future of retribution and new departures.

MARIA LUISA NUNES

September, 1978

Introduction

I. Life and Times

Lima Barreto, 1881–1922, a gifted Brazilian writer of the early twentieth century, came closest of the great Brazilian novelists to being a ''black'' writer. There are many Brazilian writers of African ancestry but there are few ''black'' Brazilian writers possessed of a consciousness or concern for the black man in Brazilian society who have managed to incorporate this consciousness into their art. In part because of Brazil's racial hierarchy in which varying degrees of white admixture, class, education, money, and other factors determine social race, because literary life in Brazil has traditionally been elitist, and because black artists have often been accepted individually by a society that may consider them exceptional, there is no body of Brazilian literature by blacks reflecting the experience of ''black'' Brazilians.

An exception to this rule is Afonso Henriques de Lima Barreto. Born in Rio de Janeiro in 1881, he spent his childhood on the Ilha do Governador where his father was in charge of a mental institution. He completed his secondary education at the Colegio Pedro II and attended the Escola Politecnica for three years. Lima Barreto initiated his literary career as a journalist. He earned his living for the greater part of his life as a civil servant in the Ministerio da Guerra [War Ministry]. Burdened with the care of his father who had become incurably insane, Lima Barreto struggled in poverty. His nonconformance to the Brazilian racial hierarchy in which a poor, dark-skinned mulatto ranked low always caused him difficulties. In addition, the tedium of his civil service job combined with the mediocrity of Brazilian literary life drove him to a bohemian life style and the excesses of alcohol, which carried him to an early death at the age of forty-one.

Lima Barreto's uniqueness in Brazilian society and letters manifests itself in many ways. He was never deceived by a Eurocentric social hierarchy that denied full equality to some individuals because of their color. He was fully aware of his own intellectual superiority among human beings. In his *Diario Intimo* for July 5, 1908, he stated that his greatest satisfaction was in being a highly intelligent person even though he was a mulatto, disorganized, and misunderstood. ''Humanity lives by intelligence, through intelligence, and for intelligence and I, an intelligent man, am a part of humanity, the great humanity to which I wish to belong.''[1] His proud feelings often made for humiliations resulting from racist episodes. On one occasion, he

1

had been invited to a reception on board a visiting American fleet. He observed that of all the guests, he was the only one asked for his invitation.[2] What was interpreted by his biographer, Francisco de Assis Barbosa, to be a nostalgia for whiteness — "It's sad not to be white"— was in reality a protest against discrimination.[3] A common occurrence in Brazilian society even today, the automatic identification and assigning of blacks and mulattoes to inferior status repeatedly angered Lima Barreto. For example, he was asked more than once at his office in the Ministerio da Guerra if he was the office boy. He commented:

> Why do these people continue to identify me as an office boy, why? Because ... what applies to the white race is not true for the others; I, a mulatto or black man, am condemned to being taken for an office boy. But I am not vexed, my life will always be full of this sorrow and it will make me superior.

> It would be interesting to ask if Argolo, dressed as I am, would be taken for an office boy: the only difference is that it would be true in his case even though he is white.

> When I evaluate myself, I'm nothing.

> When I compare myself, I'm superior.

> Enormous consolation.[4]

In personal terms and in his art, he came to grips with a perennial problem of Brazilian and other multiracial societies, sexism combined with racism. As a black man, he did not have free access to any woman who might attract him, particularly not to well-educated women. On the other hand, white men felt perfectly comfortable taking liberties with and sexually exploiting black and mulatto women. Lima Barreto feared for his own sister in this regard and was later to make the theme central to his novel, *Clara dos Anjos*. In a letter to Esmaragdo de Freitas of October 15, 1911, he explained why the protagonist of *Recordações do Escrivão Isaías Caminha*, a mulatto, marries a white woman. In conformance to the Brazilian value given to whitening the race, Isaías wished his children to be lighter so that they might enjoy greater opportunities, and he simply did not find a woman of color as well educated as he.[5] Lima Barreto was not deceived, however, by the underlying prejudice of the Brazilian ideology of "whitening." In a letter to Veiga Miranda of October 29, 1917, he wrote:

> As for color prejudice, you say that it does not exist among us. There was always an aversion that was equal to a prejudice when Rio Branco tried to "make elegant" (whiten) Brazil. This can't be proven, I know; but if I don't have judiciary proofs, I have a lot of other evidence to go on.

> Why, there in São Paulo and in Campinas as well, are there societies of men of color? They must have arisen because of the social milieu since there are none in the rest of Brazil.[6]

As Assis Barbosa has commented, everywhere that Lima Barreto went, he found someone telling him that black men were not admitted, particularly ''uppity'' black men. This ''uppity'' stance was his original sin; he would pay for it.[7]

Extremely anti-American, Lima Barreto objected to the economic imperialism of the United States as well as to the treatment of blacks in America. In a letter to Oliveira Lima, of June 29, 1919, he asked if a black Brazilian could ever accept the influence of the United States over Brazil in view of the racial policies of the former.[8] In *Marginalia,* he comments on the segregated trains encountered in the United States by the French journalist Jules Huret. According to the Frenchman, black passengers were seated in cars resembling chicken coops. Lima Barreto was shocked at this despicable brutality of despotic white domination.[9] For the Brazilian, the American determination to effect complete segregation was excessive; he quoted Booker T. Washington's assessment of train conductors' ''Hamletism'': ''Is he or is he not a Negro?'' Cases had occurred when Italians had been thrown out of white cars and this had troubled United States diplomatic relations with Italy.[10]

In his esthetic judgments, Lima Barreto was extremely enlightened, particularly in the Brazilian context where African cultural expressions have been so disparaged. In his *Diario Intimo* for March 1919,[11] he stated that he would view the Winged Victory of Samothrace with the same emotion he would experience viewing an African idol. He desired to create a novel in which the work of blacks on a plantation was the subject. It was to have been a black ''Germinal.'' His great love for black people inspired him to write such a book, but he delayed writing and finally never wrote what was to have been his masterpiece. He feared the work would bring him bitter trials he might not be able to overcome.[12] On the other hand, he hoped that the realization of this work would bring him glory and even fame in Europe. It was to have been a *negrismo* parallel to the Indianism of the romantics, which might incur general disfavor, but the immense service he would perform for his people and for one of the races to which he belonged would inspire him to persevere.[13] While he felt a great deal of sympathy for the blacks of Brazil, he was aware that they did not understand his artistic identity or aspirations. Ultimately, he was an artist and his raised black consciousness was simply a part of this identity. He rejected the Parnassian art of the preceding period; indeed, his magazine, *Floreal,* of 1907, had objectives similar to the modernist magazine, *Klaxon.*[14] He felt that the Brazilian past was nil and not equivalent to that of Portugal. For Brazil, there was only the future with which Brazilian literature must deal in a literary way:

> We must communicate with each other, to understand each other. We
> must address ourselves to the qualities that each one of us has, in order to
> bear the burden of life and our destinies. Instead of praising gentlemen of
> suspect nobility and ladies descended from an aristocracy of wholesale
> dealers, because they live in Botafogo or Laranjeiras, we should show in
> our works that a black man, an Indian, a Portuguese or an Italian can get
> along in the common interest of all.[15]

Thematically and stylistically, Lima Barreto showed an originality far superior to his predecessors. He had great admiration for Monteiro Lobato and his regionalist literature in which the men of the backlands were not simply picturesque but sought the truth of their significance in a language free from "the perfection of superior art." Lima Barreto's Gonzaga de Sa has affinities with the art of Monteiro Lobato in this respect.[16]

Lima Barreto did not like to be compared to Machado de Assis whom he considered stylistically overly indebted to the Portuguese tradition. In a letter to Austregesilo de Ataide of January 19, 1921, Barreto said that he was happy that Ataide separated him from Machado de Assis. While he acknowledged Assis's merits, Lima Barreto disliked the aridity of his soul, and his lack of sympathy and of generous enthusiasms. He, Barreto, had never imitated Assis nor had he been inspired by him. Maupassant, Dickens, Swift, Balzac, Daudet, yes, but Machado de Assis, never. Even Turgeniev and Tolstoy supplied models but never Machado de Assis.[17]

Thanks to the organization of *The Complete Works of Lima Barreto* by his biographer, Francisco de Assis Barbosa, the Editora Brasiliense has facilitated access to Lima Barreto's literary output. Today, he is enjoying a vogue in Brazilian literary life and recognition fifty odd years after his death. It is fitting as well that his work should appear in English translation and it is desirable that novels other than those included in the present volume be translated and published in the future.

II.   The Life and Death of M.J. Gonzaga de Sa

The narrative structure of *The Life and Death of M.J. Gonzaga de Sa* is particularly striking and experimental. In the "Foreword," Lima Barreto's implied author addresses the reader directly to inform us that he is the publisher of a biography written by his friend Augusto Machado. Machado wished Barreto to make revisions, which the implied author considered unnecessary. Although he felt uncomfortable with the classification of biography that Machado had given his work, Barreto encourages Augusto Machado's literary vocation. For Barreto, the classification of biography was not exact if it implied a rigorous exactitude for certain data and a minute explanation for certain parts of the main character's life with careful attention to dates. Machado often speaks more of himself than he does of Gonzaga de Sa and this frequent appearance of the "author" disturbs Barreto. In reality, Lima Barreto's implied author of the "Foreword" is giving the reader a premonitory indication of his character's identity. Augusto Machado is the young mulatto writer of plebeian origin who rejects the gaudiness of the new upper classes to identify himself with the grandeur of Brazil's tropical nature and its history of four centuries of slavery in contrast to the imported intellectual and cultural legacy of Germany and Greece. Gonzaga de Sa is the elderly, white scion of an old noble family, a skeptic, a privileged Voltairean whose characterization is a contrast to the venality of the new republican bourgeoisie and to the dull bureaucracy at which he works. Both are one moral and spiritual entity. They enjoy perfect communication and are equivalent to what is good in Brazilian society, artistic ability, racial tolerance, intelligence, nobility of the spirit, critical wit and self-analysis, and originality in their vision of Brazil. W.J. Harvey refers to this process of psychic intimacy between disparate characters in a work of art:

This process, wherein our sense of duality between Self and World is diminished and in which discrete identities merge into the unity of a larger spiritual continuum, we may call psychic decomposition. By this I mean that process whereby an artist's vision of the world is such that it decomposes and splits into various attributes which then form the substance of disparate characters. But the relative solidity of individual characterization does not quite conceal the fluidity of the original vision, so that characters exist not merely in the context of normal human relationships but also unite in their common reference back to the single imaginative vision from which they emerged and which, so to speak, still envelops and overflows their individual outlines.[18]

Augusto Machado is an "I" narrator purporting to write a biography of his friend and mentor, M.J. Gonzaga de Sa. While Augusto Machado's irony is sensed from the very beginning of his narrative, it has specific objects of attack. Among the moral norms of the implied author, Augusto Machado's satire, and the dialogue between Machado and Gonzaga de Sa, there seems to be no ironic gap. Rather, Machado's metaliterary awareness expresses itself in his nonconformance to the established rules. Instead of writing a biography about a minister, he will write about the minister's secretary. He claims to lack the necessary erudition for such a literary undertaking, but his every reference belies his feigned modesty. We know just how witty his attack on the conventional forms is when he tells us that biography as moral literature is equivalent to a pharmaceutical remedy.

The spectrum Machado–Gonzaga de Sa focuses on various aspects of Brazilian society as objects of attack. The Brazilian bureaucracy, much concerned over the number of cannon volleys due a bishop as his ship enters the harbor, or the quantity of arrows a representation of Saint Sebastian should have, is a crew of dullards who might have been mentally agile before the attrition of civil service eroded that feature. The government of Rio Branco is comparable to the art of a seamstress for whom form is much more important than substance. The Brazilian bourgeoisie are nouveaux riches, uncultured foreigners who frequent Petropolis, a "chic" suburb of Rio de Janeiro. Gonzaga de Sa would produce an inversion of all "chic" norms. To the banality of Petropolis, Gonzaga de Sa contrasts the historical Rio de Janeiro with its blacks, mulattoes, and aristocrats.

The sharpest attack focuses on Brazilian racism. Not only is the attack not satirical, but it coincides with some of the narrative's themes. The value system of the new bourgeoisie is under attack as Machado–Gonzaga de Sa comments on the presence of European prostitutes who are the "refiners" of the Brazilian mixed race and who are the recipients of the new money. When Machado and Gonzaga de Sa go to the opera, the mulatto ponders his feeling of inferiority among the disdainful spectators. He concludes that it is his African ancestry that they despise, but, he reasons, if they all have African ancestry as well, what is the explanation? Implicit in this query is the answer that the Brazilian's disparagement of blacks and mulattoes is a particularly vicious aspect of man's perversity. Gonzaga de Sa observes that the old families and the blacks who had been together in Brazil for four hundred years would have come to an understanding. The new post-imperial rich would never understand the old values and the blacks would eventually have to use force with them in order to gain respect.

Still attacking racism, this time coupled with sexism, Gonzaga de Sa comments on the character of his dead *compadre* who had married a black woman, thus removing her from the social role reserved for women of color in Brazil, that of somebody's mistress or a prostitute. Gonzaga de Sa resolves to educate their mulatto son, but Augusto Machado foresees the prejudices the boy will encounter in life. Machado's premonition is a shadow of his own existence in which learning was for nought since the larger society would not recognize him in his own face but only as a stereotype. Finally, Gonzaga de Sa views racist attitudes from America and Europe as especially influential in Brazilian life.

Among the important themes of the narrative are death and the meaning of existence. Machado tells us that the way a man dies tells more about his life than his official history. To Gonzaga de Sa, death comes as he leans over to pick a flower against the backdrop of the beautiful natural setting of Rio de Janeiro with its light, mountains, and water. There is later a contrast of death to the life force that continues in man and nature. This force itself is the meaning of life in the face of the human condition with all its suffering. Art and invention are closely tied to it as we see by means of Gonzaga de Sa's text, which Augusto Machado inserts in his narrative. It serves to reveal Gonzaga de Sa. After attempting to construct a flying machine, Gonzaga de Sa is confronted with the discovery that it will not fly. He concludes that fortune plays no favorites. Invention as a metaphor for art gives the artist his *raison d'etre* and the opportunity to ponder and to delve into the meaning of existence. For Augusto Machado, European culture helped him to know himself; for Gonzaga de Sa, this exposure was complemented by a reading of obscure, provincial newspapers as a ''means of knowing the young minds of my land.'' Stylistically and thematically, *The Life and Death of M.J. Gonzaga de Sa* is an innovation in Brazilian letters that captures the true image of Brazil by means of original narrative techniques in the literary context of the times. It shows a transition period between the traditional and the modern eras and brilliantly and subtly delineates the origins, essences, and contradictions of the Brazilian myth of racial democracy.

III.   Clara dos Anjos

Clara dos Anjos is Lima Barreto's reaction to the Brazilian stereotype of the mixed-blooded woman as the sexually promiscuous, easy target of a ''macho'' dominated society. His heroine, Clara dos Anjos, is far from the mulatto temptress so often depicted in Brazilian culture — from its literature to its samba lyrics.

The first version of *Clara dos Anjos* appeared in 1904. The definitive version was published in 1923–1924 in sixteen issues of the *Revista Sousa Cruz.* The action of the narrative consists of the seduction and abandonment of a young mulatto girl by a dimwitted, more upper-class, white seducer. Contrary to the stereotypical *mulata,* Clara is an overprotected daydreamer who has a very sentimental and idealistic idea of love with no basis in reality.

The novel is set in one of the lower-middle-class suburbs of Rio de Janeiro where there is free intermingling of individuals of all races and racial mixtures. Throughout the work, there are autobiographical references to a fictional mulatto artist, Leonardo Flores, who has suffered greatly because of his artistic aspirations as a man of color in Brazilian society. Like the creator of *Clara dos Anjos,* Flores abuses the consumption of alcohol and is subject to bouts of insanity.

The narrator of *Clara dos Anjos* maintains that all girls of color and humble origin are condemned by society *a priori.* He focuses on Clara's tragedy in its racial overtones but the question of class is also present. In reviewing the affairs of the seducer, Cassi Jones, the narrator informs us that he always got off free because the girls he dishonored were of humble social status and of all colors. His choice was dictated by their lack of protection or influence that might vindicate them. His mother, with her aristocratic pretensions, did not wish to see her son married to a black servant, a mulatto seamstress, or a white but illiterate washerwoman. Race, however, was still the most important factor in social relations according to the narrator. In the poor but integrated society of the Rio de Janeiro suburbs, the accident of color was a reason to judge oneself superior to one's neighbor.

The portrayal of Clara dos Anjos reflects Brazilian shade consciousness as the narrator tells us that Clara was light-skinned like her father and had straight hair like her mother. The more important aspect of her characterization is her psychology, however. One of the few outside influences in her life is that of the *modinha,* a melody conveying a simple-minded amorous sentimentalism. On the basis of the *modinhas* she heard, Clara built up a theory of love believing that it conquers all. Because of it, there are no obstacles of race, fortune, or class. Her cloistering fosters a life of daydreams, reinforced by the *modinhas* she hears. Furthermore, her curiosity about the outside world increases as a result of her excessively sheltered existence. On the basis of her lack of experience, penchant for daydreaming and fantasy, and her taste for the *modinha,* Clara becomes an easy prey for Cassi's attentions. Although, inwardly, she questions the racial difference between them, she concludes that it does not matter. Naively, she believes that even if Cassi's bad reputation is true, he would respect her father's house. She is convinced he wants to marry her but her godfather, Marramaque, deflates that dream by telling Clara's father that Cassi would not choose a poor *mulata* if he desired to marry. After Marramaque is found murdered, Clara fears that Cassi is responsible, but she rationalizes the act as one of madness provoked by the seducer's love for her. Eventually, she allows him into her room when her parents are asleep and Cassi achieves his goal.

Cassi's character is more of a caricature than a characterization. His negative traits are drawn with such a heavy hand that he emerges as a somewhat comic figure and, to those of particularly warped sensibilities, as an anti-hero.

After she has become pregnant and Cassi has run away, Clara realizes that her innocence and lack of experience blinded her. Cassi chose her because she was poor and a *mulata.* She fears ostracism and scorn from her family and friends and further exploitation by others worse than Cassi. She envisions her end as similar to that of a local prostitute, suffering from shameful maladies and the excesses of alcohol. In the company of a strong-willed neighbor, Dona Margarida, Clara goes to Cassi's family. To Clara's appeal to Cassi's mother that he marry her, the older woman responds: ''What are you saying, you nigger?'' Clara's initiation into life is tragic and her final words in the novel are:

> — Mother, Mother!
> — What is it my child?
> — We're nothing in this life.

Interspersed throughout the story of Clara's seduction and abandonment are criticisms of women in Brazilian society. Not only are they kept from a real knowledge of the world, but they often forget their educations entirely once they are married, as was the case of Clara's mother, Engracia. Furthermore, they have no desire to master any skill which might be useful to them and their families. They pass from the protection of father to that of husband and they have no aspirations for self-realization. The narrator's advice to Brazilian women is to train the character, acquire will, like Dona Margarida had, to be able to defend oneself against the likes of Cassi and fight against those who oppose one's social and moral elevation. Nothing made black Brazilian women inferior to the others except the general opinion and the cowardice with which they accepted it.

Barreto is reversing stereotypes and explaining the social conditions that give rise to the widely accepted image of the moral corruption of the mulatto woman. Because of his own marginality in the society, he is able to enter the psychology of the character with a great deal of sensitivity. We understand the victim's mentality and the social forces acting upon her. Although race and class are inextricably bound up in this society, Barreto makes it clear that race is the critical factor.

NOTES

1. Lima Barreto, *Diario Intimo* (São Paulo: Editora Brasiliense, 1956), p. 135. Hereafter, all works of Lima Barreto are from his *Obra Completa* (Sao Paulo: Editora Brasiliense, 1956).
2. *Ibid.*, p. 130.
3. Francisco de Assis Barbosa, *A Vida de Lima Barreto*, 3rd ed. (Rio de Janeiro: Editora Civilizacao Brasileira, 1964), p. 87.
4. Barreto, *Diario Intimo*, p. 52.
5. Barreto, *Correspondência*, Tomo I, p. 239.
6. Barreto, *Correspondência*, Tomo II, p. 24.
7. Barbosa, *A Vida de Lima Barreto*, p. 175.
8. Barreto, *Correspondência*, Tomo II, p. 39.
9. Barreto, *Marginalia*, (São Paulo: Editora Brasiliense, 1956), pp. 197, 198.
10. *Ibid.*, p. 198.
11. Barreto, *Diario Intimo*, p. 206.
12. *Ibid.*, p. 84.
13. *Ibid.*, p. 84.
14. Barbosa, *A Vida de Lima Barreto*, p. 308.
15. Barreto, *Impressoes de Leitura* (São Paulo: Editora Brasiliense, 1956), p. 71.
16. Antonio Arnoni Prado, *Lima Barreto, O Critico e a Crise* (Brasilia: Editora Catedra/MEC, 1976), p. 96.
17. Barreto, *Correspondência*, Tomo II, p. 256.
18. W.J. Harvey, *Character and the Novel* (London: Chatto and Windus, 1970), p. 124.

Bibliography of the Works of Lima Barreto

Francisco de Assis Barbosa collected the complete works of Lima Barreto as *Obra Completa de Lima Barreto* (São Paulo: Editora Brasiliense, 1956). All the following references are found in the complete works with the earliest date of publication included when possible.

Recordações do Escrivão Isaías Caminha [*Memoirs of the Clerk Isaias Caminha*] 1909.

The first person narrative of the young mulatto, Isaias Caminha, who leaves a small town to go to Rio de Janeiro where his dreams are shattered and he finds only disillusionment. In order to "succeed," he must descend to the corrupt moral level of the powerful men of the world of journalism, the object of the narrator's satire. Of particular note in the novel are the tribulations of a man of color in early twentieth-century Rio de Janeiro.

Triste Fim de Policarpo Quaresma [*The Sad Ending of Policarpo Quaresma*] (Serialized in 1911 in the *Jornal do Comercio;* published 1915).

Policarpo Quaresma, idealist and super-patriot, traverses three phases: first, he is a self-styled preserver of Brazilian customs, literature, history, food, and traditions. Second, after a bout with insanity, he becomes a cultivator and proposes to reform Brazilian agriculture. Finally, he becomes an active major in the 1893 Naval Revolt against Floriano Peixoto. Although active on the side of the dictator, he is executed by Floriano's forces for treason. Policarpo's odyssey highlights the contrast between the real and the ideal while satirizing the bureaucracy, Brazilian agricultural policies, and the ministry of war.

Numa e Ninfa (1915).

The ascent of Numa Pompilio de Castro to the heights of political success as a result of his marriage of convenience to Dona Edgarda (Ninfa), daughter of a well-established political boss. A satire of the political customs of Rio de Janeiro during the first decade of this century. Like Emma Bovary, Ninfa wants Numa to achieve greatness, which she will enjoy vicariously. To that end, she writes his successful political speeches. Numa discovers that Ninfa does so in adulterous collaboration with her cousin but accepts the dishonor as the price of greatness.

Vida e Morte de M.J. Gonzaga de Sa [*The Life and Death of M.J. Gonzaga de Sá*] (1919).

The meditations on the perigrinations in Rio de Janeiro during the early part of this century of the elderly aristocrat, Gonzaga de Sá, and his biographer, Augusto Machado, a young mulatto. The Brazilian bureaucracy is the object of satire as are many other aspects of Brazilian life, not the least important of which is the Brazilian version of racism. As the title suggests, life and death are important themes particularly in relation to art and creativity. An experimental narrative perspective characterizes the novel's form.

In the same volume is a collection of short stories concerned with the subjects of bureaucracy and corruption, political customs, marriage customs, the outskirts of Rio de Janeiro, the irony of the appearance of virtue, the venality of the journalistic profession, carnival tricks, the follies of the *nouveaux riches,* and racial discrimination.

Clara dos Anjos (serialized in the *Revista Cruz e Sousa,* 1923–24; published 1948).

Clara dos Anjos recounts the seduction and abandonment of a young mulatto woman by a more upper-class white seducer. A rich source of detail on the background and customs of early twentieth-century Rio de Janeiro suburban life. The narrator makes a strong appeal for the self-assertion of Brazilian women, particularly those of color, who are judged to be immoral *a priori* by the society in which they live.

The volume includes a series of short stories concerned with incest and miscegenation or the mores of Portuguese immigrants in Brazil, paternalism, avarice, charlatanism, the national adulation of white foreigners, and the follies of Brazilian science from grammar to the treatment of the mentally ill.

Histórias e Sonhos, contos [*Short Stories and Dreams, Short Stories*] (1920).

Short stories treating the subjects of the poor blacks of Rio de Janeiro's suburbs and the reaction of a sensitive young black boy to racist taunts. Another story satirizes the unintelligible literary output of Java's (Brazil's) medical doctors, schools of higher education, and the plight of the intelligent nonconformist. There is a satire of United States–Latin American relations set in interplanetary imagery with an emphasis on America's treatment of its black population and its exploitation of Latin America. Other subjects treated are carnival, African influence in Brazilian life, and the São Paulo oligarchy's coffee policy. Brazilian science is another object of satire. The theme of *fin de race* and regression to brutishness emerges in the symbolic act of book burning. More psychological stories portray the interior life of a romantic, and guilt and expiation. *Clara dos Anjos* here takes the form of a short story. Other subjects are the prostitute with a heart of gold, the customs of Rio de Janeiro, the exploitation of black women, the price of an artist's unique identity, and art versus nature.

Os Bruzundangas, sátira política [*Trifles, Political Satire*] (1922).

A satire of Brazilian life in the guise of that of an exotic country with the same foibles as Brazil. Its literature is suspiciously Parnassian like Brazil's, its finances are chaotic, its population reveres academic titles, and its politics and politicians are corrupt. The rotten core of the country resides in its coffee oligarchy, education, diplomacy, the constitution, the powerful, the armed forces, its electoral practices, and its racial prejudice. In addition, literature, art, and society are all objects of satire.

In the same volume are the "Adventures of Doctor Bogoloff," a Russian immigrant who enjoys the prestige of his race and title. As Director of National Pecuary, he has political adventures in the provinces during a *coup d'etat* in which he is mistaken for the new boss. Charlatanism is the key note of his characterization along with his disdain for the Brazilians.

Coisas do Reino de Jambon; sátira e folclore [*Matters from the Kingdom of Jambon; Satire and Folklore*] (1953).

Essays satirizing Brazilian political life, the bureaucracy, and feminism. Upper-class women who want to be civil servants and to vote are the object of attack. Their values are "feminine" such as excessive attention to clothes, they are intellectually inferior to men, and incapable of creating great literature. All Brazilian charlatans are under fire, the worst of whom are painters. Other objects of criticism are the presidents of the Republic, and Brazilian racism as expressed by her diplomats who dislike foreigners' referring to Brazil's large black population. In addition, there are short essays on agriculture and animal husbandry as well as folkloric selections on dreams, animals, religious celebrations, totems, tales, superstitions, prayers, and orations, and the "animal game" (*jogo do bicho*), a kind of lottery.

Bagatelas, cronicas [*Bagatelles, Chronicles*] (1923).

Journalistic essays including one of the best Brazilian discussions of the Russian Revolution of 1917 and its importance for the common people of Brazil. There is criticism of academic titles, corruption in the professional schools, and privilege for the titled and the oligarchs. Other essays express Barreto's opposition to uxoricide as a punishment for adultery, and his concern for the preservation of Rio's architecture. Furthermore, he opposes bourgeois capitalists. He also treats the subject of Machiavellian women, anti-Americanism, the Brazilian theater, the Versailles Treaty, and World War I, as well as responding to Renan's ideas on slavery. There is an essay on Barreto's experiences in a mental hospital.

Feiras e Mafuás, artigos e cronicas [*Fairs and Amusement Parks, Articles and Chronicles*] (1953).

Inevitably, Barreto repeated himself to some extent in his essays. This volume contains discussions of popular street fairs, and Rio's architecture. There is a critique of Machado de Assis, a discussion of the ideas of Taine as an esthetic program, and commentaries on advertising, legal complications, and the intellectual limitations of medical doctors. There are childhood memories of the Naval Revolt of 1893 and a critique of Marinetti and *Klaxon's* futurism as well as a rejection of Coehlho Neto's Grecophilia. North American racism, soccer, city slums, and higher education are all subjects of Barreto's essays. In others, he is pro-labor and against the bourgeoisie and its ally, the Church. World War I failed to resolve anything in Barreto's astute opinion.

Vida Urbana; artigos e cronicas [Urban Life; Articles and Chronicles] (1956).

Journalistic articles commenting on life in Rio de Janeiro. Once again, Brazilian women are the subject. They are inferior to men in musical creation, nevertheless, the laws against abortion are unjust. The press, Rio Branco, *machismo,* race consciousness, academic titles, and military schools as well as the condition of the streets, United States imperialism, the judicial system, uxoricide for adultery, the marriage of convenience, and all injustices are the subjects of Barreto's criticism. He also discusses the plight of the literary man who cannot live from his literary production.

Marginalia, cronicas, impressões de leitura, folclore urbano [Marginal Notes, Chronicles, Literary Criticism, Urban Folklore] (1953).

Lima Barreto apparently never tired of certain subjects such as racism, soccer, the corruption of Republican Brazil, the Grecophilia of Coelho Neto, anti-Americanism, academic titles, feminism, and segregation in the United States. In addition, he discusses the Brazilian mania for claiming Indian ancestry, popular dances, censorship, the preservation of Rio's architecture, and housing for the poor (read nonwhites).

In the same volume is a series of stories about charlatan doctors, suicide in style, political foibles and venality *cum* adultery, and death, the leveler, among others. There is also a sketch for a play about black slaves who have escaped from a plantation.

Impressões de Leitura [Literary Criticism] (1953).

Lima Barreto's criticism of other authors' works often points to his own aesthetic criteria. La Brunetière was one of his principal influences but he rejects ancient Greek culture, then very fashionable in Rio de Janeiro. For him, literature was to facilitate fraternity, justice, and understanding. Barreto himself practiced militant literature with the aim of reforming society. He had nothing but praise for Monteiro Lobato. He believed that Nietzsche inspired World War I. Barreto never claimed to understand poetry and believed that women writers lacked great ideals. Interspersed in his literary criticism is a discussion of slavery in the ancient and modern worlds and the role of the Church in this matter. Again, anti-Americanism makes an appearance as well as Barreto's favorite target, Coelho Neto, a much acclaimed contemporary writer who, like Barreto, was a mulatto. Soccer is still in disfavor. The northeastern droughts merit a serious discussion by Barreto.

Diário Íntimo [Intimate Diary, notes from his personal diary] (1953).

The intimate diary of Lima Barreto contains the beginnings of unfinished novels, outlines for the study of philosophy, the plans for *Clara dos Anjos* and *Negrismo* as well as one for *Triste Fim de Policarpo Quaresma.* Personal matters such as family problems, finances, anxieties about color and women, feelings about blacks, racial slurs received, and a preoccupation with drinking and madness are part of the diary. In addition, there are the usual complaints about the Republican government, and discussions of Bovarism, Patrocínio (an abolitionist leader), racism in the United States, and football. The diary contains an incomplete version of *Clara dos Anjos* with an emphasis on class and the abuses by the upper classes of their privileges in relation to poor blacks.

Cemitério dos Vivos [*The Cemetery of the Living,* unfinished novel about experiences in a mental institution] (1953).

The first part is called *Diário do Hospício* (*Diary from a Mental Hospital*) and contains notes on Lima Barreto's incarceration. The first person narrator comments on treatment received, the treatment of other patients, the organization of the hospital, the manias of the patients, and the doctors' personalities. There is a slight attempt at fictionalization when the narrator refers to his wife.

The second part, *Cemitério dos Vivos* [*Cemetery of the Living*] is a fictionalization of the above materials including the character of the wife, a mother-in-law, and others. The volume contains an inventory of Lima Barreto's library as well as official medical documents on Barreto's internment, the result of delusions brought on by alcoholism.

Correspondência I, (*Correspondence,* first volume).

Letters about literature, and letters to family and friends. Some subjects covered are art, theater, travel, bureaucratic irritations, financial problems, the Naval Revolt of 1893, and religion.

Correspondência II, (*Correspondence,* second volume).

Literary matters receive more attention than in volume one and include Lima Barreto's comments on his own production. There is a great deal of literary criticism. Some of the issues discussed are color prejudice in Brazil, North American racism, soccer, and academic titles. The letters also refer to Lima Barreto's publishing relationship with Monteiro Lobato, a contemporary writer much admired by Barreto, the mores of Botafogo (a chic section of Rio in the early twentieth century), and the problems Barreto had obtaining his pension. His letters project reading lists of Comte, Spencer, Kropotkin, Hamon, and Reclus. There are also letters referring to Lima Barreto's candidacy for election to the Brazilian Academy of Letters, a distinction which he never achieved.

Selected Bibliography of Works about Lima Barreto

Amora, Antonio Soares. "O Homem da Cabeça Furada" [The Man With a Hole in His Head]. *O Estado de São Paulo*. June 2, 1962.

Through his reading of *Vida e Morte de M.J. Gonzaga de Sá,* the author claims to penetrate the authentic psychology of the man of color in Brazilian Society.

————. "O Mulato que se Despiu" [The Mulatto who Undressed]. *O Estado de São Paulo.* June 23, 1962.

A summary of *Recordações do Escrivão Isaías Caminha* underscoring the theme of the young mulatto who does not achieve fulfillment but whose creator had the courage to "undress" or reveal himself through his creation for all the world to see.

António, João. *Calvário e Porres do Pingente Afonso Henriques de Lima Barreto* [*Calvary and Binges of the Straphanger Afonso Henriques de Lima Barreto*]. Rio de Janeiro: Editora Civilização Brasileira, 1977.

Although there is no real analysis of Lima Barreto's works, the author claims to have given rhythm and breath to other people's works. Essentially a guide to the Rio bars frequented by Lima Barreto based on the testimony of one of his acquaintances, Carlos Alberto Nobrega da Cunha, who at the time of the interview was in the Muda Sanatorium in Tijuca and was seventy-two years old, the text cites Lima Barreto and works about him.

Barbosa, Francisco de Assis. *A Vida de Lima Barreto* [*The Life of Lima Barreto*]. 3rd ed. Rio de Janeiro: Editora Civilização Brasileira, 1965.

A compassionate biography of Lima Barreto taking into consideration all known aspects of the writer's life — his origins, childhood, education, character, journalistic activity, literary production, problems, and all other pertinent information. The biography is constructed on the basis of the historical period in which Barreto lived, the works of Barreto himself, and testimonies from relatives, friends, and acquaintances.

————. "Prefácio" [Preface]. *Recordações do Escrivão Isaías Caminha*. São Paulo: Editora Brasiliense, 1956.

The bohemian, literary, and intellectual background of Rio de Janeiro in the 1900's. Lima Barreto, the writer of militant literature, was influenced by Taine and La Brunetière. Although he was affected throughout his works by his condition as a mulatto, Barreto also left a rich description of the Republic and the bourgeois mentality reigning during its early years. Barreto was the true initiator of the modern novel in Brazil. The preface contains a history of Lima Barreto's publications.

Barreto, Plínio. "Um Grande Romancista" [A Great Novelist]. *O Estado de São Paulo.* October 5, 1952.

Lima Barreto was a great novelist whose works are characterized by satire. A social critic, Barreto was, nevertheless, different from the satirical Machado de Assis. Each was great in his own way. Barreto was a rebel who left a record of his revolt. Close to the poor, he was against the powerful and mighty oppressors of his day.

Bosi, Alfredo. "Lima Barreto e Graça Aranha" [Lima Barreto and Graça Aranha]. In his *O Pre-Modernismo.* São Paulo: Cultrix, 1967.

Despite Lima Barreto's opposition to the construction of skyscrapers in Rio de Janeiro, soccer, and the ascent of professional women, he was a premodernist. His was a sentimental conservatism. He had an aversion to oligarchies, he ridiculed nationalism, and he was anti-Parnassian in his natural and colloquial use of language. His intelligence was an active force. The author finds much that is autobiographical in the works of Lima Barreto who was also a coherent and astute observer of Rio society and a precursor of the best moments of modernist criticism.

Brayner, Sonia. "A Mitologia Urbana de Lima Barreto" [Lima Barreto's Urban Mythology]. *Tempo Brasileiro.* 33/34 (1973).

Using a structuralist vocabulary, the author discusses space in the works of Lima Barreto including the geographical, the politico-administrative, and the literary. As in naturalist literature, the characters are linked to their respective spaces.

Candido, Antonio. "Os Olhos, o barco e o espelho" [the eyes, the boat, and the mirror]. *O Estado de São Paulo, Suplemento Cultural.* October 17, 1976.

For Lima Barreto, the writer must be sincere and directly transmit his feelings and ideas, and he must emphasize human problems in general and social problems in particular. His mission is to liberate man and better his condition. The author asks to what extent the personal circumstances of Lima Barreto are projected in his vision of man and society and to what extent do they affect the very mode of his realization as an artist. Lima Barreto is a lively and penetrating writer who aimed at revealing society and his own emotions, but he is less well realized as a fiction writer, with high and low points, frequently incapable of going beyond the autobiographical and the social to the strictly literary level. Barreto had a deeply personal commitment to literature in which his militancy left aside "the beautiful" for "the real." The author examines samples from Barreto's nonfictionalized writings and shows how the writer transforms the episodes described into art. The author observes that Antonio Arnoni Prado was the first to show how Lima Barreto used the quotidian as fictional material. He united personal experience with his vision of society and artistic consciousness. The author concludes that this convergence makes his personal literature, his diaries, etc., of great interest. His is a personal element that is not overwhelmed by personalism, but is channelled into a courageous representation, militant and rebellious, of his world. He made his pain a vehicle for an assault on the world, instead of isolating himself because of it.

Dimmick, Ralph. "Social Satire in the Novels of Lima Barreto." In *Proceedings of the International Colloquium on Luso-Brazilian Studies.* Washington, D.C., October 15–20, 1950.

Lima Barreto was a brilliant satirist. The objects of his attack were the bureaucracy, politics, the armed forces, the press, and Brazilian education. His view of the society stems from his inferior status as a mulatto in Brazil. Consequently, his vision of society is one-sided.

Duggan, Vincent. "Social Themes and Political Satire in the Short Stories of Lima Barreto." Unpublished Ph.D. Dissertation, City University of New York, 1976.

The author examines the essential structural elements in each work in which there is a political or moral message to be conveyed. These didactic works illustrate a preconceived social thesis. A thematic analysis of the social issues in Lima Barreto's stories strikes at the heart of his very personal concept of literature in society. The dissertation includes background on the short story in Brazil, a biographical sketch of Lima Barreto's life, and Lima Barreto's position in Brazilian literature as a short story writer. The author concludes that Barreto sympathizes with society's victims and satirizes the oppressors.

Figueiredo, Jackson de. "Prefácio" [Preface]. *Feiras e Mafuás.* São Paulo: Editora Brasiliense, 1956.

Despite his unkempt appearance, Lima Barreto was one of the greatest intellects of his day. He was a social analyst, combative, and active. He pointed out the falseness of other writers' language. There was a conspiracy of silence surrounding at least two of Barreto's novels despite their excellence. Figueiredo, a contemporary of Barreto, protests against this silence.

Freyre, Gilberto. "Prefácio" [Preface]. *Diário Íntimo.* São Paulo: Editora Brasiliense, 1956.

The author cites Lima Barreto's unrealized desire to write a black "Germinal." He asserts that Lima Barreto was lacking in disciplined or systematic scholarly habits even though he possessed an imaginative grasp. Lima Barreto's problems were those of the dark-skinned mulatto in Brazil. While Barreto felt superior to other blacks, he was sociologically one of them and unable, like Machado de Assis, to become "white" for practical purposes. The author concludes that Brazilian prejudice is one of class more than of race.

Gicovate, Moises. *Lima Barreto Uma Vida Atormentada* [*Lima Barreto a Tormented Life*]. São Paulo: Edições Melhoramentos, n.d.

A biography of Lima Barreto designed to inform the younger reader about the existence of Lima Barreto and to convey a general impression of the writer's works. Lima Barreto's lifetime, 1881–1922, was an era of profound social transformations. The grandson of slaves, Barreto's militant literature aimed at the criticism and reform of society. He was the writer of Rio de Janeiro and his existence was undermined by his addiction to alcohol. The biography gives the background of Barreto's parents, details about his childhood and education, and information about his adult life as writer and bureaucrat as well as his gradual decline under the effects of alcohol.

Gomes, Eugenio. "Lima Barreto e Coelho Neto" [Lima Barreto and Coelho Neto]. In *A Literatura no Brasil.* Vol. II. Edited by Afranio Coutinho. Rio de Janeiro: Editora Sul-Americana, 1955.

A pessimistic appraisal of Lima Barreto and his works. In the author's opinion, Barreto's was the novel of personal resentments created by a neurotic alcoholic. Although he felt called upon to champion nonwhites in Brazilian society, there were many who succeeded fully. Barreto's fiction is uneven and an arm of combat against a society that disdained him. Influenced by the great, nineteenth-century Russian writers, he turned toward radical socialism and desired social reform. His production hovered between the esthetics of the novel and journalism.

―――――. "Prefácio" [Preface]. *Cemitério dos Vivos.* São Paulo: Editora Brasiliense, 1956.

Lima Barreto was a precursor to the modernists in his stand against the sterile concept of art for art's sake. A sincere idealist, Barreto produced art that was militant literature written in simple language comprehensible to all. Citing *Recordações do Escrivão Isaías Caminha* and *Clara dos Anjos,* the author criticizes the limitations of those works. To Barreto's credit, the author compares him to Manuel Antonio de Almeida, creator of a well-known Brazilian picaresque novel, *Memórias de Um Sargento de Milícias.*

Grieco, Agrippino. *Evolução da Prosa Brasileira* [Evolution of Brazilian Prose]. Rio de Janeiro: Ariel Editora, 1933.

Lima Barreto was the greatest portraitist of Rio de Janeiro. He focused on the common man and his work was the best in decades. He was not offensive, he was passionate. A great writer and an objective novelist, he eternalized Rio de Janeiro.

―――――. "Prefácio" [Preface]. *Marginália.* São Paulo: Editora Brasiliense, 1956.

Lima Barreto was the greatest and most Brazilian of all novelists. He loved Rio de Janeiro and its outskirts. Although he was not honored by the Brazilian Academy of Letters, he was a creator of souls and the writer of the Brazilian people. In praising Lima Barreto, the author shows himself to be something of a detractor of Machado de Assis. Lima Barreto was superior to all those novelists who preceded him and could only be compared to Manuel Antonio de Almeida, author of *Memórias de um Sarjento de Milícias.*

———. *Vivos e Mortos* [*The Living and the Dead*], 2nd ed. Rio de Janeiro: Livraria Jose Olympio Editora, 1947.

The same article as found in *Evolução da Prosa. . . .*

Herron, Robert. "Lima Barreto's 'Isaías Caminha' as a psychological Novel." *Luso-Brazilian Review,* 8 (1971): 26–38.

Lima Barreto was generally thought of as a social novelist. The mental processes of his characters in society are most important. An obsession with the social world indicates the psychology of Barretian characters. They are concerned with their place in the world, how the world affects them, and how they can influence the world. In narrating his memoirs, Isaías sets out to disprove the notion that people of color have declining intellectual powers in their later years. It is society that stultifies them. The author maintains that Isaías's claims of racial prejudice cannot be proven. Ultimately, Isaías's quest is one individual's unanswered search for a meaning in life within the framework of the individual–society relationship. It is the procurement of an explanation and strategy for living, a formula by which he might know the best way to face his existence and the proper way to act in order to obtain the maximum of satisfaction. The author concludes that there is existential anxiety in the mind of the narrator-protagonist which makes *Recordações do Escrivão Isaías Caminha* primarily a psychological novel and not a sociological novel following a dogmatic thesis.

———. "Lima Barreto y Clara dos Anjos Su 'Mulatismo' erroneo y su Feminismo" [Lima Barreto and 'Clara dos Anjos' His false 'mulattism' and his Feminism]. *El Comercio.* Quito, Ecuador, January 23, 1972.

Lima Barreto's error in *Clara dos Anjos* was to think that only mulatto girls are seduced and abandoned. Clara was atypical as was Cassi. Furthermore, a seducer could be black or mulatto as well as white, and Cassi seduced white women too. Therefore, Lima Barreto's main thesis, the vulnerability of mulatto women, is not valid. Lima Barreto's most valid criticism is of a society which does not provide a good education for all Brazilian women.

———. "The Individual, Society, and Nature in the Novels of Lima Barreto." Unpublished Ph.D. Dissertation, University of Wisconsin, 1968.

The first systematic analysis of all the novels of Lima Barreto including the unfinished *Cemetério dos Vivos.* The critical approach is that of the psychological method, by which the author means that the work of literature is a reflection of Lima Barreto's psyche. The dissertation includes a summary of Lima Barreto's life and literary output, the theoretical bases of the study, and their application to the individual, society, and nature in their interrelationship. There is a section on the chronology of Lima Barreto's works followed by the author's conclusions. The bibliography is the most extensive in all the secondary literature on Lima Barreto. Herron's reading of the texts defuses Lima Barreto's accusations of racism in Brazil and ascribes his bitterness to his own failures and shortcomings.

Holanda, Sérgio Buarque de. "Prefácio" [Preface]. *Clara dos Anjos.* São Paulo: Editora Brasiliense, 1956.

Lima Barreto was not the genius his admirrers believe him to have been and cannot be compared to Machado de Assis. His work is confessional. The novel *Clara dos Anjos,* for example, missed being transformed into art. The author, who met Lima Barreto during the last year of the latter's life, comments on Barreto's wounded sensibility on the subject of racial prejudice and discrimination. Unlike Machado de Assis who sought out a fashionable white neighborhood, Botafogo, Lima Barreto went to live in the poor, nonwhite suburbs. His sympathies for their inhabitants were not always distanced enough in his novels to achieve an artistic level.

Houaiss, Antonio. "Prefácio" [Preface]. *Vida Urbana.* São Paulo: Editora Brasiliense, 1956.

Lima Barreto always used the instrument of language effectively in the militant communication that is his art. He was accused of incorrectness and bad taste in writing, but in reality, he was always on top of the subject of grammar and style. His writing is rich in communication and expression. Throughout his works, the question of language is present. He was disdainful of the purists of grammar but his own use of language was a continued effort at assimilation of resources, faculties, and possibilities for the utmost efficacy. He did not accept the standard rules completely. With a combative attitude, he sought all means — diversity, variety, equivalences, syncretisms — to show that the fixedness of authoritarian grammar was far from corresponding to the living reality of language in its infinite potential. He was well grounded in grammatical and philological rules. His publishers, often of the second rank, were responsible for many of the errors in his texts as was his terrible handwriting. The author asserts that the Brasiliense edition is an attempt faithfully to establish the original texts, and he discusses the problems involved in this process.

Kinnear, J.C. "The Sad End of Lima Barreto's Policarpo Quaresma." *Bulletin of Hispanic Studies,* 51 (1974):60-75.

Policarpo is a martyr to a society that doesn't understand him. He is ridiculed as a nationalist and it is shown that his outlook has a destructive effect on the nation. The novel entails a critique of exaggerated nationalism, inspired in part by Afonso Celso's *Porque me ufano* [*Why I'm Proud*], a popular book at the time expressing a hysterical and emotional nationalism. Barreto mocks Policarpo, an unbalanced idealist in a vicious society. His end is therefore ironic.

Lima, M. de Oliveira. "Prefàcio" [Preface]. *Triste Fim de Policarpo Quaresma.* São Paulo: Editora Brasiliense, 1956.

The author, a contemporary of Lima Barreto, asks why the press has not given due attention to *Triste Fim de Policarpo Quaresma.* The novel is one-hundred times superior to Graça Aranha's much acclaimed *Canãa.* Policarpo is a Brazilian Don Quixote. The author defends Barreto's style as innovative, simple, and unaffected. After an analysis of Barretian characters and a commentary on the 1893 Naval Revolt, which provides some of the background for the novel, the author compares Lima Barreto to Manuel Antonio de Almeida.

Lima, Alceu Amoroso. "Prefácio" [Preface]. *Vida e Morte de M.J. Gonzaga de Sá.* São Paulo: Editora Brasiliense, 1956.

Lima Barreto was the greatest writer of his time. Independent of any school, he was the writer of the *Carioca* (of Rio de Janeiro) masses. His works are modern and genial. His life, however, was difficult and ungratifying. A solitary and forgotten man, he experienced none of the usual joys and pleasures of life. Nevertheless, his works are keenly humane. He wrote to free himself, he wrote out of love — not hatred or ambition — in order to give his testimony. A caricaturist and a humorist, Barreto is the creator of unforgettable characters. His was a painful vision of the ills of society. The author believes he is deserving of universal recognition.

_____. "Um discípulo de Machado" [A disciple of Machado]. In *Primeiros Estudos. Contribuição à História do Modernismo. O Pre-Modernismo.* Rio de Janeiro: Agir, 1948.

Lima Barreto's disenchantment with life found its expression in a gallery of social caricatures. Barreto was a humorist of the intellectual stripe of Machado de Assis. He was the creator of truly Brazilian characters. While his irony was often directed toward the bureaucracy, he had a sorrowful vision of the evils and foibles of society.

Lins, Osman. *Lima Barreto e o Espaço Romanesco* [Lima Barreto and Novelistic Space]. São Paulo: Editora Atica, 1976.

Lima Barreto courageously took his stand as a black man. He was a defender of the weak, he denounced Yankee imperialism, and he has been ostracized by certain classes of Brazilian society. One of his principal themes is that of isolation or lack of communication. In his novels, there are different varieties and functions of space. The author views *Vida e Morte de M.J. Gonzaga de Sá* as a series of meditations on human destiny. In this novel, spaces of exterior scenes are preponderant — the sea, the hills, architecture. Rarely are interior spaces mentioned. There is a conversion of space into what the author calls "full thematics" or examples of space indicating the essence of a character. The essay contains many interesting insights about the art of Lima Barreto.

_____. "Narração e personagens nas 'Recordações de Isaías Caminha!' " [Narration and characters in "Recordações de Isaías Caminha"]. *Estado de São Paulo, Suplemento Literário.* June 6, 1974.

The author maintains that the novel, *Recordações do Escrivão Isaías Caminha,* is the revelation of a curious spirit. Lima Barreto inaugurated the modern theme of the difficulty of communication in Brazilian letters. The author views Isaías as a precursor of the protagonist in Camus' *l'Etranger,* Meursault.

_____. "Policarpo Quaresma ou Os Perigos da Ação." [Policarpo Quaresma or the Perils of Action]. *O Estado de São Paulo, Suplemento Literario.* June 2, 1974.

As in *Recordações do Escrivão Isaías Caminha,* the theme of alienation is central to *Triste Fim de Policarpo Quaresma.* The novel's social nuclei have no effect on each other. Action in fact is dangerous and when the protagonist first acts, he is taken off to the mental asylum. His next action, directed toward Brazil's fertile lands rather than toward any social organization, is equally disastrous. The author compares the metaphor of action in Lima Barreto to Joseph Conrad's use of the same metaphor in *Victory.* Policarpo's final action in the Naval Revolt of 1893 leads to death. The author asks if thought and dream distance can deepen the abyss already present that this melancholy and sarcastic book accentuates as if by chance.

Loos, Dorothy S. "The Brazilian Novel: 1870–1920." In *Proceedings of the International Colloquium on Luso-Brazilian Studies.* Washington, D.C., October 15–20, 1950.

A taxonomy for the study of the Brazilian novel. The author includes Lima Barreto under the psychological novel.

Martins, Wilson. "Lima Barreto ou o Falso Boemio" [Lima Barreto or the False Bohemian]. *Província de São Paulo* (1955): 118–120.

Lima Barreto was not impelled to true bohemianism by his "spiritual youth." His disordered life resulted from an inferiority complex. He could have triumphed despite his condition as a mulatto as did others if he had had the will. His biographer, Barbosa, blames society, but Lima Barreto, like Verlaine, was a false bohemian enslaved by the vice of drink. Barreto, unlike true bohemians, was a solitary man who went off alone to drink. The author concludes that the novelist was much greater than the man.

Montenegro, Olivio. "Prefácio" [Preface]. *Coisas do Reino do Jambon.* São Paulo: Editora Brasiliense, 1956.

Lima Barreto was a rebellious writer. He was much affected by the fact that he was born a mulatto seven years before abolition in Brazil. In the author's view, Barreto coincides with his characters. His art is confessional. Barreto's color complex became a weapon unlike Machado de Assis's aristocratization. These two Brazilian novelists were different in every way.

Pereira, Astrogildo. "Prefácio" [Preface]. *Bagatelas.* São Paulo: Editora Brasiliense, 1956.

Bagatelas consists of political and social criticism. Barreto was one of the best Brazilian journalists of his time as well as a great novelist. He alone recognized the importance of the 1917 Russian Revolution and his vision of post-World-War-I problems was most astute. He was not a Marxist and in an eclectic way, drew on positivist materialism, Spencerian liberalism, and Kropotkinian anarchism. His writing embodied a sincere attempt at achieving liberation for the masses. He was for "maximalism" or the maximum in reforms. The ruling bourgeoisie was an oppressor to Lima Barreto. These plutocrats included not only great capitalists but also the great landowners. Barreto was for agrarian reform and against the latifundia. His interest in the United States stemmed from that country's treatment of its black population. He had read the theories of Gobineau, Lapouge, and other racist ideologues. Barreto keenly sensed Brazilian racism. He was particularly critical of United States dollar diplomacy and Brazil's role as a United States protectorate. He predicted a future Latin American coalition against the disguised oppression of the Yankees. Through *Bagatelas,* Lima Barreto survives and participates today in the struggle for peace, democracy, and independence. That is his claim to glory.

Pereira, Lucia Miguel. "Prosa de Ficção de 1870 a 1920" [Prose Fiction from 1870 to 1920]. *História da Literatura Brasileira,* Vol. XII. Rio de Janeiro: J. Olympio, 1950, pp. 284–313.

The author compares Lima Barreto to Machado de Assis in terms of their commitment to fiction, of their characters, and of their questioning of existence. Although Lima Barreto did not like being compared to Machado de Assis, both used the vehicle of the novel to express themselves. For both, literature was servitude rather than a gift, a fatality of temperament more than a grace of the spirit. Both were mulattoes, neither completed his education, and to Machado de Assis's epilepsy, the author compares Lima Barreto's alcoholism. Machado de Assis's life was a harmoniously ascending curve while Lima Barreto's life led to destruction in a catastrophic rhythm. The author maintains that Lima Barreto's drunkenness was more harmful to his destiny than was his color. Like Machado de Assis, Lima Barreto always delved beneath the surfaces. The author discusses the works of Lima Barreto employing a biographical method and often finds Lima Barreto himself in his characters. Lima Barreto's themes focus on the problems of mulattoes in a multiracial society. His relationship to Rio's outskirts is lyrical and he is the novelist of Rio de Janeiro's panoramas. A skillful short story writer, he is comparable to Manuel Antonio de Almeida in his treatment of the common people. Lima Barreto was a man of his time and of his country.

———. "Prefácio" [Preface]. *Histórias e Sonhos.* São Paulo: Editora Brasiliense, 1956.

The same article as the previous entry.

Pimentel, Osmar. "Prefácio" [Preface]. *Os Bruzundangas.* São Paulo: Editora Brasiliense, 1956.

Lima Barreto is of the greatest interest to contemporary Brazilian critics. A great humorist, he was a novelist of the city and its suburbs. Two of the themes of his works are pity for the oppressed, and attribution of efficacy to the power of intelligence and idealism for a possible ethical organization of the city of men. Policarpo Quaresma is more than a caricature of a nationalist. He is a great man and an alterego of Lima Barreto. The theme of the man of color is most insistent in the works of Lima Barreto but for him, race is a corollary of spirit. Lima Barreto spoke to future generations of Brazilians. It was unfortunate that he went for so long without recognition.

Prado, Antonio Arnoni. *O Crítico e a Crise [The Critic and the Crisis].* Rio de Janeiro: Editora Cátedra, 1976.

Elaborated within the limits of premodernism, Lima Barreto's work confronts tradition and is not free from certain decisive contradictions even in the definition of this moment of Brazilian literary life. The liberation of the writer and his approximation to marginalized groups lead to a debate of parallel problems, with a thematic renovation and the valorization of an authentically national literature. Barreto's nonconformity is more of a protest against exclusion than the historical consciousness of an order in crisis. Lima Barreto was independent from foreign models and influences. His reformist sentiment was directed towards a defense of human dignity, and to the right of all to happiness and satisfaction. Impotent before the marginalization of his truth, the nonconformity of Lima Barreto imposed itself as a contrast that does penitence, revealing at each stage a conscious reply to the deceit that disfigures it.

Proença, Manuel Cavalcanti. "Lima Barreto." In *Augusto dos Anjos, e Outros Ensaios.* Rio de Janeiro: José Olympio, 1959.

Lima Barreto's style was called incorrect but he was a rebel against purism and heralded modernism. The author analyzes Barreto as a stylist and claims that Lima Barreto's concern was for the goals of literature. He was critical of the Parnassian, Coelho Neto. He was influenced by Taine and La Brunetière and believed that the destiny of literature was to make the great ideals of the few accessible to the common man. Stylistically, his desire was for clarity. Barreto was intellectually honest in his fidelity to his models. He prefigured the modernists and he achieved success in Brazilian letters because of his complete love and dedication to literature despite much opposition.

——— "Prefácio" [Preface]. *Impressões de Leitura.* São Paulo: Editora Brasiliense, 1956.

Same article as previous entry.

Quadros, B. "Prefácio" [Preface]. *Correspondência, Tomo II.* São Paulo: Editora Brasiliense, 1956.

The author, a contemporary of Lima Barreto, describes the writers' circle in 1908 and the cafes Barreto frequented. Barreto did not show at that time "the sorrow of the pride in being black." The author gives the history of the publication of *Recordações do Escrivão Isaías Caminha.* He discusses the "à clef" character of the novel, for which it was criticized even though Afranio Peixoto's "à clef" novel was not. The author concludes that with the passage of time nobody remembers the real models.

Rabassa, Gregory. "The Negro in Brazilian Fiction since 1888." Unpublished Ph.D. Dissertation, Columbia University, 1954.

Lima Barreto deserves universal attention. He is a link between the nineteenth century and modernism. The author comments on *Clara dos Anjos, Vida e Morte de M.J. Gonzaga de Sá, Recordações do Escrivão Isaías Caminha, Numa e Ninfa,* and the short stories. A black man writing about blacks, Lima Barreto has an outstanding place in Brazilian letters. He has direct experience of what he writes.

Ribeiro, João. "Prefácio" [Preface]. *Numa e Ninfa.* São Paulo: Editora Brasiliense, 1956.

Numa e Ninfa mirrors the vices and customs of Brazilian political life. A mediocre adventurer becomes notable in his profession because of a fortunate marriage. The author reviews the interesting characters and comments on the creation of milieux. He finds the end of the novel defective. Lima Barreto was a great urban writer, an astute observer of society, imaginative, and a stylist.

Santos, Antonio Noronha. ''Prefácio'' [Preface]. *Correspondência, Tomo I.* São Paulo: Editora Brasiliense, 1956.

Lima Barreto practically never left Rio. As a result, his letters are rather limited and to the point. They project naturalness and fluency as well as humor. The letters follow the writer's development. Largely addressed to his father and friends, the letters recount his domestic drama, Lima Barreto's aspirations for a degree, and the tribulations of being a bureaucrat. Some refer to the publication of books, and others give advice to young writers.

Sayers, Raymond. ''The Negro as a theme in the Novels of Lima Barreto.'' In *Proceedings of the International Colloquium on Luso-Brazilian Studies.* Washington, D.C., October 15–20, 1950.

The author compares Richard Wright's *Black Boy* to Isaías Caminha. Until 1888, the main problem for the Negro was abolition. Literature treated the life of slaves. The psychology of the free Negro was little studied. *O Mulato,* by Aluisio Azevedo, was an exception. Lima Barreto was the first to write about average Negroes. *Clara dos Anjos* is one of the most interesting accounts of Rio de Janeiro during the early part of the century. Isaías Caminha is important as a description of a society of Negoes struggling to overcome the difficulties of poverty and lack of education. The solution for Lima Barreto's society is racial amalgamation.

Translations

THE LIFE AND DEATH OF M.J. GONZAGA DE SA

Translated by
Rosa Veloso Dwyer and John P. Dwyer

Contents

FOREWORD

My old schoolmate and now my professional colleague, Augusto Machado, gave me the task of publishing this short work of his. Beforehand, he asked me to revise it. Even though nothing in it had to be retouched, I still felt somewhat uncomfortable with the classification of biography that my friend Machado gave to the piece.

To merit such a classification, a book must have a rigorous exactitude for certain data, a minute explanation for certain parts of the main character's life, as well as important dates relating to it. This work is lacking in all areas; but it's not only because of these factors that I feel this way — there also exists the fact that the author appears quite often, at times too much so, throughout the course of the writing.

During many passages, Machado has more to say about himself than about his subject.

But since I felt that these shortcomings were relatively insignificant in light of the real literary merits of this book, I did all I could to get it published, certain that by doing so I could help to encourage the outstanding literary vocation that assuredly manifests itself on the following pages.

April, 1918

LIMA BARRETO

Seul le silence est grand: tout le reste est faiblesse.
A. DE VIGNY.

La plaie du coeur est le silence.
BOURGET.

A NECESSARY EXPLANATION

The idea of writing this monograph occurred to me when I read Dr. Pelino Guede's biographies. They are biographies of ministers, all of them, and I thought to write a few about ministerial scribes. For now, I am subsidizing only one; later, perhaps, I will write the two dozen I have planned.

In this endeavor, there is no censure intended toward the illustrious biographer, nor any socialist nor revolutionary plans of any nature. Absolutely not! I followed, quite unintentionally, at first, the law of the division of labor, and with that, I can say without false modesty, I happened upon a small discovery for which the world will thank me.

The sages, by any information I have, had not yet noticed the lack of any proof of this law in the field of biography.

Nevertheless, it was evident that since our world's strange requirements for orderliness demand that some doctors practice medicine and that others practice law, it was also necessary to have a biographer for ministers and one for scribes.

In that manner, we, Dr. Pelino and I, are admirable proof of the complete generalization of that great scientific assertion of the division of labor; therefore, far from being a whim, the publication of this small book is a manifestation of a great and inevitable law to which I bent and will bend, as with all laws independent of my will.

Believing myself to be justified, I hereby give my public testimony of gratefulness to that writer, and if in the length of this publication I add anything about myself, the blame, apart from my incorrigible and basic egoism, falls solely upon me because I did not know how to imitate stylistically the telegraphic conciseness of the model I adopted and its superb, department-report impersonality.

All things considered, I do not judge myself by the truth. God forbid such a thing! Actually, because I chose such a different activity, I never did become accustomed to the studies required by literature. I do not know Latin or Greek, I have not read Mr. Cândido Lago's grammar text, I have never worn an academic gown nor have I to date been able to converse for five minutes with a well-tailored diplomat. Instead, I follow the example of the severe and melancholy mechanics professor from the Polytechnical Institute, Doctor Licínio Cardoso, who studied advanced mathematics for many years in order to cure homeopathy.

His demonstration was always a productive one for me. The failing grades I received were fair. Before me, everyone who passed turned out marvelously; afterwards...oh, then...!

His judgement was like that of Minos, inflexible and rigid, drawing its own inflexibility from the order of the Cosmos, and if in my life's actions I have once been just, I owe it to him — and only to his example, which I always had before me during my troubled adolescence.

On my knees I thank my lucky star for having found such a rare and model example in my career....

Throwing myself to the fates by publishing this meager, unworthy tome, perhaps I will be as happy as my worthy professor friend was with homeopathy; or perhaps I won't be and will suffer the consequences. Even though it may be unpleasant, the insults will give me reason to live, something which is quickly fading in me.

It is a stimulant that I am looking for and an imitation I am attempting. Plutarch and Dr. Pelino, both masters of the school, will have to forgive my plebeian design of wanting to transform such a superb genre of moral literature — the biography — to a type of pharmaceutical remedy.

October 8, 1906   AUGUSTO MACHADO

I

THE INVENTOR AND THE FLYING MACHINE

It never occurred to me that my friend Gonzago de Sá would ever become involved with air balloons. Unless that certain paper he left me among others was intended to communicate another thought, I find it hard to believe, given the friendship we shared, that he would hide from me that noble preoccupation of his mind. I have always respected people who wished to fly.... Well!... Let's get on with the story.

I met Gonzago de Sá once, when in the line of professional duty, I was sent to the Department of Religious Affairs. It concerned the number of salvos due to a bishop. The bishop of Tocantins, upon entering the port of Belém, onboard a steamship, received only a seventeen volley salute from the respective fort in the harbor. His most reverend complained. He was due eighteen volleys. Thick, leather-bound lawbooks were quoted by high church authority to substantiate his case.

The claim was registered with the secretary of religious affairs, and in the lengthy report it issued, there were allusions to the matter of investitures, to those of bishops in the days of the Empire, and to top it off, to canon law, without resolving anything definite.

The State Department was heard, and judicial protocol respectfully and wisely interpreted did little to get the case moving. They then appealed to the procedure established by the legislation of countries whether they were civilized or not.

China's rules were completely omitted, but those of Montenegro gave a twenty-four gun salute to a bishop.

Wise transpositions were made from one religion to another, in the fine shades of delicate international issues, so as to establish a correspondence between the respective authorities.

A very useful and well delineated chart was drawn up, upon which the names of all the clergymen of each religion were written, respecting the original spelling in their own native languages.

Catholicism, Buddhism, Judaism, Brahmanism, and the Protestant sects all met each other placidly in the sphere of bureaucratic and ceremonial conventions.

Witch doctors, muezzins, bishops, lamas, Buddhist nuns and dervishes were all neatly laid out, side by side, as if by a valet.

The State Department recognized that by clarifying in this manner the relationship between clergymen of all sects and religions, it would be easier to interpret the legislation relative to the case in each country on the globe. That is, the customs of Burma, Tibet and Turkey would come to the rescue of the distressing conflict in which the Brazilian administration found itself.

Nothing of the sort, however, succeeded in making heads or tails of the problem. By that time, an opinion was sought from the secretary of defense, who came to decide it as if he were Solomon.

It was his impression that, in order to avoid future claims and to satisfy all parties from then on, there would be given a salute consisting of seventeen shots from a number fifteen canon, and one shot from a number seven-and-a-half cannon. Apart from being solomonic, mathematical or perhaps a combination of both, he had made from eighteen discharges, seventeen and a half, satisfying the prestige of the government and the pique of the prelate.

This resolution was adopted once everyone had heard the great technical reports of the ministry, whose technical know-how regarding the matter was beyond measure.

A report from the artillery division superficially outlined the theory of the separation of powers: The Justice Department, therefore, abandoning laws and treaty writers, based itself only on the theoretical matters of artillery and developed figures to substantiate the complaints made by His Reverence.

The matter was being decided once and for all when an agonizing doubt concerning the cardinal's case arose. Was His Eminence a Brazilian ecclesiastical authority? Should he receive only a bishop's salute or more? If he were a foreign ecclesiastical authority, what salvo should he be given? If he were a national one, how many? Etc.

And in this manner the questioning continued in the Department offices, when my director, to avoid more delays, decided to send me to the Department of Religious Affairs to submit to its qualified personnel the agonizing question—the cardinal one.

Few people know the Department of Religious Affairs or have heard of its services. It is surprising that this should be so because, in my opinion, if there is any office that deserves the respect and consideration of our people, it is that of Religious Affairs.

In a country where it is so easy to produce miraculous fetishes, terrestrial idols and omnipotent gods, it is amazing that the Department of Religious Affairs would not be as well known as that of Transportation. It has, nevertheless, in its museum and registers, many interesting things worthy of investigation.

It was by coincidence, that following my director's orders, I happened to meet Gonzago de Sá, drowning in a sea of paperwork in the ''Ornaments, Vestments, and Images'' section, reporting in all seriousness the Vicar of Sumaré's advice concerning the number of arrows Saint Sebastian's statue should have.

Gonzaga de Sá was a tall, old man, not yet completely gray, but getting on in years, very lean, with a long fowl's neck, a protruding Adam's Apple, a certain soothing quality in his deep voice, and a faraway look of gentleness and suffering in his energetic eyes. His complexion was sallow, almost like the yellow wax used in some candles during pilgrimages.

I greeted him with complete respect, which even more than to beauty is due to old age. He seemed pleased with my consideration, looking at me with a poorly concealed interest beneath his ''pince-nez,'' propped up in the abyss of his bureaucrat's desk.

I immediately perceived that he was an intelligent, old man of keen insight that encompassed a vast realm of society. I sensed his being illustrious and of an extremely benevolent nature. I don't know why I also guessed that he was of noble birth and that the history of his ancestors' arrival in this country did not date back to the Republic nor to the early years of the Republic's stock market speculation boom.

My impression was not wrong, because later when I was still going to the Department of Religious Affairs about the "shots" due a bishop, I asked him, in the midst of the transaction:

"Mr. Gonzaga, you are not married, are you?"

"No."

"Nor did you ever wish to marry?"

"Twice — once to a viscount's daughter at a dance given by a marquis."

"And the other?"

"Son, you seem envious."

"Perhaps," I said, quickly answering his question.

"Well, let it be known: the other was with my laundress."

From this response, I guessed what kind of youth he had had.

In addition, he was a skeptic, privileged, Voltairean. As I later discovered, in order to be up to date with his God, he used to attend religious services, but not like the republican bourgeoise, so as to endorse the monks, priests, nuns and Sisters of Charity nor to become rich ignobly, criminally and cynically, without charity or love but rather for pompous display. He was anticlerical, but not a Mason.

To understand a man well, one should not try to discover how he officially lived. It is to know how he died, how he received the sweet pleasure of embracing death and how she embraced him. After I relate this great event in the life of a friend, I will decipher his intimate ways and explore his insignificant deeds. I believe there can be no error in proceeding this way.

Lord Bacon's official life history is contemptible and villainous but look at his works, his thoughts, and above all, his death — how fine they are, and how they overshadow his other life!

Having suddenly thought that snow might prevent the spoilage of meats, Bacon stepped down from his carriage on a very cold day (he was an old man by then) and went into a straw hut to conduct an experiment. He bought a chicken, had it killed, and with his own hands, he himself stuffed it with ice. He caught a cold, and some time later in a stranger's home, since he didn't even have the strength to return home with the carriage, the daring inventor died, the philosopher of the experimental method, the author of the scientific and industrial greatness of our days.

As for Gonzaga de Sá, I will give an account of his personal affairs, and describe to you, first of all, how he died, in order to highlight certain fragments and details that will be retold later regarding his fascinating obscurity. Let's narrate the events.

We had planned to meet on the terrace of the Public Park to watch that certain shade of green which the sky sometimes becomes in the late afternoon. I hurriedly went to meet him, to converse with him and to admire him. I rarely watch the sky, hardly ever the moon, but always the sea. Although he was not there yet, the sight of the sea distracted me. But let me narrate these things in detail.

When I reached the terrace of the Public Park, the quarries of Jurujuba and Niterói had lost the violet tinge that I had observed covering them during the trolley ride. Nevertheless, a stream of dense, luminous clouds still hovered above the

Armação, from which, as usually seen in religious paintings, the angels and saints of our faith arise.

It was an undefined afternoon, with an irregular light and a threatening storm; but my secret correspondence with the environment had informed me it would not rain. As soon as I arrived, I sat on a bench jutting out from the wall, directly in front of the new staircase leading to the famous Beira-Mar Avenue. I immediately pulled out a cigarette and began to smoke it with a passion, watching the mountains stifled in the heavy clouds, embedded into the indigo horizon, a shred of purple that extended over the islets and beyond the bay.

I also noticed the calm appearance of Guanabara, lightly curled, maintaining a certain kind of smile during the conversation it struck up with the sober austerity of the granite hills in that moment of tenderness and trust.

Villegagnon floated in the water's calm with its white walls and solitary trees.

I noticed then the harmony between the sea and the mountains. The dark coast of Sugarloaf melted into the gentle waves of the cove; and because of the mysterious darkness of the sea, Boa Viagem was saddened.

They became one and the same in nature and touched each other benevolently.

The reflective and flowing sea accentuated the majesty and the stability of the mountain ridge, and by virtue of its magnificence, at times solemn, the complacent smile of the gulf had a celestial bond.

The poet was right! This was truly the magnificent Guanabara that I was viewing.

The Glory at the top of the mound, with its entourage of projecting palms compelled me to contemplate and recall my life, whose evolvement, according to the desire my godparents expressed during the baptism — depended upon the noble and valiant protection of Our Lady of the Glory. And when something reminds us about that dim and solemn ceremony, past events come to mind, memories that we are losing.

Of course I didn't try to see if I had already reached the point my blessed godmother planned. One should wait until he is closer, and if I am not yet a thousandth part of the way, I shall never arrive there.... I was not upset; I made a detour through my feelings, trying to see how my life had evolved according to the mysterious plan of this fragment of the planet on which I was born. For one half hour I examined in detail my past deeds and I gathered their analogies to my native environment.

They had been varied in appearance and as careless as the irregularities of my birthplace. I smiled with the bay, vacillating between sadness and joy; and underlying that smile was a wave of energy from those ancient rocks.

Looking towards the Órgãos mountain range, as a youth, I sensed its yearning to rise higher in hopes of touching God, and it was then that I learned to despise the vain gaudiness of the upper class and to see only the crushing stateliness of its stolid crests.

I was good and tolerant like Guanabara Bay, where the boat, the canoe, the galley and the battleship are welcomed; and like it, secure in the protection of friendly mountains, I sought refuge in the shade of impartial friends.

I wanted to live life fully; I had ambitions and dreams on those clear May mornings, but the scorching summer sun taught me (before Mr. Barrès had a chance to do so) to suffer in resignation, and to yield to the teachings of nature, always good, and to those of men, sometimes evil.

I saturated myself in that palpable melancholy, that elemental sensibility of my city. I live in it and it lives in me!

And in this way, I began to feel proudly that the circumstances of my birth and the direction of my life were in harmony — one assumed the limitations of the other. And it was also with great pride that I could substantiate not having lost anything acquired from my grandparents from the time they loosened their ties with Portugal and Africa. I was already a rough sketch of what I would become years from now, a man created by this community. For that reason, I already rely on the things that surround me in a familiar way and the scenery that faces me is no longer strange: it tells me the public history of the city and the lengthy elegy of the pain that it witnessed in the preceding fragments of life that gave origin to mine.

I couldn't have cared less about the Germans and the Greeks! The State and Art! Other people and their dreams, neither of which do I understand, are the author of these tyrannies.

I have my own dreams, similar to those of my dead predecessors and my dreams are more beautiful because they are imponderable and ephemeral....

At that moment a group of Englishmen passed by, observing the surroundings with the same gaze used by all guides, and carrying with them boughs of shrubs. I saw foliage that the jequitibá tree never does.

I felt an impulse to shout, "Idiots! You think you carry the luxuriant tumult of my jungle in that garden plant!"

"Do as I do: suffer for four centuries the climate and plantation toil so that you may feel in the deepest cell of your organisms the beauty of this lady — the disorderly and delirious nature of the Tropic of Capricorn!... And go away — because this belongs to me!"

Then I remembered my authors — Taine, Renan, M. Barrès, France, Swift, and Flaubert — all from there, more or less from the same country as these people! I reminded myself that some of them had given me the sacred knowledge of knowing myself, of being able to attend that rare performance of my own emotions and thoughts.

I witnessed at the moment an unutterable and limitless awareness.... I looked upon those fools with veneration, in homage to those of their blood who taught me and made me realize that I, a nitwit or a genius, wise or unwise, have the power to influence the mechanism of life and the world.

Humiliated, I lowered my head.... My old friend was arriving. The afternoon, however, was not favorable, and we did not see the display we expected.

We remained there for a short time, conversing on the terrace of the Public Park.

Gonzaga said to me, upon seeing yet another group of Englishmen pass before us:

"I can't stand these English! How quickly they walk! It is not quite that late in the afternoon.... Walk slowly, slowly.... You should not run, not even to death, which I love.... Let's have supper at my house even though my aunt is not at home.''

I was twenty years old and had a passionate desire to be a director. My hair had stood on end before that invocation of death.

I accepted the invitation, in spite of it all.

''Let's walk, and take the longest path.''

We headed towards Barbonos, through the venerable shaded trails of Italian neighborhoods that lead to Santa Teresa. He didn't say anything. Soon we passed by an uncivilized looking mansion. Gonzaga asked me, pointing to the Convent of Saint Theresa.

''Do you know who lives there?''

''Nuns.''

''A count lives there also, and princesses, I believe.''

''Dead?''

''Yes, dead. Don't you see the sign of death there?''

''No, it is smiling and happy.''

''And that mansion there?''

''It is here, abandoned.''

''Dead, isn't it? Do you know why? Because it keeps no dead.''

We continued to go up.

Upon arriving at the garden of his house that looked out on the Lapa, The Gloria, the Armação and Niterói, he contemplated the silent sea, and leaned over to pick a flower for me, but he fell, and died. It happened just like that. Days after the death of my friend, I found a double sheet of legal paper written on both sides entitled ''The Inventor and the Flying Machine'' among the disorderly papers and books that he had willed me. I read it and saw that it was a complete chronicle.

Although it does not give a complete picture of my dear friend's spirit and his concept of the world, I will publish it so that those who did not know him can in some way appreciate my intellectual companion and mentor, whose judgements of men and things has greatly influenced the choice of paths my mental activity has trodden.

Gonzaga was one of those men whose thoughts were transmitted poorly in written form or in any other medium of communication created by mankind. His intellect was not capable of leaping from his mind to the paper; only his living word, even in a public speech, could express what was properly and profoundly his.

Nevertheless, as I have said, I will publish these sheets I found among the papers he left me, in the hopes of giving a slight idea of who my old friend Gonzaga de Sá, official in the Department of Religious Affairs, really was. Here it is:

''For ten years, not a second went by in which he did not think of his machine. Sometimes, pouring over the pages of the Canson, he would occupy himself sketching and crossing out the retracing, to the point of wondering how the pitch dark of the night had transpired quietly and unnoticed into the morning light. Pages and pages of paper, at other times, piled up with closed equations and other algebraic expressions; and in his leisure hours as he gazed distractedly upon them, they would appear before his eyes in crude Greek letters, the '*phi*'s,' '*mi*'s,' '*gama*'s,' or '*pi*'s.'

Those miniscule light characters, subtly curved, like a staccato of fragile thoughts moved by the "integers" in disciplined formation, marching forward, forward.... He consulted magazines, discourses, and abstracts, skimming them thoroughly, and nights upon nights with his feet soaked in water to ward off sleep, he would pour over his pages, reading, comparing them with each other, categorizing and completely absorbed in their teachings, meditating, imagining the impossible for his apparatus, probing the obstacles he should conquer and the laws by which he should abide."

"Then one fine day, after laboring hours on end, it appeared on paper, marvelously drafted in colors. And the inventor checked and rechecked it many times, lengthening a certain line, softening another angle, or a junction, and finally the machine was complete, perfect, exactly as he had pictured it in his mind and as it had been forming, little by little, day by day during a gestation period of twenty years."

"He rested on that happy day unequal to any."

"He was able to sleep a deep, refreshing and calm sleep. But already on the following day he began to think about the materials he would need to construct it. He considered the resistance each one provided, the specific weight, the price; everything was taken into account with acumen and wisdom."

"He combined one with the other, considering their qualities, advantages, and defects, always mindful of the effect he desired; he selected motors, delicate, but strong engines, and then he went with all these meticulous and serious thoughts to the office where he planned to build the flying machine."

"Not for one minute during working hours did he leave his workers' side. Piece by piece, he followed every step of the construction; from time to time he would weigh them and ask that they be sharpened or polished further, so that they be the exact weight calculated to the milligram. Not one screw went by that he did not check for a slight difference in size that might upset the rigid system and abort his expectation of the invention. It was ready, and attractive; swift as a dragonfly."

"It would soar, it would ride the sky, go beyond the mountains, lift itself far from the land, exist ephemerally almost outside the earth's destiny, become intoxicated with the blue and the celestial dreams in the height of the rarefied stratum...."

"The experiment would be conducted in the morning, and that night he could not sleep. It was as if the following day he would meet the love he had dreamed of, and in order to be able to consummate it now, he had waited many years in anxiety and hope."

"Dawn arrived and he saw it for the first time, with an interested gaze of passion and enchantment. He put the finishing touches on it, adjusted the levers, started the motor, and took his place.... He waited ... the machine did not rise."

This is what was on the yellowish sheets of legal paper I found last year among the papers Gonzaga de Sá left me.

At first I did not understand the significance of this tale, but referring back to this and that aspect of his life, I well understood that he meant that Fortune, more than any other God, is capable of upsetting the most erudite plans that we may have developed and can mock our science and our will. And Fortune plays no favorites....

II
PRIMARY INFORMATION

Manuel Joaquim Gonzaga de Sá had a bachelor's degree from the Imperial College of Dom Pedro II. He was a bright student and had a solid foundation in both upbringing and instruction. He knew classical psychology and metaphysics from all historical periods. He would compare the teachings of the Viscount of Araguaia with those of Teixeira Mendes.

His romantic background is limited. He never married, and simply put the thought out of his mind, even though he did have two romances: one, the viscount's daughter he met at the marquis' dance; and the other, his laundress, even though he doesn't remember exactly when.

You should keep in mind that this information came directly from him.

Following his favorite introspective method, he studied detainedly these two cases of emotion and, after a detailed analysis, found them to be identical in appearance and in and of themselves.

He added to this a stoic disregard for notoriety, or rather for the comfortable public status associated with it. As the son of an official general of the Empire, he could have become a ''somebody,'' but chose not to. It was a case of studying to be a doctor, receiving his degree, pulling strings, practicing hypocrisy and suffering the solemnities.... A complete bother, in short, which he refused to endure. Instead, he became an apprentice and went about his business. He was a diligent and competent worker. On the day the Republic was announced, he was one of the few working in the department, drafting a decree by the Religious Defense Office, when he was informed: ''My dear Mr. Gonzaga, today no one works. This morning Deodoro has proclaimed the Republic at Campo de Sant'Ana.''

''But, which one?'' he asked.

His recall of history failed to form immediately a clear idea of what might be a republic. He knew of many, each so different, that his question was not insincere. He told me that on that very morning of November 15 he was reading his *Fustel de Cou-langes,* coincidentally, the passage regarding the aristocratic definition of civilian rights.

It must come as a surprise to the reader that Gonzaga de Sá, an official in the Department of Religious Affairs, would have anything to do with such books.

There are many people who without any special vocation for medicine, law or engineering, have other intellectual pursuits, a fact that the Brazilian public, in its ignorance, fails to appreciate, encourage and sustain. They are the philosophers, essayists, students of social problems and pursuers of other intellectual interests. Our people who read have not yet turned to them. They don't admire the elite, and have no voice in the nation because of the astounding gap to be found between the great Brazilian intellects and their reading public.

With the knowledge that those talents can not afford them a living, those unfortunately born with such talent, if poor, seek employment in the Civil Service, escaping our imbecilic and instigating intellectual elite. They are not many; they are a rare sight in each department, but considerable in the total Civil Service of the government.

At first they do so to maintain their integrity, and to work for the basic necessities of life, but the anger, the mental depression caused by their surroundings, their isolation from their peers, and the stupid disdain which is shown them, all this, little by little, begins to parch their vitality; they lose heart and even the will to study. With the years they become dull and degenerate.

I was friends with a clerk who knew Zend and Hebrew in addition to the other areas of common learning.

His father, who had money, sent him to Europe as a young man of fourteen.

There, where he had spent approximately 10 years, he became interested in religious criticism and studied those ancient, sacred languages. Having lost his fortune, he returned to the streets of Rio de Janeiro only to find himself with his priceless and useless knowledge.

At that time, the feuilleton was in vogue, as was the repetition of certain base things that dealt with mathematics.

Our clerk-to-be was not cut out for writing newspaper fillers; he decided to declare himself a ''know nothing'' and took the civil service exam for scribes. And went his own little way.

It was like a geometry student who decided to live in a hamlet inhabited by grasshoppers. And he died fifteen years later, leaving a void in the department. ''Poor fellow,'' they would say, ''he had such good handwriting!''

Gonzaga de Sá wasn't exceptionally talented but he compensated for it with his own personal insight. Furthermore, in comparison to that other scribe, he was more intelligent in being able to resist the mental depression generated by the Department of Religious Affairs, a state, in all departments few officials can overcome.

Once, he told me in an off-handed manner some of his theories on South American civilization; and I asked him:

''Why don't you publish them, sir?''

At that time I called him 'sir' and it wasn't until much later that I began to address him with greater familiarity.

''Heaven forbid! And what about the newspapers?''

I couldn't believe that this childish reverence prevented him from publishing; there must have been a deeper and more significant reason.

He was a person whose quest for the latest thoughts of the day and long hours of difficult reading probably would have generated an entirely original work of his own, especially since he never repeated findings of others and he had his own way of seeing facts and commenting on matters in his own particular style.

I think he had his own plans along those lines because in spite of being a middle income employee and having job security, he would not let himself become lax; he was constantly thinking and had an agile mind, although when I met him he was past his sixties. He never ruminated.

On the contrary, he never ceased adding to his knowledge, sharpening and polishing it, extending it into remote and tedious fields. What was the reason for all this work, if not to create?

It is true that this could be attributed to his own personal tastes, totally apart from intellectual matters, lacking an objective or pressures from the task or a profit of any kind.

Later on, however, I became convinced that it was simply intellectual curiosity that stimulated and encouraged him in his arduous reading, simply because there was no possible explanation, given the obscurity which he had voluntarily inflicted upon himself.

He, like Mérimée, did not have anyone to whom he could offer pearl necklaces. Gonzaga, alone, without children, a member of a soon to be extinct family: to whom would he leave his glory?

Not having taken any professional courses was like having eluded the programs so as to read the authors with greater orderliness and method, in the manner of someone about to write his memoirs, or a Felix Alcan worth seven francs and fifty. He completed his coursework in ancient studies by taking isolated courses, abandoning the consecutive series of the medieval universities, a tradition that, dominating our universities, establishes the most absurd chain of subjects and courses in its years or series.

Gonzaga da Sá liked journals very much. The variety of instruction he received and his polychromatic tastes allowed him to pursue, without effort, the anarchy of his articles. He subscribed to the ''Revue,'' the ''Mercure,'' the ''Revue Philosophique,'' but above all the ''Revue des Deux Mondes'' was the one he preferred and quoted.

He did not appreciate ours, so *chics,* he told me. He would, however, glance through some with exception to the unknown ones and to illustrated newspapers of meteoric fame. Later we shall come to know more of his opinion on these.

Through books, he kept up to date on his country's literature, with a lively interest but not with a passion.

He read ''Figaro'' and repeated in French by memory several anecdotes by ''Masque de Fer.''

. . . .

By my first meetings and with the assistance of information gathered from here and there, this was what I first perceived about Gonzaga de Sá. For months I had this *croquis;* later the sketch became more complete, the profile defined itself more clearly, and I believe I obtained a reasonable portrait.

It is not proper then, to exclude the narratives of the first *boutades* that I heard from him.

I will narrate them as I continue with this unpretentious sketch of his biography.

Right now I'm going to tell one of the stories that struck me as amusing.

III
PUBLIC EMBLEMS

Our lack of talent in the art of drafting is apparent. It is not so poor in its execution, but in what relates to creativeness, there is no doubt about its insufficiencies. The symbols of states, our cities, the stamp on our coins, all prove my point.

I can't open the *Garnier Almanac* and see the maps of our provinces with their respective heraldic emblems without becoming horrified at the figures that flank the ridiculous shields, complete with mountains and inscriptions, beside groves and parrots, everything of the most extravagant and hideous nature that can pop into the head of a madman and of the least artistic person possible in this world.

The arms of the Republic, then! They are of stunning ineptitude. That gigantic sword! That huge ribbon! What a sight, my God!

With the exception of the seal on the coat of arms for the city of Rio de Janeiro, which is in fact elegant, well proportioned, heraldic, representative of the city, few of our public emblems can be saved from drowning completely in ugliness or complete idiocy.

How they differ from those in colonial days! Just look at the hooped sphere intersected by the Cross of Malta — the symbol of the Realm of Brazil, and conferred by I don't know which king of Portugal — it's enough to show how there used to be better taste then than there is today in high places.

Gonzaga de Sá told me this once in the Paço Square while he looked at the Mestre Valentim Fountain. Then he continued:

"This fountain is ugly, it is too massive, but the spherical hoop that tops it adds a certain majesty, a certain grandeur.... But it was once beautiful."

"When?"

"When the sea reached its feet. It had that shape, or better, that 'repoussoir,' and possessed a certain beauty. I knew it that way...."

Night came and all fell dark upon us.

We then felt our souls completely submerged in the shadows, and our bodies asking for love. We became quiet and watched the stars in the dark sky for awhile.

The park swelled with tired sailors and ladies; girls of modest and intimate class, mistrusting, passed by hurriedly.

"What is the reason, Machado, why all women in this land fear men?" Gonzaga asked me.

"That is because the men are not good."

"I agree. Here it is not the woman who wants to deceive man. It is the men who want to deceive women."

"I agree with you, sir, and the proof lies in newspaper articles. It is men who rob their mistresses. It is the husband who transfers the wife's dowry into his pockets. It is the fathers that defraud their daughters' legitimacy. It is the brothers who steal their sisters' jewels, and it is the men who always manage to stay afloat!''

''In the light of that, adultery is worthless. Let's go.''

We left the park and I attempted to go home to write a few letters to relatives in Minas: and the next day, when I entered the post office to mail them, needing first to correct one of the addresses, I headed for one of the counters where there were pens and inkwells to be found. Since they were all being used, I decided to wait for a free one. I stood nearby only to find, when I looked closer, that Gonzaga de Sá was the person using the stand. Instead of writing, he was examining a handful of stamps spread out on the surface of the table.

''Oh, Gonzaga da Sá. Hurry up, now!''

''Why, it's you!''

''I'm just waiting for you to finish.''

''Have you seen these new stamps? Did I not speak to you yesterday about emblems? Did you notice?''

''Some of them.''

''It's good to point it out. Some of these are worth ten réis, twenty, fifty, one hundred, two hundred and four hundred.''

''Do you collect them?''

''No, I like famous men, and the stamps bear the faces of some of my favorites. Here we are: Aristides Lôbo, Benjamin Constant, Pedro Alvares, Wandenkolk, Deodoro and Prudente.''

''Nice idea!''

''It's a shame the stamps don't come with a few biographical facts on the side so that future generations may know who these men were, along with good moral sayings for the edification of our contemporaries and future generations.''

''That's an excellent idea.''

''That way we could have had a Brazilian Plutarch on postage stamps. Even without all that, however, these stamps are thought provoking. When you look upon Aristides Lôbo, ten réis, you will say to yourself: 'There is a man who was born for 10 réis, something that did not happen to Benjamin, who attained twenty. Lucky guy! Lucky guy!' Go on your way because you are probably getting a local letter. Here comes Wandenkolk, with rooftile coloring, one hundred réis. You think to yourself — how far he has gone! And that's not all ... If we had a Deodoro also, greenish, two hundred réis, a Pedro Alves, only five hundred réis, and the others? Those were my thoughts on these stamps, and thinking about stamps is one of the most modest intellectual pursuits. Don't you agree?''

''Indeed.''

''Good. Go on with writing your letter, now.''

IV
PETROPOLIS

Gonzaga used to tell me:

"The most stupid Brazilian obsession, the most foolish and imbecilic is that of aristocracy. Open any cheap publication, the cartoon type, and you'll soon find one of those very black clichés ... note that nobody wants to be black in Brazil! ... You'll find very somber clichés with captions reading: 'Sousa and Fernandes wed' or 'Costa and Alves wed.' Do you think they refer to great noble families? Nothing of the sort! They are social climbing doctors that quite naturally marry the daughters of rich Portuguese. They are descendants of bankrupt ranchers without nobility and the bride's grandparents are still pushing the plowhandle in the old glebs of the Minho, thriving on the evening lard soup there. You well know that I don't have any superstitions regarding race, color, blood, cast, or anything. For me there exist only individuals and I, more than anyone else, because as a descendant of the Sás who founded this city of mine, could be only that way. But I recognize what makes people have those superstitions. In order to consider myself a member of the nobility, my grandparents would have had to uphold all the rules of the aristocracy. They married with whom they pleased and did what they felt like doing, and now it's just like me to go out in the main street and shout foolishly: I'm a Sá, a noble, a son of the aristocracy, an esquire and all that rabble just because my family name is Sá. That's what I'll say because I'm a Sá. Now imagine just any Fernandes with such haughtiness! ... An institution is valid only as long as its rules are maintained. The noblemen here have degraded themselves because they did not respect the rules of lineage.... Do you understand even what it means to say "degrade" in the code of nobility?"

"Of course I do! It's to go back down to the third rank, once rules of lineage are ignored, to where, for true nobility, the bourgeoisie is located. The Colbert family, the ancestors of the great ministers...."

"They degrade themselves by their own will, choosing to be carpet dealers in Lyon, I believe," concluded my friend.

It was four o'clock and we had pleasantly wandered off to Pedregulho. Looking off in the distance toward the Jockey Club, toward Leopoldina Station, Gonzaga suggested:

"Shall we go to the Engenho da Pena?"

"Where is it?"

"All you people know is Tijuca and Botafogo. Rio has other pretty places, you know. It's over there."

And pointing in the direction of Órgãos, he then continued:

"It's at the edge of a canal, maybe two miles in length, that separates Governor's Island from the mainland. It looks like a river when you see it flow smoothly by the surrounding land, with boats sailing on it, swift canoes and smooth riding steamers in parade with flickering candles passing lovingly by. The Galeão is opposite Governor's Island. Also the Fundão, another island, and both with marvelous mango trees.... Imagine beside those struck down by storms are several dozens of trees, all manicured and dating back to Dom João IV.... The mental hospital that they shaded was the home of the unhappy simpleton king.... Let's go!''

We caught the train. It was going to Petrópolis. It was full of the types of people Gonzaga had just described to me. We brought first class tickets to Bom Sucesso, but quickly moved to second. My friend bought a newspaper and began to read. I watched the mangroves go by, desolate and solitary.

We arrived, got off the train and entered a bar, asked for a beer and Gonzaga teased me:

''You will have to walk a little.... As Fontaine said: Aucun chemin de fleurs ne conduit à la gloire....''

''Let's go,'' I said.

A little distance from the bar, he stopped me and said the following:

''I ran away from those people in Petrópolis because to me they are foreigners, invaders, more often than not lacking culture, and always pillagers, be they national or foreigners. I am a Sá, I am from Rio de Janeiro with its mixed bloods, its blacks, its mulattoes, mestizos, and its ''Galicians,'' as well....

We continued walking and soon he resumed talking with the usual gentleness.

''Have you noticed there is nothing more trite than the news in Petrópolis?''

''I hardly ever read it,'' I replied.

''You really should, because we should be concerned about our individual fulfillment. Don't you see it clearly? Become interested in Petropolis, man!... Trivialities that it might be, their news deserves our attention..... It's only who is promoted, who 'steps down'; there is no doubt.... I don't criticize an ordinary reporter who concerns himself with who is promoted, but imagine, with those who step down! That's not his job; he should leave it to Sister Paula.... And that is not all! What is worse is that the news is like that elsewhere—common, boring.... What a deficiency!...

''What type of news did you expect?''

''Me?''

''Common scandals?''

''What! That is mundane! I would want reforms, revolutions, inversions of the *chic* norms.''

''How?''

''Imagine an audacious philosopher from the guidebook of civility — he's probably a zoological species that should flourish in the beautiful mountain city — who suggests inverting the consecrated in the ''Don'ts' and that, accepting his bold ideas, Petropolitan society is obliged to relate to us, with serious consequences for the cities of Nova and Catumbi, the following pleasantry: now, in Petrópolis one can eat with a knife and weddings are performed in pyjamas. Oh! What delight! In addition, everything has been inverted, shuffled, changed from white to black, only the 'savoir vivre' remain the same!... It's not possible! It requires an inversion in such transcendental rules, don't you agree?''

"That's true. But the fault does not lie with the newspaper men, then. It is with Petrópolis."

"Why?"

"It has no history and little imagination."

"What lucky people!"

By then we had arrived at the sea. We had crossed small plantations of cassava, sweet potatoes, and squash. The road was flanked by grasslands and hedgerows. People were plowing on the hilltop and the person guiding the oxen was a Portuguese girl with a large cocoa straw hat and a red Alcobaça scarf at her neck. The sea....

It actually seemed to be a river. Ahead, on the left side, the insane asylum with its ancient mango trees like ladybugs and its flat, sandy field. There was a small island in the middle of the canal and the four walls of a house were still standing. I asked Gonzaga what it had been.

"It is the Cambambe. Those walls belonged to a house several stories high, with the ground floor a store."

"There? What for?"

"Before the railroad existed, communications with the interior were transmitted under the bay, through Inhomirim, the port of Estela, now in ruins, and from there to the Mineiros docks in small boats that passed through here. This one's crew members maintained the general store which operated fifty years on that island without trees."

Gonzaga then reminded me that Estácio de Sá died of an arrowhead wound during combat on Governor's Island, nearby, just ahead of me.

Looking out over the canal, I saw the centuries old mango trees in Galeão, and stared at the blackened walls of the island and when I noticed the canal's gentle waters, it was as if I saw Estácio da Sá's canoes with his archers and musketeers veer off course, taking the conquistador to his death....

V
THE STROLLER

The thing that fascinated me the most about Gonzaga de Sá was the way he abused his ability to move about. I found him everywhere and at the latest hours. Once, as I was riding the train, I saw him on the dreary side streets that border the downtown area; another time, on a Sunday, I saw him on the Flechas Beach in Niterói. I was no longer surprised to see him on the city streets. He was on all of them, both morning and evening. Once I followed him. Gonzaga de Sá would walk a few meters, stop in front of a house, look and then continue on. He climbed steep grades, descended hills, always slowly, smoking voluptuously, with his hands behind his back, holding his cane. I imagined when I saw him with those grimaces that during the course of the day he'd recall at the spur of the moment: "I wonder what shape the house I first saw in 1876 is now?" And he would continue along down the streets only to once again contemplate an old roof or a balcony and see in them again features that no longer were objects ... I was not mistaken. Gonzaga de Sá thrived on the nostalgia of his garrulous childhood and anguished youth. He would seek out houses, balconies and roofs so that by looking at them his recollection of things he knew would not fade away along with the past episodes and experiences of his life. I sensed that in this act, he saw before him a parade of thoughts that would build up behind an unknown dike to grow with the passing months and overflow, making life a bit more bearable as it did. One day he failed to show up for work (as he later told me) in order to contemplate in the mid-day sun a shack in Castelo that he had seen about fifty years ago at the same hour when he had played hooky in primary school. Poor Gonzaga! The house had been razed. What sorrow! Thus, living every day in the minute details of the city, my kind friend had been able to love it completely, except for the suburbs, which he did not accept as being either the city or its outskirts. He felt for the city the same love one feels for an art object or in the way city dwellers value country life. So much so, that it was a pleasure listening to him talk about the old things of the city, especially the sad, detailed episodes. He had a very flexible memory, relatively exacting but imaginative and had no need for leases, deeds or land allotments, nor did he favor such documents. He would liven up his narrations by dotting them with witty, erudite ponderings and unexpected estimations. He was an artistic historian and just like the first poets of the Middle Ages, he related tales orally, just as they told the epics. Of these matters, two or three points bothered him intensely and he would construct another finer and more lively version to tell. Once, I don't remember why, I mentioned to my friend the following:

"This Rio is very strange. It extends over here, over there; the pieces don't fit together well, they live so segregated that no matter how much the population grows, it will never have the appearance of a densely active, large capital."

"To think that all cities should have their own features, that of all cities being the same, is an idea that comes from the United States. And may God prevent such a plague from infecting us. Rio, my friend Machado, is logical in and unto itself, as its bay is with itself, being a submerged valley. The bay is beautiful for that reason, and Rio is also beautiful because it is in harmony with the location upon which it was placed. Let's contemplate it awhile.

"If we consider Rio's topology we shall see that the conditions of the physical environment support what I am saying. The mountains and hills push back and separate the component parts of the city. It is true that even with our present means of rapid public transportation, it is still difficult and delaying to go from Méier to Copacabana: it takes almost two hours. Even from Rio Comprido to Larangeiras, places so close on the map, the time is not much less. São Cristovão is almost opposite Botafogo; and Saúde, Gamboa, Prainha — thanks to that chain of granite hills Providência, Pinto, Nheco — are very far from Campo de Santa Ana, which is on the opposite slope; but with the perfection of the transit system, new tunnels, etc., all the inconveniences shall be remedied."

"That crowding together of hills, that sprinkling of mounds and the Tijuca ridge with its foothills packed under various names, gives to the city an appearance of many cities connected by narrow pathways. The city, nucleus of our glorious Rio de Janeiro, is connected with Botafogo, Catete, Real Grandeza, Gávea and the Botanical Gardens only by the narrow path squeezed between the sea and Santa Teresa. If we wanted to make a more detailed survey of the city, it would be easy to show that there are half a dozen communication lines between the outskirts and the actual center of the city."

"That's because Rio de Janeiro was not built according to the established theory of perpendiculars and obliques. It suffered, as with all spontaneous cities, the influence of the area in which it was built and the social changes it underwent, as I think I have already mentioned."

"If it is not in accordance with a surveyor's geometric order, it is, however, in tune with the hills that characterize it and that make it unique.

"When created, on the summit of Castelo, it was no more than a white reef rising in a turbulent sea of forests and swamps. Growing, it descended down through the venerable hill; it slithered through the lowlands in narrow roads. The necessity of an external defense, in some form, obliged them to be that way and the reciprocal laws of the inhabitants against possible criminals made them continue in the same fashion, after there was no longer a need to fear pirates."

"The runaway slave and the pirate helped design the city, and surprised by the discovery of gem mines in Minas, which it drained, old São Sebastião quickly covered several swamps in order to grow and stretch out, and all this material was helpful for that purpose."

"The population, too lazy to climb upward, constructed on the dusty ground. I think Dom João came to discover beaches and enchanting environs whose existence he never suspected. One thing offset another as soon as the Court wanted to establish itself and attain a serious nature...."

"Anyone looking at a map of Rio can get information from its ancient topology that perfectly defines the lazy twisting of its streets and the unexpected turns that they offer."

"There, a peak of mountains pushed them; here, a march divided them in two symmetrical trails, leaving it intact, waiting for a slow embankment."

"Let's go to the homes and neighborhoods. A perceptive observer does not need to read up high between the stucco ornaments to find out when one of them was built. That house we look at now on the Rua da Alfandega or General Câmara, dates to the first years of our independence."

"Look at its obvious security, as if wishing to appear even more secure than a Gothic cathedral; the extra strength of its walls, the thickness of its doors ... whoever made it had been through the War of Independence and the first Reign, and was certain of owning his own land upon which an entire generation of offspring could live."

"The slave traffic imprinted upon Valongo and the hills in Saúde something of an African field, and the melancholy of the Mineiros docks reflects a longing for the rich feluccas, with cargoes of merchandise that no longer arrive from Inhomirim and Estrela."

"C'est le triste retour...."

"The streetcar then disturbed that orderly distribution of the social stratum. Today (not considering the improvements) the urban geologist is concerned by the overturned appearance of the neighborhoods. No areas seem planned out; different social strata are interspersed; deposits are shuffled; and the distribution of riches plus the new social institutions help out the streetcar in an endeavor worthy of Plato."

"Nevertheless, the streetcar widens the city even more and forces the wealthy to live with the poor, and the poor with the wealthy. Neighborhood lines are dissolved."

"What's bad is the separation between them; it's how little mutual exchange there is, causing them to be actually neighboring cities, asking that the proper channels communicate to the appropriate authorities their needs and wishes, but once traffic is set up, that whole problem will disappear."

"But even if topography caused those difficulties, it still gave to our city its poetic and dream-like form and its grandeur. And that, in itself, is sufficient."

I had no choice but to say that he was entirely correct.

VI
THE BARON, THE SEAMSTRESSES
AND OTHER MATTERS

Having nestled himself comfortably on the hard bench, his many years full of thoughts and dreams, Gonzaga de Sá informed me:

"This morning the Baron received a poet."

"And so?"

"The poet, extremely uneasy and visibly embarrassed, came to ask him if the word love should be capitalized."

"And Rio Branco?"

"That it wasn't advisable in the middle of the verse; but that it was necessary in the beginning."

"It gives me great satisfaction to see the superb manner in which the Baron is influencing our letters."

"And with spirit! . . . Ah, the baron!"

Gonzaga de Sá could not allow himself to remain in the ecstasy provoked by that title, in spite of the fact that he found Paranhos, as he sometimes called the minister, to be an outstanding mediocrity, an anachronism, always thinking about diplomatic foolishness rather than things of immediate importance. Paranhos was a fool whom magazines consecrated and the babbling of the masses deified. What surprised Gonzaga was the title bestowed by the emperor. At that time, as I thought about this matter, there passed by in an open-air coach the powerful Minister of Foreign Affairs, with his protruding stomach aiming toward the heavens. Watching the Baron pass by, obviously carsick but still arrogant, from across the garden's rise, Gonzaga told me:

"This Juca Paranhos (it was yet another name for the Baron of Rio Branco) turns Rio de Janeiro into his own private country house. . . . He doesn't explain himself to anyone. . . . He thinks he is above the Constitution and the law. . . . He deals out the Treasury's funds as he sees fit. . . . He's a Robert Walpole. . . . His system of government is corruption. . . . He lives in a State palace, without legal authorization; he puts aside all laws and regulations to provide all ministry jobs to the puppets who fall in his favor. When there's an absence of diplomatic complications, he invents one, purely to show off his cleverness like Talleyrand, or his Bismarkian astuteness. He is an autocrat, a Khédive, because "this" is truly a future Egypt. . . . It's true he studied the question of boundaries but he never spoke about Joaquim Caetano, nor about old Teixeira de Melo. Purposely, he forgot them; and he made the newspapers forget them, also. When the Emperor read the *L'Oyapock et L'Amazone* by Joaquim Caetano, he said that the book was worth an army of six thousand men. Juca wins the argument about Amapá, receives awards, pensions and likewise for his sons; meanwhile, Joaquim de Caetano's daughter lives in misery.... It's just that! This Rio Branco is an egotist, vain and an ingrate. His ideal as a statesman is not to make life easy and comfortable for everyone; its is all grandeur, gold filigree, the courtly solemnity of old European monarchies — it's all theatrical form, the presentation of a Chinese ceremony, an observance of the court manners and all the ancient nonsense associated with a Versailles. It's not exactly a Louis XIV that he's in contact with; he imitates Dom João V, without Odivelas, perhaps, but he still imitates him. We even had a cardinal that cost us a fortune. He was like the monstrous bell of Mafra that was the pride of the Portuguese king.

We were seated on a bench in the Campo de Santa Ana. We had arranged to meet there so that he could show me exactly where the "Provisorio Theater" was. After completing his promise, we remained seated, admiring the afternoon and conversing.

At a certain moment, there suddenly appeared in front of us an available "pretty maiden," accompanied by the notable complacency of the aged mothers of the maidens. We were surprised by the visitors to the Campo de Sant' Ana, and the "pretty maiden" slowly passed by us, glancing scrutinizingly at the few frequenters of the abandoned park. She was a stray sheep; she didn't belong to the crowd seen at times in the park. She smelled of the Rua do Ouvidor and the counter of Botafogo. Nevertheless, not even Gonzaga de Sá's decrepit gaze and my heady, vulgar gaze were forgiven. She took them home when she slowly paraded in front of us. I was grateful to her from the bottom of my heart....

"Up to this date," Gonzaga said, as he lost sight of the two ladies, "and I count more than sixty years of existence, I regret not having had a long and perfect friendship with a seamstress."

Having had a close relationship with such a precious and exceptional superior hierarchy that would allow me to have an insight into his mental process, I began to draw wild conclusions from his small displeasure:

"It would have been in fact very instructive since you would be (I already addressed him familiarly) perfectly fit to be a judge of ladies' fashions and thus, you would obtain an accurate standard for establishing a personality scale. And furthermore, the qualifications for this trade must give these shop girls a certain special and rare intelligence. They automatically have to compare their rich client's nude hips and thin arms with the fascinating, resonant and robust aspect that their bodies will assume once they are wrapped around with rich fabrics and padded accessories. They must also keep in mind the unjust dual nature of the passion that their clients inspire in men.... My God! What a marvelous influence the muslin exerts on our feelings! This is purely a case where weavers provoke strange psychic reactions. All this, I continued to say with enthusiasm, must come as excellent sarcasm worthy of someone with a broken heart."

"You are right, lad. With the scissors of their humble trade, they create the beauty of professional women where pride, once it is struck by the perception of its own reality, gives way to sarcasm."

I was surprised at the mathematical manner in which Gonzaga de Sá summarized my words, but I soon saw that it was in jest when he said, with that skeptic half-smile:

"We are, from what I gather, carrying out a pretentious contemplation of a seamstress. And it is not without value," my sorrowful friend added, "in our cloaked society, to meditate upon such a curious agent, minute and ignored, which really shows the grandeur and majesty of the representative upper classes. To prove how beneficial, important and productive the actions of these pale infusoria are, imagine for an instant all the great ladies of the 'upper ten thousand,' poorly dressed, simply "patched-up" or nude. Reduced to the minimum, or nothing, their beauty overcast, by inference, we would examine the basis for their greatness as it is managed by their husbands and fathers. Criticism, with such a stimulus, would extend itself and the masses of contagion, and swelled by an anarchical and demoralizing disrespect, would drown society. The rest would not require so much justification, today's knowledge slashes the infinitesimals, the minuteness.... There is a point of contact between the universal suffrage politicians and the men in the laboratories."

"A point of contact excessively honorable for both," I then said.

"It wasn't quite that about which I wanted to speak," Gonzaga de Sá corrected, his calm voice resounding with gentleness and kindness.

"I regretted not having a long and perfect friendship with a seamstress, with any seamstress, because I've remained ignorant to this day about attire, lace, styles, types, kinds and varieties of hats and outfits. All his life, Darwin regretted not having learned algebra. I regret not having learned the technique of 'Notre Dame.' "

When Gonzaga de Sá told me that he knew nothing about such a transcendental branch of life, that he didn't have the slightest notion or awareness so necessary to the philosophy of love, to the science of behavior and to the analysis of social crystallization, my admiration for him diminished, the same admiration that had been so tumultuary since the beginning of our relationship.

Gonzaga de Sá had fallen in my estimation. Plato not knowing the styles of the ladies in Athens — was it possible? How can one understand the strong motives leading to the difficulty in nominating a delegate to the Conference on Repression of Dog Vagrancy in Italy if one does not know of exactly what fabric the skirt Mlle. Zeddin danced in was made at the chic ball given before her departure to Europe, shortly before the nomination? A dress has always had an immense vibratory power in our society; it is a state of mind; it is a manifestation of the unfathomable majesty of our nature, provoking different ones in other people. And Gonzaga de Sá, a wise man, a thinker, a subtle commentator on life, how had he not studied natural history?

"Finally," he said to me, "it can be that in the search for fabrics and laces, in that torturous adjustment of materials to the body, there is a longing for an ideal shape, superior, ethereal and imponderable, beyond our bodily vulgarity, that has throughout something detached, spontaneous, from itself and back, but — what? Do you know what for?"

"What for?"

"To get married, have four children, and raise one more social climber who, in addition, is rude, cruel and demanding. Despicable! Some, to top it all, even learn to play the violin...."

It was then that I regretted having misjudged my excellent and witty friend. He did not stop with details. Perhaps he did not know the meaning of *voile, nanzouk,* "plaid," *soutache* and other tailoring vocabulary, but he grasped the basic law, the prime philosophy of women's fashion — and who knows? — male fashions also. Only one objection could be made. Why did loose women dress well? Everything boils down to the notion of marriage, to keep its general formality, to slightly change its duration. That done, Gonzaga's principle is perfectly exacting and true. But the look the "pretty young lady" mercifully gave me decidedly moved me. I quickly defended the ladies against Gonzaga de Sá's fine bluntness.

"Oh Gonzaga! What deviltry! Don't act pious, you are breaking my heart...."

"No, absolutely not. Individuals move me; that is, the isolated person suffering; and that is all. Those abstract creations, classes, masses, races, don't touch me.... If in effect, they don't exist!? And according to literary, philosophical, sociological and religious thought, women. I even have a great fondness for them, purely intellectual — be it well understood! — so that there will be no contradictions."

"Fondness?"

"Certainly, and it is infinite and all inclusive."

"You amaze me."

"Don't accuse me of inconsistencies. I feel sorry for the person who suffers. I already told you, but certain of our intellectual biases are incapable of provoking deep feelings toward people; nevertheless, they are real enough sometimes to awaken in me a sympathy or indifference in the appropriate field. I detest anthropology and love religious critique. It was my wish when young, soon after reading Renan, to go to Europe and study Hebrew, Sanscrit, and Zend but ... it wasn't possible. It's because some of our human intellectual creations are organic, itemized and perfect. They aren't the results of guesses, the arbitrary choice of certain dice or the carelessness of others; they are not the results of war strategies. You must have noticed that the mathematical law of averages enslaved everything. It is a strong and reasonable resource for certain aspects of our activity, but completely inappropriate to characterize a class, a people, or even to express the determinants of intelligence or character; and feelings, as society imagines, are tyrranically individual. The genius is Rousseau, not the Swiss.... You could say, on the average, in Rio de Janeiro each year a certain number of people are born, since that deals with numbers. But you would be grossly mistaken to say that on the average the Cariocas are happy. Happiness, such a changeable sensation, instable, irreducible from man to man is something different and does not concede to averages covering hundreds, thousands and millions of human beings. Imagine that Mme. Belasman, from Petrópolis, has a bunion, a hideous defect from which she suffers excessively; and the factory worker Felismino, from Mortona, takes pride in having a talented son. Mme. Belasman lives despondently with the copiousness of her bunion. She spent her childhood suffering from it, her adolescence was anguished and such an insignificant growth on her foot was reflected in her mind as permanent, continuous, with the most incredible and appalling display. Meanwhile Felismino, as he pounds rivets, smiles and looks in expectation to see what effect a fragment of his blood will cause upon society. His colleagues thought he was crazy and because once he had enthusiastically referred to his son's brilliant qualities, that act created two or three enemies for him. He is sanctified — who is happier — I ask — Mme. Belasman or Mr. Felismino? And in view of that, could you say that all the ladies in Petrópolis are happy and all the foundry workers unhappy? Is there a possible average for the happiness of classes? We modern men keep forgetting that these stories about classes, peoples, and races are typical of gossip columnists, invented for the needs of certain logical structures, but kept from them, they completely disappear: Isn't that the case? They don't exist, we can understand the ''sphere,'' ''cube,'' ''square'' in geometry, but outside of that it is impossible to obtain them. And that deceit is disturbing my opinion in such a way that it seems to me that it will revive the famous scholastic debate of the ''universals.'' You are familiar with it, aren't you?''

''Barely.''

''The Middle Ages was filled with this question: are certain general ideas a reality? Do they exist or not outside of the individuals who conceive them? For centuries, there was divided opinion, and the debate was prolonged; among the knowledgeable there were passionate factions — realists and nominalists, as today, with our hobby horses there are the blues and the greens among their clients. The modern debate has not yet been settled; however, be it as it may, I am a ''conceptualist'' like Abélard, and therefore, I feel sorry for Mme. Belasman in view of the pride of Felismino, the foundry worker from Mortona....

Night was rapidly falling. The dubious evening hastened its descent and did not offer us more than the single-colored, overcast twilight of theatre flies. An open calash passed by us, dirty and ugly, balancing an extremely heavy pair that did not seem to fear the approaching storm. We had left the park and were slowly descending the Rua da Constitução, also without any fear of the afternoon's grim aspect. Behind the calash, a light ''charrette'' came whipping by, passing us impertinently in that silent atmosphere. For several minutes, the two of us remained in the Largo do Rossio without speaking, still, looking from side to side, until Gonzaga smiled and said to me:

''Let's go to Garnier because I want to buy the Poincaré — 'La Science et l'Hypothése.' Then we will go have a snack.''

We descended the avenue toward the Rua de Ouvidor.

VII
COMPLETE CONTRACT

When I went to the Department of Religious Affairs to discuss the problem of the cardinal, I first spoke, as expected, with the general director, the Baron of Inhangá. He was an old official from the days of the Empire who had become director and baron, thanks to his birth and experience as an official. An intelligent man, but lazy, he never understood these matters or anything else. He began as head of the department and during business hours the extent of his job was opening and closing his desk drawer. He became the director, and as soon as he settled in his position, he tried to find another activity. For lack of something more useful to his country, the baron would sharpen his pencil point at every opportunity and moment. It was a waste of pencils that was endless; but Brazil is rich, and appreciates the dedication of its sons. When he completed twenty-five years of service, he became a baron. As I was saying, I first spoke to him and he sent me to the head of the Department of "Ornaments and Vestments." As soon as I entered the room I was struck by how Gonzaga de Sá stood out. The department head was a mediocre person of the most banal type. But with Gonzaga de Sá, I felt he was strong willed in his actions and had a definite air of confidence in his tall figure. After explaining the purpose of my visit to the director of the department, he took the "paper" I was carrying and wrote at the top of one of the pages:

"To Gonzaga de Sá for information and consideration."

We went, the office boy who accompanied me and I, to the designated room. I was glad to see that it was the same office boy to whom I had taken a liking upon entering. I noticed that, before writing, the magnificent head of the "Ornaments and Vestments" shook his pen as if he were a fencer and it seemed to me as if the ink were about to drip on his humid, red nose. His cursive writing, at the end of several minutes, in its meagerness, looked fancy and flowery, with great respect to Chaldean style. I followed the "paper" to Gonzaga de Sá's desk where I explained the atrocious problem. Considering the slow reading of the process, the kind informant handled the case well, and soon, smiling with the moist mouth of a young girl, he asked me:

"Why don't we listen to the Ministry of Information in Rome?"

Immediately then, taking his pen to trace out in exaggerated script, he began to fill out the form with the appropriate solemnity. The difference between one manner of action and the other was so brusque and this revealed so much of his two personalities that I immediately felt that hidden behind those quick formalities was the quick thinking of a lively mind that had adapted itself superbly to the spiritual trappings of where he lived and to his own weakness for practicality. It was truly on this occasion that our relationship began. During the following months we found ourselves rapidly complimenting each other with the strongest 'pledge' of affinity. Unintentionally, as these meetings lasted more and more, I was better able to understand that hidden under this habitual imitation was a great, compassionate soul. At first I thought he had organized bitter memories of some minor disappointments in order to create a temperament all his own, but with time I noticed that there was nothing contrived or insincere, everything about him was structured and his originality had come about naturally, built by the slow labor of the sediment of time, isolation, goodwill and personal suffering. Then I suspected that a great heartache had upset him in his youth, and that heartache, because he never confessed to it, because he didn't admit its presence, remained indefinite, vague and fleeting. I tried to decipher it and to form a hypothesis. It wasn't a result of love; that would have been too commonplace for Gonzaga de Sá! Anyhow, I can't guarantee it.... For my beloved friend, criticism preceded any action, and in this way, love does not err. Well ... had he always had that talent? He himself confessed to me that, so to speak, he had forgotten to marry. And that only crossed his mind on the two occasions I have already mentioned. Would his heartaches have been from one of these two? I don't know. Nevertheless I caught him once or twice acting strangely.

When I entered the department of vestments in the morning, I saw Gonzaga de Sá was drawing. When he realized I was there, he awkwardly hid the paper. It wasn't an action appropriate for his upbringing, and I could see at a glance that it was a human figure. One afternoon, in a bar in Copacabana, I found my old friend scribbling in his notebook. He was taking notes, he said, and I believed him.

Aside from these incidents, there were no other indications that he had bruises from any clash with life. One might try to explain his state of mind by guessing that his heartache was dispersed in the imbalance of his personality, in the variety of his interests, without any one being preponderant or victorious, reflected in his bitter and bruised outlook on life and his longing for the absolute. Did he have within him a conflict of organization and intellect, or what was it?

As you will see, I formulated all sorts of hypotheses, but none ever satisfied me; meanwhile, not to tire the reader, I will remind you as Poe did (I believe it was he) that the truth always lies in the simplest hypothesis, to which Comte adds: the kindest one. Each one to his own opinion, according to this advice.

On a clear Thursday afternoon, I was recalling such things as I was walking through the path leading to my friend's house. I was accompanied in these pleasant memories by an enormously exuberant happiness surrounding my soul. The contract was going to be complete and it would unite our souls perfectly. I walked as if toward a nuptial room.... More than just to have dinner followed by some aquafortis, which was the pretext of the invitation, I was going to his house because of the sincere curiosity to know how he really was and to have a taste of his intelligent, paradoxical and somewhat sententious way of speaking. In our country of expected submission, the paradoxical is fascinating, even in its positive aspect. I slowly walked up an elevated road on the Candelaria, and I knocked with respect on the garden gate of his old house, almost at the top of St. Theresa. An old black man came to open the door, one of that race of old blacks that had to suffer paternally the whims of our past generation.

"Sir Gonzaga de Sá?"

"Sir?"

"Yes, my old man."

I entered into the main room of the house, which Master Gonzaga had converted into his study. It had a stucco ceiling with rectangular pyramidal shafts and the bookshelves, except for those on the window bays and doors, were small, the height of the window sill, and they decorated the wall on all four sides. Above them, like a long console, were busts, pictures and a collection of worthless minerals, and on the walls, aside from two or three small oil paintings, a reproduction of Botticelli's "Spring" and a Rouget de Lisle singing the Marseillese for the first time. Also, there was a bust of Julius Caesar on the desk and nailed to the wall on which it leaned, a magnificent portrait of Dante, in an ordinary frame. Under it, in Gothic letters, this verse from the *Inferno* was written: "Amor, che a nullo amato amar perdona." Hovering over the entire room was the transcending gaze of a bronzed owl, perched on the "banner" of the door-way. All this, in perfect order and without excess; only the large table at the center was disorderly, with books, magazines and papers shuffled about informally. A rocking chair was destined for long, vague meditations; to the right of the table, a stork with an outstretched neck and the aloof tilt of the head so characteristic of that longlegged bird, elegantly and untrustingly presided over Gonzaga de Sá's laboratory of dreams and thoughts.

Vases with small palms and ferns were scattered among all this. Standing with a small newspaper in his hand, he welcomed me.

"Right on time. Five o'clock."

"I thought I might not find you yet. Did you go visit your godchild's father in the suburbs?"

"Yes, I did. The poor man! He is in poor health; after becoming a widower, he has worsened."

Gonzaga de Sá lowered his head slightly and then brusquely, as if wanting to remove this bad thought, he added:

"I went. Each time the suburbs become more interesting. Extremely loving and feminist."

"Feminist?"

"Feminist, Why not? The intellectual activity of that section of the city, upon entering the train, seems to have been handed to the girls.... Such is the number of those carrying books, violins, music cylinders, that one begins to think that we are in the reign of the "Grand Duchess." Do you know the "Grand Duchess?""

"No."

"It is an operetta by Offenbach where the women are men, make war, have armies.... I saw it with Vasques.... How funny that thief was! He spoke well, with malice, — if the baby cries, who will let him be nursed? Oh, that Vasques!... How I miss him!... In the suburbs, one feels like asking: who will nurse the future sons of those girls?

"There is no problem," I said, "when they get married they will close their grammar books and burn their music, and they will repeat the same dull story as all bourgeois marriages.''

''It will be so because the eternity of our species seems to rest on solid bases. What do you think?''

''In complete agreement,'' I replied. ''It doesn't matter what the women's conditions be, they don't think about anything else, and they want it so desperately to the point of making the human race the most wretched of all the races, species, genus and varieties of animal and plant life on this planet. I blame them!''

''Sometimes, I think that way, without a natural doubt, but then something happens, that ... two hours ago, in the Piedade station ... But ... Venus is a revengeful goddess, they say.''

I had sat on the couch, near the entrance and master Gonzaga de Sá did so on the rocking chair. Between us, in its entire length was a large center table. It was within the reach of my friend's hand, while I was slightly further. Through the open windows, the gentle afternoon breeze entered, and brought with it the garden's fragrance, dispersing it throughout. Looking at the delightful figures of the melancholy Sandro, my kind friend's thoughts flowed:

''Two hours ago in the Piedade Station I was waiting for the train. Finally it was announced. In an instant it appeared at the time a man crossed the track a bit before the station platform. Warnings ... screams ... gestures ... the train whistles. The man becomes dizzy, loses his presence of mind, and is caught ... but in what manner, my God? The front of the train lifted him, threw him on that platform — prow type — do you know the kind I mean? The animal clings to an iron post and the locomotive finally stops, very close to the station, bringing the poor man, with a broken head, humiliated, bleeding, but alive, dumbfounded, crushed, completely overcome by terror before that bestial paleontology that he himself had invented. The eternity of our species rests on solid bases, Machado.''

Hearing a voice in the room, I turned around.

''Machado, my aunt, Escolastica,'' Gonzaga de Sá introduced me.

What a charming, elderly lady she was. Very light-skinned, with tiny green eyes and a small profile like a child. All was candid and kindness in that unmarried lady. The whiteness of her jacket stood out in an extraordinary way, immaculate, and her white hair, with a tint of yellow that comes with age, was parted in the middle and held with a black net. I couldn't linger any longer in regarding the septuagenarian. Gonzaga de Sá excused himself and went with her inside the house to arrange something. He returned soon. There was time therefore for me to look discretely at a piece of scribbled paper on the table. There were about eight or ten noses drawn successively by an unqualified hand that had forced itself to sketch a figure that he had seen but still recalled in his mind. What a strange obsession, my God.''

''You can't imagine,'' he said upon entering, ''how much work those pigeons require.''

''You raise pigeons?''

''Yes, I like birds, especially pigeons, their flight, the shiny feathers of their necks, their gracefulness, their intermediate nature between land and air.... My cat's savage ways frighten them, but the poor things fly towards the sun.... Are you hungry yet?''

''No.''

''I sent for some Bucelas white wine. Do you like it?''

''It is delicious.''

Soon the old black man, Inácio, entered with two glasses and the bottle on a tray.

''Leave it there, Inácio.''

Even though Gonzaga de Sá spoke with utmost kindness, the poor old man almost let the bottle fall down.

''You can't imagine, lad, the treasure of dedication in that man. I don't know where he gets it from, nor how he has developed such great sentiments. He was born a slave, a few days before me. My father liberated him in the baptismal font because of it. He has accompanied me since the first days of my birth. He is a foster brother. He saw me at my humblest; he thought well of me even during repugnant moments. He was present at the collapse of our family's greatness; meanwhile, not being as he appears to everyone, lacking in critical intelligence, I am to him the same, the very same person who was formed in his mind those first few days of light in his life. I don't completely understand him. I find him obscure; but he fascinates me — he's great!... Sometimes, I confess, he seems a dedicated, subordinate animal. At other times I also confess, he seems a divine sentiment.... I don't know, but I love him.''

It wasn't without emotion that Gonzaga de Sá told me this; there was a slight tremor in his voice and perhaps to disguise it, he picked up a small newspaper from the provinces and quickly looked through it.

''Do you read the 'Gazeta de Uberaba'?'' he inquired.

''I do. A friend, a politician from there, sends it to me.''

''That he sends it to you is not surprising, but the fact that you read it!...''

''I read it. I like obscure newspapers, the ones put together by beginners. I like the way they begin stories, the obscure struggle between intelligence and words, the peculiarities, the extravagances of the free or contrived invention of beginners.''

''You're like my friend Domingos Ribeiro, Jr., who said: 'All that is triumphant is trite.' ''

''I agree with him, but only in my narrow, personal point of view.''

''Certainly.''

''I subscribe to 'Pesquisa' by Cascadura. There is a copy right here. Take it,'' and he pointed to a bookcase near me.

''This one?''

''Yes. Read the summary.''

I had ''Pesquisa'' by Cascadura in my hands. On the cover, ugly and dirty, which enclosed the seventy-page pamphlet, I slowly read: ''Topics below — ''Teixeira de Sousa, the stylist and the novelist,'' by Gualberto Marques; ''Halos'', poetry by Beltrando F. de Sousa; ''The painter, Manuel da Cunha and native colorists of the 18th century in Rio de Janeiro,'' by Aimbiré Salvatore; ''The Nature of Science'' by I.K.; ''Hindu and Arabic Mathematics and Differential Calculus versus Greek Geometry'' by Karl von Walposky da Costa; ''On the necessity of corrupting the Portuguese language spoken in Brazil'' by Bruno Uricuri Furtado; ''On the material disassociation and impassive science,'' by Frederico Balspoff de Melo; ''Monthly topics and commentaries,'' chronicle by Baldônio Flaron.

Immediately, I leafed through it, reading here and there the pages of the suburban monthly publication. I didn't do it without a certain surprise. It was a wonder that in such a detractive suburb there should be so many new and different thoughts. Gonzaga remained quiet, without missing any of my reactions. He was enjoying the whole thing.

''Cascadura is setting a fashion, eh?''

''That is true.''

''In view of our great newspapers and elegant magazines, 'Pesquisa' by Cascadura is a good, intellectual publication.''

Once again I leafed through the pamphlet; I read passages here and there and said,

''It is strange that there are so many unknown people capable of writing about such lofty topics. Do you know any of them?''

''None, but why does that surprise you?!... There is a lot of talent among us. What there isn't is publicity, or rather, the existing publicity is humiliating, aside from completely lacking any sort of higher vision.

''How's that?''

''Very simple.... Let's analyze it: what are the publicity media?''

''Newspapers and magazines.''

''...and books,'' concluded Gonzaga de Sá.

''And books, also.''

''A newspaper, a major one, you well know what it is; it's a firm of powerful people needing constant flattery, secure only in those minds already signed, registered, sealed, etc., etc. Besides the limited and restricted point of view of those firms doesn't allow publications for any but the average readers that want to hear of politics and assassinations. Their owners do well in giving the public what it wants.... If they don't consult the average people, they have to gratify the rulers, the upper class, cater to them — people in general, completely removed from the subtle Brazilian spirit, who don't want to know anything about impartial ideas.... Besides that, a thousand twists and turns are needed to reach the large newspapers, and when they are reached, in order not to scandalize the average man and the great bourgeoisie, where they have their clientele, it's necessary to remove the best intellectual parts.''

''And magazines?''

''It's the same thing, having only more photographs. There isn't among us,'' he continued, ''that demand that stimulates the wit of foreign editors and other publishers, that of alive and young minds. Nothing of the sort! Our book and journal salesmen are satisfied with routine, and for variety they look for news in Portugal. They restrain our minds because whoever doesn't appear in the newspaper — doesn't appear in books, nor on stage nor anywhere — dies. It's a dictatorship.''

''You should divide the blame.... And what about the public? And the authors?''

The public is flexible, easy to manage. The authors, these are indeed culpable. Meanwhile, I found a way to join with the young minds of my land: I read obscure magazines and some newspapers from the provinces. If the pain of the rhythm or meter increases the beauty of poetry, the lack of space greatly enhances the articles in small magazines. One must guess much of what the authors could not say, inventing also much that never even crossed their minds. What does this suggest?

It's possible that you have different emotions upon reading small magazines, but newspapers from the provinces — so full of politics and intrigue!''

''An error! This issue of 'Gazeta de Uberaba' is proof to the contrary of your claim.''

''Bah! A petty question!''

''Petty question! My goodness! Lofty social matters, my friend! It takes care of the grazing industry as well as diplomacy!''

Upon saying this, Gonzaga de Sá rose bit by bit, finally standing up, making as if to read, with the newspaper at eye level.

I looked for a moment to the window. The clouds played on the mountain tops and were diversely covered by the soft light of sunset. Here it was orange, there purple, gold, indigo, gray; now they covered each other; now in knots, in ribbons, in stripes taking on the most capricious and changing forms with the most beautiful colors of beautiful skies.

Gonzaga de Sá did not have time to pronounce a word. Illuminated, with the light of a tabloid by the connecting door, the aunt appeared to summon us:

''Come and eat.''

We went. Gonzaga de Sá took the newspaper.

VIII
THE DINNER

Dona Escolastica asked me to walk in front of her, and Gonzaga de Sá followed with the newspaper in hand. We entered the adjacent room where I paused a bit, looking at the family portraits. The master had not broken the tradition requiring that these be placed in the parlor. There they were, and not in the study. There was a gallery of over six venerable portraits of men of past decades some trimmed with braids, and all heavily decorated, and some ladies. Without moustaches, bearded, with collars, and an imperial look, with heavy eyebrows, it seemed to me one of them was about to raise his arm above the golden frame to underscore an order meant for me. I thought he was going to demand: 'give him the cod-fish.' I turned my face to rest my gaze upon the untouchable figure of a young lady with a raised coiffure with many large combs in it, very white, in an expensive dance outfit of a past era.

"Who is she?" I asked.

"My grandmother, as a young girl — my father's mother. She lived in France, and was there during the Revolution."

I was detaining my gaze upon the picture and my feelings changed. The benevolent look of the girl, tender, irresistably meek, made me forget the frown the old man with the collar had given me.

"Did you like it? She resembles Escolastica, don't you think?"

"Yes, it seems so."

"When she was young, she was exactly like her, my father used to say, except in her eyes. Escolastica's tend toward green, and hers were deep blue, like Minerva's. She doesn't resemble in any other way any of my other grandparents, whose physical appearance made them seem as if they had an executioner's outlook on life."

"You came up with such suggestions, Manuel. You seem crazy.... He was always like that. He could never be understood," the old aunt told me.

"It's not a lack of respect.... Each one in his own era," Gonzaga reflected. "Much as I wouldn't want it, as someone in between, my picture for posterity's sake should have something in common with that man on the nail. The money-lender, disguised as this or that, is the most representative man of the time...."

We continued to the dining room, but not until I had gazed detainedly on those old pieces of furniture of jacaranda wood so ample and strong that one would say they were made for another race of man, not like ours, those that we see in streets, in theaters, at horse races, wretched and sordid.

Dona Escolastica sat on the left, Gonzaga de Sá at the head, and I to his right. Through the windows at the two extremities of the room, I could see outside. From the flank of the abruptly lighted quarry, I could see small, black clouds of people coming down; to the left on the hilltop plateau, I saw a palm tree bent by the winds.

"Did you like the house?"

"I did."

"It was my father's.... What a sacrifice to keep it! Don't ever get involved with lawyers because they usually are the only heirs. Fortunately, I did keep it."

"It was the only time I saw you active," Dona Escolastica reflected.

"No wonder! I loved the surroundings, the views, the roof, the walls...."

"It has scarcely changed," observed the aunt.

"Some, that palm tree for instance," Gonzaga de Sá explained, pointing to the window, "is new."

"New! It's over twenty years old," remarked Dona Escolastica.

"New, yes! Since it did not see us born...."

I took another look at the tall elegance of that tree, there up high, vacillating over the entire city, and kissing the radiant clouds. For more than twenty years it suffered the inconsistent violence of the winds; for more than twenty years it had escaped the treacherous vengeance of lightning; for more than twenty years it had withstood the inoffensive roar of the thunder.... All these negations, and others coming from the cruel granite and poor earth made it taller, more dignified, gave it more pride and called to it to flaunt its height. Today, on the same level with everything, with the city, above the ungrateful granite, it looks compassionately and scornfully at the poor and well pruned trees that decorate the streets. The dinner was beginning to be served by a butler who was about 18 years old. After having the soup, Gonzaga de Sá, who had the small newspaper in his hand, said to me:

"I don't want to delay the delight I had promised you."

"Which one?"

"The reading of these beautiful chronicles from the 'Gazeta de Uberaba!'"

"Let's hear it."

"It's about the arrival in Uberaba of..."

"Some poets?"

"No."

"Of naturalists?"

"No. It refers to the arrival of zebu breeders. The newspaper covers the event in three columns and begins this way: "Once again Uberaba had the opportunity to confirm what the initiative of its sons is capable of, etc., etc.""

He continued reading, and at another point said to me:

"Note this sentence, 'explorers in a new crusade,' etc."

He continued reading and in a given moment, he called to my attention:

"Look at this piece: 'in spite of the early hour, large masses of people, approximated at 500, etc.' What a crowd, eh?"

He began reading again but soon he interrupted it to emphasize a certain passage:

"Notice that there was music; 'then (when the cows and bulls arrived) the Saint Cecilia band broke into a brilliant military march and continuous acclaims were heard?' Long live the cows," added Gonzaga de Sá.

He continued his reading and at a certain point said,

"Observe this piece: 'some handsome bulls arrived, one of which was outstanding in his beautiful posture and exceptional beauty....' "

He lowered the paper and considered:

"Imagine how many amorous cows awaited him in Uberaba."

The aunt chided him at that moment,

"What is this, Manuel? Finish dinner."

Dinner from thence onward went calmly, without interruption from the zebu stock. Taking advantage of the incident, Dona Escolastica began to tell me the peculiarities in her nephew's life. He didn't seem old, he kept no special hours, he had no method. He ate at all hours, he would get up late at night and go out; he would spend days away from home with this one and that one. He seems truly a gypsy, like those who have the attitude that God will provide.

"I still don't know how you live," she concluded, with that natural and unctuous air about her.

"Bah," he said.

"A few days ago he came here," continued Dona Escolastica to me, "at midnight ... And without having had dinner! I don't know where he goes.... He returns tired.... And that is not all: some nights he doesn't sleep a wink, reading, reading...."

I was surprised by the affectionate interest with which she followed her nephew's life.

She showed a daily devotion, minute by minute, from morning to night....

"You don't understand me, Escolastica, in spite of having raised me...."

"Yes, that's certain. Those strange ways ... those vagrancies of yours...."

And the dialogue continued in that manner, with a young freshness of pique as if between a brother and sister in their twenties.

"It's true that Manuel was always extravagant. One time (she began to tell me), my brother (his father) caught him in the attic window. Get down Manuel. Get down! What are you doing there? Do you know what his reply was?"

"I...."

"I want to fly, Daddy!"

"My brother scolded him harshly and Manuel cried all afternoon."

"That was my father," Gonzaga de Sá recalled. "Tall, meticulous, very serious and solemn. Did you know him?"

"No, nor could I have."

"That's right."

"Was he in Paraguay?"

"No, he wasn't able to go. After the war against Rosas in 1852, he took a teaching post as a college professor at the Central School." Gonzaga de Sá explained to me. "He was too weak by then, in 1865 when the war against López broke out."

"You had a brother who died in the campaign?"

"Yes, I had, Januário, the eldest."

"And the others?"

"All died without heirs. Only a sister, Maria da Glória, who still lives in Bahia, where her husband is a retired judge of the High Court, had sons, four I think; that must have given her grandchildren by now. I haven't seen her in thirty years, nor written to her in five."

"Is she the youngest?"

"No, I am. She is a year or so older than I am."

"And your mother, did she die young?"

"No. At a good age. I was eight years old. The one who raised me was Escolastica."

Upon saying these words there was a slight tremor in my friend's voice; meanwhile it was trivial whatever he recalled, and the dinner had progressed to the dessert during that conversation. Coffee was served in the living room, with the windows open and facing Niterói, which had begun to light up. The room still didn't have its lights on and there was a great peace outside. The houses on the hill began to turn on their lights and they all seemed to be contemplating us with kindness. The palm tree, standing firmly, was asleep. A cicada chirped in the garden and we were quickly absorbed. The cicada became silent, we smoked, Gonzaga and I, and looked out at the hill but could distinguish little.

"How is Romualdo?"

"How is he doing?" asked Dona Escolastica.

"Very poorly. And Aleixo Manuel at 8 years old, so alive, so exceptional ... Poor thing ... Without maternal tenderness; and now his father ... How his soul will always be full of angels...."

"Has he gone to school?" asked the aunt.

"He attends it. He is an extraordinary child, very much so; he already reads with speed and can do mathematics. Ah! If he becomes the genius we expect! Who can tell?!"

Gonzaga began to look about, questioning. The room was almost in complete darkness, and in the indefinite outline of his head, I only saw the wide-open stare that completely enveloped me, breathing prophecies of kindness. Dona Escolastica rose from her chair, looked a while at the window, then turned around and said, with emphasis on each word:

"It's dark, Manuel. Turn the lights on Manuel."

And the gas lamps were slowly lit. The old Érard piano, monstrous, huge, appeared in its entirety in the lighted room like a fantastic animal. No sooner did the lights blaze than the external peace broke. There were slight whispering sounds and things came back to life.

"You don't play, Dona Escolastica?"

I asked this only out of politeness, given that her old age must have already separated her from the old instrument.

"It's been almost 30 years."

"You became disenchanted with it?"

"After I heard Gottschalk, I couldn't sit at the piano. Only those who have never heard him!... It was so smooth, what a thing! I don't know what he had in his hands...."

And the old lady wanted to find words, expressions that would transmit the immense impressions that the pianist and his music had made upon her, and with her effort, her emerald eyes took on more brilliance, with a brief, youthful lightning spark through them.

"You never heard pieces by him?" Gonzaga de Sá asked me.

"One or another."

"They are worth listening to. They are very different from the European masters — dry, cerebral, without roots in our American sensibility. Gottschalk was fantastic, sorrowful, violent.... Here he provoked a general ecstasy."

"You liked it very much, didn't you, Manuel? I remember you went to all the concerts with your father. You would talk a lot about "The Dead Woman" or "The Poet.""

"Savana," "Bamboula," "Creole Eyes," concluded Gonzaga de Sá. "What enthusiasm it caused me. And we were at war with Paraguay ... didn't you go, Escolastica, to the monstrous concert?"

"No, but I went to the Stoltz benefit. There was never a benefit here like hers. Manuel was a child, he was eleven or twelve. I went. Today when I recall it, I seem to see the Provisorio Hall, beautiful and overflowing with ladies and young women. The aria "Oh! mio Fernando" from "Favorita" was followed by a burst of applause, flowers and toasts. The Duchess of Abrantes, sitting upon a pillow she had embroidered herself, sent her a crown of flowers. The hall became delirious, "Crown yourself! Crown yourself!" Flowers, shouts, flowers, shouts.... Stoltz hesitates and finally puts the crown on her head. What a lady! Even if she were a queen, she couldn't be more noble!"

And I thought about the ingenuousness of that society; and Dona Escolastica continued:

"It seemed like one pair of hands clapping — all in unison....""

"Months later, came the rebuke, the idle talk, the epigrams. Was it not so, Escolastica?" observed Gonzaga.

"It's true. Everything here is that way! Much festivity, and much festivity, then...."

"There were even some verses," continued Gonzaga, "that became famous. People said that Francisco Otaviano had written them:

"What does it matter that they say she is old, that she is ugly, that she dyes her hair, and makes up her large face."

Gonzaga de Sá had tears in his eyes and the aunt looked up at the ceiling, filled with happiness. I was surprised and said,

"How well you remember!"

"Why!... The city knew them by heart for ten years."

"Lyrics were always our weak point," I reflected.

"Imperialistic influence. The Provisório Concert House cost rivers of money. A hall was needed, a meeting place for the high society. We didn't have palaces, there was no worldly education.... High society lacked culture. Unless they had received a good education during their youth, the rich, the planters, the big business men, and even the politicians could only understand music and opera in the theater — a place where little is spoken. An elegant house was needed to refine them with the aid of art. Opera has this advantage — it is easy, understandable, popular, in spite of the tycoons wanting to make it transcendental. Whoever, during twenty, thirty years became removed from intellectual matters, can understand it without effort. The Emperor's idea, when forming an aristocracy, was to take advantage of that music to gather them, to oblige them to meet, to insure that they speak to each other and that they marry among themselves. But it all failed. A nobility wasn't created, and the Lyric Theatre degenerated in an idiotic manner — always with the same narrow-mindedness but always surrounding everyone. Find, for example, today in the Lyric Hall the great names of fifty two. Where are they? Where are their sons, their grand-sons? No one knows....

Dona Escolastica remained silent. Naturally, she didn't understand those infer-ences her nephew made at all. I was surprised, although Gonzaga de Sá had prepared me for everything. Around eight o'clock, I took leave and came down the hill slowly. I had penetrated the past, the live past, tradition. In the presence of those kind elders that had spoken to me of vivid events in their youth, I had an instant perception of the feelings and ideas of the generations that preceded me. Listening about that legen-dary Provisório Concert House, grotesque and formal, that they had evoked, I could see the ancestor's works and virtues and also their errors and crimes. I descended ... I had taken root once more. I was firmer against external pressures. I also felt that I had sipped a drop of poison. I caught a streetcar, I sat down on the first seat and began to go over my thoughts. I crossed Rua do Catete and the rococo Largo da Glória which was filled with people. I saw that the old Passeio was crowded. I had reviewed my thoughts. There is not a civilization exempt of crimes and errors, I concluded. I reached my station, and jumped off.

IX
THE GODFATHER

One afternoon, in the Café Papagaio, as I was looking out on Rua Gonçalves Dias, I saw several great foreign ladies passing by, up and down, from one side to the other, covered with jewels, with extravagant, high feathered hats like sails billowing in the wind propelling large schooners. Seeing them pass by on foot, by car, burdened with precious stones, gold and sweeping silks that drew the gazes of the judges, deputies, serious heads of family, honorable ladies and innocent girls, I recalled a remark Gonzaga once made: The loose woman is the center of life. I recalled that all those women had arrived empty-handed, with some second-hand dresses and many rattling suitcases, but they had come with their polar whiteness, with their crimson faces, with their strange blue eyes and with the prestige of their original race. They left Bordeaux or Havre "comme un vol de gerfauts," they arrived with strange features of marble consecrated by the centuries and their golden hair made the air, the houses and the souls of the city tremble. The docks also felt their walk and softened at their feet, and granite mica tried to assume the sparkle of diamonds. From there they went, transforming everything along the streets. The ancient vice-regal palace polished itself: it wanted to be dignified, dandified. It began to shine up the niches in forgotten dark alcoves in order to uncover any riches. The statue's bronze in the sunlight resembled gold and the ladies stopped to admire the fascinating shine. On the Rua Primeiro de Março, the stalls of the money-changers almost burst at the fragrance of the foreign perfumes of the recent arrivals and opened lavishly, giving them coins and money in large amounts. They continue.... It's the Rua do Ouvidor, then it is vertigo, all the souls and bodies are swept away and jolted by the vortex. There is a powerful energy in them all and in what they wear. There is an attraction, a fascination that makes one forget who he is, a shutting out of one's personality in the brilliance of their eyes. It is magical and supernatural. Patiently acquired savings are drained, inheritances that caused so much pain disappear, estates and bank deposits are drained away. Minds work, imaginations work up plans for larceny, embezzlement and thievery ... And everything ends up with them; it is for them that ancient riches go into faraway lands, plump cattle, thriving plantations. Salaries and subsidies go to them — and also the fruits of burglaries and the casino profits. An entire population, an entire country converges upon those beings in fleshy bodies. And they continue prancing grandiosely, protuberantly, like ancient vessels tugged by the great high feathered hats imitating sails blowing in the wind. They come two by two or in fours like fleets, those fleets of the past, armadas of ships, of caravels, of galleons that come to America looking for silver in Potosi and gold from Brazil's heart. Civilization is formed by such varied and obscure means that it seems to me they, like the venerable galleons they bring to mind, brought to the Brazilian shores the great conquests of European activity, the result and slow evolvement of the millennia. I then recalled one of Gonzaga de Sá's sayings. He said to me once in the Colombo Tea Room:

"Do you see those women?"

"I do," I answered.

"They are troubling themselves in order to refine us."

In fact, they brought us fashions, the latest bits from the "boulevard," the walk "dernier cri," the high point of fashion — fleeting things to be sure, but no one can calculate the reaction upon the nation's minds. Their mission was to refine our society, remove the coarseness that had remained in the people, given the dullness and the swindling of the slaves who formed us. It was to bring to the intellects the idea of correct features, in spite of it all, the regular and classical features of that Greek formula they dreamed of. How many of them inspired beautiful verses and how many lived in periods surrounded by them! That is not all! The husbands that followed their teachings, took to their homes upon the advice of these foreigners the most modern plays, the latest "Bibelot," the latest furniture, cloth, hat and lace. In this manner, they would spread commerce and stimulate the contact between our land and the large world centers, thereby perfecting good taste and luxury. They would return with gold, at least those lucky enough to get through customs: but they would spread throughout Brazil a malicious aspect — hard to believe — but they would spread it.... And civilization is formed by such different ways, varied and obscure, that I seem to see in those French, Hungarian, Spanish, Italian and Polish protuberant women, so large with their pompous hats like sails billowing in the wind, continuing in some way the conquistador's mission. As usual, I would meet some of our friends in that café. As they began to arrive, I'd slowly remove myself from these thoughts to listen to pleasant matters they wished to discuss. We came to the café to talk. The conversations varied and rarely stayed on the same theme. There were times when we would begin by commenting on the latest scuffle in the Casino and end up examining the advantages of a large social reform. We were all reformers. We intended to reform literature and morals by degrees, starting with women's fashions and high button shoes. On that day, in the first table by the door, little by little, four of us met: Amorim, Domingos, Rangel and I, the "Splendor of Clerks" was almost complete, for that was what we called our meetings, in view of the occupation of the majority — clerks that had their greatest hours of satisfaction and jocund pleasure there, around that table, a disorder washed down with coffee between the discontent at the office and the unpleasantness of problems at home. Rangel, a future water-colorist but presently a talented painter for worn out labels in commerce, arrived last. There was still running in the Tragedia Playhouse a Japanese theater piece he had created, long drawn out, with hundreds of acts that always ended up in Rua da Carioca, in Zé's Steak House. Zé was an excellent host and hotel owner, gentle and good that gave out lunches for six hundred reis, something hard to find in Rio. Pedreira passed by with his familiar coat of fluttering flaps and a long chicken-like neck, a mixture of a clipper in the wind and a rooster that eats corn grain by grain. Rangel wanted to leave, but with insistence, remained listening to our high-ranging conversation.

"There goes Lord Max...."

"Do you know where he gets his English mannerisms?" asked Amorim.

"No," someone said.

"He was a translator for his students in Cruz Alta. He graduated with a list of meanings written on his cuffs."

"I don't know," said Rangel, "umph."

"A superman!" added the jealous Domingos.

"Who the devil are you calling superman?" said Rangel.

"A citizen who is beyond Good and Evil — it is simple."

Rangel was satisfied with the explanation and listened to Domingos who spoke, moving his aging figure of an ancient Roman, the outline of a displeased Seneca, who might not have been a prince's instructor. He said:

"The way I look at it, in this business of love, the preliminaries are important, the preliminary states of the soul, the agony of acquiring or not the loved object. But when it is touched...."

"The soap bubble bursts," concluded Amorim.

We couldn't go beyond the development of that old theme any longer that somehow had come up in our conversation. Unexpectedly, my dear friend Gonzaga de Sá entered the café. The arrival of the old official at our noisy table surprised me. He didn't have that false hatred of cafés usually found in all cold and infallible know-it-alls. From a conversation I had had with him I concluded that he felt them a necessity to the enlightenment of unresolved issues, the exchange of ideas, the sharing of minds, in brief, molders of a society for those who haven't one at their level, be it because of origin, luck or for those who don't feel comfortable in any. His tolerant and reflective age understood why I would go there, but the old man's misanthropy didn't allow him to take part in the noise. Gonzaga de Sá wore black, as usual, but instead of a jacket, he wore a frock coat. It was the first time I saw him in that outfit, so much in vogue with doctors and political leaders. In that fashion, my unpretentious friend seemed to have the respectability of a minister. His large eyes, soft and slow in a normal, softly curved socket, were red. The rest of his aspect was calm and his movements did not indicate any change of feelings. When the venerable old man appeared, my friends quieted down — his figure had impressed them. I got up and spoke to him apart. He said to me:

"My compadre has just died ... I came to make funeral arrangements. I need you as a pallbearer ... Come, Machado. Come, Machado. I expect this service out of compassion...."

I went, as required by my friendship and admiration for the old gentleman. And side by side we went down the street. My friend was quiet and every once in a while sighed out of weariness.... I already could see the corpse in the stark stupidity of the matter. Nevertheless, a question no one has been able to answer with certainty arose — after "this," what will we be?

I saw him step out of the house; on the casket, the funeral wreaths, the carriage, the sincere sobs, the pity, the condolences of the funeral parlor officials; then the grave and mysterious task of decomposition. And it seemed to me that his voice —

the sweet things it expressed and even the bad — the notions, the ideas, the feelings that mind had acquired in life, all had grouped together in an imperceptible existence to hide from that decomposing mass.... And the women passed by, young and old, ugly and pretty of all colors brushed past me. Never had I seen such shine on their faces, never that strange glow, with that fascination, that force of absorption.... The light was sweeter, the façades more beautiful, the pavement wasn't harsh ... and I was going to see a dead man.

We took the street car at Largo de São Francisco. The vehicle was full. I rode comfortable, suffering that human contact, trying to absorb as much of the vital heat as I possibly could from my fellow men. I was not alone in the world and all those people had to die, like me....

The train was full, too. In the row next to me, vis-à-vis, four fellows sat down. Among them was a fat man, bald like a wise man, with a commercial and a financial belly. He was the most talkative. He didn't tire of chatting, criticizing, condemning politics and the government, its expenditures, the congressmen's idleness and that of public officials, and the judges' dishonesty, turning to his companion in the front, just when the train began to move:

"Give me your 'A Noticia.' "

The other man, certain to provoke him replied:

"Would you like to give me two hundred reis for it?"

The passenger by the side of the wise politician therefore took the same newspaper out of his pocket and handed it to him.

"Thank you," acknowledged the man with the politician's belly and the wise man's baldness. "I don't need yours any longer," he told the man who asked for the two hundred reis. "Next time I ride with you, I'll take the precaution of bringing extra change with me ... I don't trust newspaper vendors...."

And unexpectedly, without the slightest motivation, all four broke out in agreeable laughter.

People who laugh easily, I thought. Well, laughter bursts in accordance with one's intelligence. The "suburban" was in motion now. I stopped observing the four strange persons. I turned my eyes and began to watch the scenery through the train window, the blue high walls, the bright green fields, the dark green of the hillside, the flashes of light, the rays of contentment in the air, the melancholy pines.... One day I would see that all this would hide from my eyes. Why am I not like that pot-bellied man, unconsciously animal-like, giving no thought to the end, to restrictions and limitations? Far from education being a comfort, it only makes things worse; it creates desires that upset me, causing rancor and even resentment! Why did they educate me, so that I wouldn't have any love in life, relatives, and perhaps friends? Ah! If I only could erase it from my mind! I'd sweep away one by one the ideas, the theories, the sentences, the laws they made me assimilate. I'd remain without the damned temptation of analogy, without the poison of analysis. Then I would fill myself with respect for everything and everyone, only knowing that somehow I would live ... But ... It was impossible, impossible! It was too late and the cause of my suffering was not my upbringing or education. It was me, myself — it was my nature, it was my pride aligned with a stupid fear. I regretted having condemned it and reconciled myself. I would cure myself. Gonzaga de Sá didn't speak to me but I felt as if half of those thoughts were his. Our friendship was so perfect, it had no need for words. Between us there existed a perfection of communication that Wells had applauded in Martians. No sooner had a thought been emitted from one of our brains than it went to the other, without any intermediaries, though telepathy. After the Rocha station where those obtuse neighbors departed and a young pair of lovers sat in the side seat, our front neighbors began to talk. At first I couldn't hear what they were saying very clearly, but afterwards I understood that they were discussing the lengthy theory of the races. One with a large, symbolic ring on his finger said:

"His mental and intellectual capacity is limited. Science has already proven that."

And the other, younger, listened religiously to such a transcendental man. The train's rusty metal workings made a deafening noise — I heard no more. We reached Engenho Novo. The train stopped. The younger one then asked, looking at the electrical transmission wires:

"Why is it that the birds touch the wires and aren't electrocuted?"

"That's because in the daytime the communications are shut." And if it weren't for the serious thoughts that absorbed me at that time, I would have laughed at that wise man of limited intellectual capacity.

At the side, the lovers continued babbling. There was a soothing quality, a happiness, a certain sweetness in their eyes that irritated my amorous abilities:

"Have you ever courted?" Gonzaga de Sá asked me in a low voice.

"Once, when I was sixteen...."

"You should go courting, son. When you become old you will regret it, if you don't do it in time. Venus is a vengeful goddess, they say."

"What! Courtship is the negation of love. I shall not regret it...."

"I will guarantee it. It would be an emotion you never tried ... experiment now, while there is time?"

And the train continued. At our station we stepped down, having exchanged with my travel companion those few words.

We climbed the street slowly, among strange examples of some fathers of families. Serious men of sad features, bent with life's weight, carrying large bundles of bread under their arms, they passed alongside us with the slow, economical, sparing pace of oxen carts. Life's road was hard: sandy here, muddy there; and further up steep and rocky.... Only their patience, only that muscular robustness that became worn out drop by drop, only that could carry the cart forward with the wives and children. With the newspaper under their arm, they would go over large combinations of small coins with the same nervous energy that any banker would use to devise a wealthy client's unjust exploitation of the funds of two or three. Unconsciously, they'd line up as I went along, observing in both directions, living examples of the theories of our curious humanity. When I was young, in the suburbs of Rio, I had seen a sight that my imagination compared to this. It was around that golden hour in the afternoon, a little earlier, but the mountains already appeared to thin out with the ethereal caress of a rarified sky. A long line of oxen carts, full of vegetables, coal and wood paraded through the street. The drivers would yell from time to time. The oxen chewed their feed; at times they flicked out their tongues, leaning upon each other, perhaps trying to divide better their effort in traction.... Oh! The solidarity of the cargo!

Slowly they overcame the obstacles and arrived at the port, to the cheerful shores of the island.... Those animals did not know their own strength. They didn't even suspect that an entire city awaited those necessary or tasteful things that only their patience and strength could drag over those unstable paths. The road came to my mind: sandy, of sliding and movable soil, but keeping indelibly the parallel tracks of the carts with choke-cherry trees on the side, sprinkled with red fruit and every once in a while, a more massive tree, a cashew or a fig tree — all of this, when the carts passed, were covered in dust upon which the setting sun cast a red hue, giving the appearance of gold. Those men, patient and slow, whom I saw in that village setting were the pillar, the base, the enormous foundation stone of society.... Workers and petty bourgeois constitute the web of our social life, an endless web, sacred deposit, fountain from whence come and will come great examples of the Fatherland, and also the corrupt to excite and ferment life in our group and not let it weaken. Perhaps they didn't know about this and if they knew, they wouldn't be consoled for their difficult burden in life. They lived on the remorse of obligation and with a vague conciliatory hope in the eternal love of their children.

"It is there," Gonzaga de Sá said to me, pointing to a clutter of houses.

We took a side street and continued on it almost alone. I still hadn't seen the house, although Gonzaga had pointed it out. The system of streets in the suburbs is delirious. A street begins wide, long and straight, we follow its path, satisfied, imagining the great palaces that will border it in several years; suddenly it strangles itself — it branches, subdivides in a shamble of crossroads that become lost in many others that multiply and develop the most overturned appearance. There is the meadow, the reflections of orchards, some garden patches, the small shed, recalling that primitive aspect of the area; there is the old master home in the plantation with unorthodox columns; there are the new bourgeois buildings with gesso ornaments, chalky and gaudy, a balcony to the side surrounded by an iron grating. All this is shuffled, confused and mixed, and it continues as the populace spreads out from the railroad tracks. The times become mixed. The years are not marked by the more lasting and perceptive things. After an old country home followed by tottering cottages, from the horse and buggy days, we walk one hundred, two hundred meters and we find a Botafogo-style palace. The chalet, therefore, is the architectural expression of the suburb. Some landowners, saving the terrace railing and valances, don't forget to give the building's roof the characteristic shape and to tie the two ends of the summit with threatening arrows. On foggy days, when it is cold, if we look upon a fragment from up high, it is as if we were in Switzerland or Holland....

Finally we hit upon Gonzaga de Sá's compadre's house. It was a chalet. From a distance, it looked like a middle class home; when we approached, I saw it separated into two residences, both having a small garden plot in the front with sad croton plants. From the road, I immediately saw the coffin, the confused mass of the body in

it and the false glow of candles at the feet and head. At the door, curious neighbors ...
The children played innocently in the street. We entered. An old colored lady came
to receive us. Gonzaga de Sá had spoken to me about her. Dona Gabriela was distantly related to her compadre's wife — she was a widow and mother of four
children.

"Everything is arranged; tomorrow at nine o'clock the funeral begins."

"The coffin just arrived. We tried to put the body in it immediately."

"You did well," said Gonzaga de Sá. "Where is Frederico, your son?"

"He went to buy some bread."

"When he returns, tell him that I want to speak to him."

"Yes, sir."

I went to the sitting room. There weren't many people. But what a variety of types
and colors — almost every type in the human spectrum was there.... The audience
was very serious; if they spoke at all, it was low, and if a smile bloomed on their lips, it
was quickly suppressed. I also sat down in a chair. And finally I could look upon the
body, the pharaoh-like color of his face, half hidden by the satin placed near his head
and by the petals of the flowers spread around him. I barely knew that man. I had met
him occasionally at work, in the Department of Religious Affairs where he was
employed. I knew him as Gonzaga de Sá's compadre and that his name was
Romualdo de Araujo. The friendship between those two men, so different in station
in life and education, was strong and deep. Although they may never have reached
complete intimacy, they loved each other in a special way, distantly, it is true, but in a
way which permitted the eternal duration of affection. Dona Gabriela, tall, silent,
with mysterious brown skin came and went, trimmed the candle wicks, straightened
a bouquet, everything very calmly, without vacillation, without fear, very familiar
with the act. Her son arrived with the bread. He was a magnificent example of a
mulatto, of a robust mulatto, confident in look and figure but light, vivacious and
flexible, without showing any heaviness or slowness in his manner. Gonzaga de Sá
suggested something to him and in a few seconds we went to eat. Night descended
and more people arrived.

I saw the night fall from the dining room, admiring the twilight from a window. I
remained during its entirety, looking at the faraway mountains to the east, the band
of golden clouds and while it lasted, I was silent, smoking, and all my mental activity
pivoted around death. Complete night fell. I had thought much, it is true, but without having reached any conclusion. Nothing remained perceptible in my mind,
everything was fleeting and escaped me as if there were a hole in my head. Everything evaporated and I only knew how to say: "Death! Death!" That is all that remained from this lengthy meditation.... Every once in a while Gonzaga de Sá came
to the dining room. He spoke very little; he would return to the corpse. Nothing in
his appearance revealed the minimum of pain and his gentle and slow eyes already
had their normal glow. I stood up and went to the back yard. Unlike my usual self, I
gazed at the star-lit sky that had its normal beauty. When I turned back to the window, a girl was sitting there. I had not seen her enter.

"Do you want your seat?" she asked upon seeing me.

"Please, sit where you wish, young lady. There are many chairs here."

I sat down immediately and like an old acquaintance; I began to talk and she responded like an old acquaintance.

"It is cooler this evening, don't you think so?"

"It is true, but it is still very warm in the parlor," she said.

"Is it true that it is very warm here? You would know, you live here, do you not?"

"A few years — two, I believe."

"Do you like it?"

"A little, but I miss the city. I lived there many years. It is something else. What activity! Cars, gardens to walk through...."

"But what is it all worth? Death comes...."

"Of course, but while one lives he should look for beauty, the theaters.... Did you ever go to the harbour entrance?"

"Never!"

"It must be pretty!"

"I don't like Botagogo. It is Buenos Aires, super civilized."

"I like it very much. Oh that I had a house there!"

"And a husband, too? Isn't it so, Miss...."

"Alcmena, at your service. I would like it, but I guarantee you that a car would be worth more...."

"But if all those things will end...."

"When?"

"When some generous men have made all of humanity work in the same way and earn the same thing...."

"Those men are evil!"

"They are good, to the contrary. Since they can't give everything to everybody, they take many things from some."

"What for!... Rather let those continue to exist with their riches because we at least have hope...."

"You must have riches, anyway, with those beautiful eyes...."

"Bah!..." She said, pushing her bust against the back of the chair until she could see the sky through the window that was within her sight.

I rested my gaze on her distant eyes and followed them to a star that shown very near our heads. In that quick position, the girl strongly attracted me. Her breasts seemed swollen; her neck, long and firm, stood out from the bodice; and the small parts drew a relief between the folds of her dress. That vivacity so far from the Rua do Ouvidor — was it comprehensible? I even saw her soft complexion, her brown hair, long and pretty hands, slightly spoiled by household chores. Then dark thoughts came to me. Vague and indefinite desires rose in turmoil, recklessly. They spouted, they rose and fell inside of me, they met, others formed, demanding satisfaction, caresses, nervous and delicious states....

We conversed for a long time, having forgotten the deceased, drunken with each other as if we were at a dance.

"Life is cruel," I told her upon a certain occasion, "everything ends in death."

"It's true. But there are certain times in life that perhaps even death does not extinguish."

"What instance of that nature do you suppose Romualdo had?"

"He is the one who knows.... Each person knows when he is happy and can't tell anyone, even if he wanted to.... It stays alive in us and only its memory can bring that happiness again.... Were you his friend?"

"I hardly knew him."

"We were neighbors for two years.... I became accustomed to seeing him always, to admire his son, and I feel ... When one is happy, he has the desire to dance, to sing — doesn't he? It seems that we have too many extra things inside us — springs, a mechanism that pushes us.... When I am sad, I also have the same urge.... It is strange!..."

"In the past, there were funeral dances, and the savages still dance them upon those occasions."

"They are right. We really don't want to, but something inside us pushes us on."

Dona Alcmena slowly raised an arm and caught with her long, open fingers, as in a scoop, some loose hairs that were falling on her forehead. We still continued to talk for some time, and I, drunk with the inebriating girl, fascinated by her strangeness, forgot very innocently that I was an enemy of courtship.

Alcmena stood up and held my hand detainedly, in order to depart.

For a few moments I remained alone, but filled with her. Her mass filled me and her words, which I don't know from whence they came, danced in my ears.

The impression soon began to disappear and the memory of the corpse returned. When I began to think strongly about it, the girl's figure returned to my eyes stronger, tall and fine, and her black eyes and the transcendent curves of her body.

After having associated these images once again, it seemed to me to be a profanity, a sacrilege, I regretted my actions. But be it a spring, a mechanism, as the girl said! How could I be blamed? Even the sweet words, the gallantries that came to me, to me so awkward with ladies! It was automatic.... How could I be blamed?

Furthermore, I also felt that it was the corpse that forced me, that pushed me towards the girl. It was his muteness, finally, that dictated the only act in my life capable of escaping the law that it bent to. Alive, to have lived, for it is strong in us to have lived, because only within ourselves do we find the reason and purpose of life, knowing that we must continue it at any price, cost what it may, in our own selves and those of our descendants.

I had yet another point of remorse, in spite of it all, because something told me I had gone too far....

Gonzaga de Sá entered, and sat on the chair the girl had occupied. He leaned back and said, looking at the sky:

"How beautiful the sky is! Eh? For it, pain doesn't exist. Those that live appreciate its beauty. Those that die leave the task of appreciating it to others...."

He became silent and then added abruptly:

"That continuity is in everything. The leaves that fall fertilize the roots of the trees from which they grew to help others grow, new and beautiful."

The observation was not new, but it surprised me, thinking that he might have heard my conversation with the girl. And he added:

"You have been in the parlor very little."

"It is very hot."

"You should go, not only because it is fitting to see death at your age but it is a chance to see how ethnologists are false and evil."

He drew a long puff on his cigarette and continued.

"Lately they said that the habits of feeling were very different in each human race, a fact that was sufficient to make these feelings incomprehensible among different peoples.... There is, in fact, more than one way of feeling, an expression proper to each race, etc., etc. Well in view of our people, so varied, I've noticed that there is nothing that can separate them deeply. And we would understand each other and fulfill our destinies if it weren't for the disturbances affected by our diplomats, bent by American opinion, wanting to spread plots and exorcisms." He continued:

"You well know how difficult it is to say where reality begins and where it ends. Man is a conceptualizing animal who is capable of making from small facts in the world a mental picture, an image, extend it, unfold it and convince others that all of it exists outside of us. Do you know the situation? Well, in Europe, universities, either through bad faith or simple ignorance (I won't say which), have decided to formulate theories on race and the human species. But the matter goes even further. The people with interest in it or affected by it go unheard, with the excuse being that they have no enduring culture, for if they had one, their station in life would be different. What happens? Assumptions are made and accepted and end up turned around. To make themselves look good, wise diplomats accept them, write newspaper articles about them, always offering the most assinine statements possible. If in the seventeenth century, religious differences separated men, it is now and in the future the scientist who will be responsible for that job.... Oh, beneficent science.... But, this is not the time to make speeches. Instead, let's pay respect to my unfortunate and humble friend...."

There were about thirty people in the parlor, more than half women. Above an old bureau, a lamp gave poor lighting; the lilies mesmerized with their smell. Gonzaga de Sá crossed the room and sat down near his compadre's mother-in-law, who was crying. She was a jet-black woman, with soft and velvety skin. I remained standing near the entrance door. There was complete silence occasionally broken with a sob from the poor woman. Her gratitude toward the dead man must have been great. He had probably given her the most pleasant satisfaction of her humble life. He married her daughter, and supported her weak female ways with his prestige of manhood; he had taken her away from the environment that closes in black girls, he had dignified her — she, whom almost all social circles, except her own peers, relegated to a future of prostitution or of being a mistress. On the other side of the room was the grandson. A noble forehead hardly yet formed by age, the arched and joined brows, his penetrating look — all of the child's aspect had an intelligent expression of curiosity and energy that his gentle nature would probably tame down. What would happen to him in life? Through the influence of his godfather, he would probably get to study a great deal and would apply himself to his books. Even after years in the false environment of elementary and secondary schools, his life won't seem what it really should be. Years will go by, along with the expectations that come from studying; he'll pass through society with its ideas and prejudices, some sound and others unfounded, good and bad — a trauma lasting and painful with which his soul will struggle. Then there would be pain, misdeeds, the crazy flights of fantasy.... It would be painful to wander as a pilgrim with one's shame for all to see, subject to the derision of the street-car conductor and the government minister.... It would always be with him, in cafés, in the streets, in the theatres, with a forerunner twenty meters ahead announcing his presence, giving everyone a chance to prepare their wisecracks, their gaping or idiotic stares ... Poor lad! Even studying wouldn't be enough; books and bravery would be just as useless; because whenever people would see him, they would say that he was incapable of knowing anything.

I felt a deep pain for him, one that sympathized greatly with that soul orphaned so many times; I was sad that such an intellect would never get to develop freely, following a course he himself would plan.... I looked at him like this for awhile, moved with pain, with sympathy and sadness. Suddenly, he began to cry a great deal, with heavy emotion, and for no apparent reason, he got up and ran as if he were being chased by someone toward where his godfather was standing. His dash and his crying happened all at once. Gonzaga de Sá picked him up, placed him on his lap and kissed him; trying to cheer him up, he said:

"What's the matter, my son? What is it, Aleixo?"

A candle flickered, and on the face of the corpse, I thought I caught a glimpse of suffering pass.

X
THE INTERMENT

On the following day, standing before the closed coffin, I felt penetrated by an icy indifference. Every now and then a twinge of annoyance passed inside me. It was a beautiful Sunday, gloriously bright and the air was exceedingly clear. Seductive, smiling widely, the day invited everyone to enjoy themselves by taking a delightful stroll....

The parlor's silence, those dimming candles, the constrained and the bewildered faces of those present seemed lacking all logic before the sunlight and cheerful morning.

I was annoyed and began smoking. Finally, it was time for the funeral. The crowd grew at the door. Some ladies cried. Gonzaga de Sá came and went, making the last minute arrangements. The coffin was shut. There was a little sound — dry and ordinary, exactly like that made by any coffin closing.... And that was it!

We took the coffin along the rocky street, staggering, taking turns, troubled and saddened below a clear and victorious March sun. Out on the walk (it was morning) the pedestrians mechanically came out, looked at the wreaths, and the entourage, surveying them well to see whose funeral it was or whose it wasn't. Girls coming from mass and others strolling happily along in an elegant manner, exuberant with life, would contemplate the cortege for awhile with a quick look of pity and then continue walking uninterrupted for a moment, indifferent, carefree, chattering, almost laughing heartily.... And the coffin continued to weigh us down until we rested it on the benches of the station. Soon a train took us and the deceased along the rails, quickly crossing through the suburban stops. The funeral car was first and when we came to a curve, I could catch sight of some feathers in women's hats through the open windows in the first class cars.... Inside, it was unbearably hot and the benches were torturous. Finally, we arrived at the Central Station. Eight of us had come, but only four would go to the cemetery. Gonzaga de Sá had not said anything until now. He had bent his body over, and his forehead was wrinkled during the entire trip as if it was holding back some fleeting thoughts. We placed the casket in the coach and took our places in the old rented car. Before departing, my friend looked at the square, the air, the houses, and the park in front of him, and when he sat on the car seat, said:

"What a beautiful day! Rather cheerful, don't you think? It doesn't even seem as if we're bearing a dead man to his grave.... It's because he didn't enjoy life. Better that way!... Dying, he in no way disturbed the life of things for others; meanwhile, as they say, society is a nice association of individuals and little separates man from the world."

Followed by two accompanying coaches, the hearse moved over the paving stones, in the direction of the Caju cemetery. We reclined in back of the coach, and I began to look into the distance, imagining, trying to see through and behind things to find a sign, a point, an indication of sorrow or displeasure of that death that must have hurt some consciences. We now turned down Rua de São Cristovão; we crossed it along with the street cars, and passing one, the master reflected aloud;

"Have you noticed, when there is no indifference, the passing of a bier provokes displeasure?"

He was silent for awhile and then continued,

"I think that if we had the courage of our convictions, we would order the construction of a special path to the cemetery, perhaps underground. Only in that manner would we avoid that constant spectacle that upsets us."

"I hadn't noticed," I replied.

I felt a tremendous mental exhaustion overcoming me. I hardly had slept the previous night and all the emotions had left me drained, with a numb body and cerebral lassitude. I answered my friend's words without any mental activity that would provoke other thoughts in my mind. There was so much perceptual resistance that the surrounding sights seemed to be moving in a different direction from my sensibility. I responded to him automatically, from mere habit of courtesy.

"Death has been useful, and will always be," continued Gonzaga de Sá. "It is not wisdom alone that reflects it, but all of civilization has resulted from death."

He stopped talking for a moment, and in rhythm with the movement of the coach, he began to look out the sides. With him, followed the decorations on the cymatiums, the grates on the balconies; up in front he would stare at a group of girls dressed up for a walk, standing in front of a bourgeois house. The car moved away and his soft and gentle glance fell upon the streetcars that passed by and the pedestrians on the street. From there it slid across to where a woman in rags slept outdoors, immobile, curled up like a forgotten bundle, and finally he rested his eyes upon the funeral coach that moved in front of us.

"Let's search out the causes," he spoke, after completing his long visual walk. "Let's search out the causes of civilization so that we can worship them like gods.... How amusing! It's as if civilization had been good and had given us happiness!"

And he didn't say anything else to me until we arrived at the cemetery gate, when he said he was going to take care of the indispensable administrative tasks to finalize the funeral. We followed the coffin through the funeral path where the workers professionally guided us. Soon Gonzaga de Sá came to join us. By now it was noontime. The sun continued bright and the skies were even clearer. The palm tree profiles stood out firmer and the cypresses would not awaken to the strong sun of that day. Soon we arrived at the edge of the deep grave ... the coffin descended quickly to the sepulcher. The chains clanked, annoyed by that task that they had repeated for so many years. I tossed in my shovel of lime, without the slightest commotion, awkwardly. Until then, I had not felt anything special; I hadn't had any thoughts or pious emotions. I had watched the ceremony without sadness, without regard to its significance nor to the great compassionate sentiments it required. Quick thoughts, far uplifted from the depression I had when I entered, passed through my mind, remotely associated with the present situation. I was reminded of my infancy, the peculiarities of the school I attended, the teachers, my classmates, the secondary school where I did my time, the painful alternatives in my life.... And thus, remembering things out of place here, I accompanied Gonzaga de Sá slowly to the cemetery gate. He walked quietly, head lowered, with his vast cranium bare to the sun. He was distracted and had forgotten to put on his hat. I didn't want to disturb his solitude by reminding him. Naturally engulfed in the sorrow of losing that obscure friend, towards whose life happy in a mediocre way Gonzaga had so generously contributed much, he looked at the top of his feet with a rigid posture and humid eyes. That friendship must have consoled him, in his own way, from the abandonment and solitude of old age without friendships. Was Gonzaga de Sá a passionate man who never was able to direct his nature towards a single object, who would remain aside, keeping his feelings to himself as much because of shyness as because of pride? Was it that, as the years advanced, now because of fatigue or now because of the demands of his nature, he had to direct his heart's sentiments here or there, to this or that object, until they arrived at the insignificance and modesty of some office boy. In such a manner, he would find in that affection a diversion of his great suffering, born when, old age brought about consciousness of his sentimental sterility? Who knows?

With his introspective nature, constantly analyzing himself, knowing well the sources of his pains and searching them out, as has already been observed, he'd be more able to understand others, to justify them at the same time, and therefore, be completely capable of sympathizing with those who suffer. I had wanted to guess that about him for a long time and was not surprised when he said to me at the cemetery gate:

"Poor Romualdo! What was it worth living if he remained in the midst of the society from which he came? Besides the inherent evils in life, to suffer this one as well, which unfolds in millions? But after all, he had no idea of this, which is important because without it, there is no suffering! All this was confusing to him and his suffering could only be created by others. I am the one who makes him suffer. He, in fact, did not suffer.... I must try to erase this from my mind...."

We slowly walked down the beach, following the cemetery wall, ambling slowly, since we had left the coach that had brought us, intending to go by streetcar. It was more comfortable; it didn't bounce on the pavement. The sea was calm at that hour, and if one were to see it from above, it would appear wrinkled. The latitudes seemed crystalline and the sun fell in streams upon the bay's surface. A gentle breeze was beginning to blow. In the distance, towards the front, the mountains rose vividly from the canvas on which they seemed painted. An islet, with its high smokestack, did not obliterate the large visual panorama that the sea offered. I swept my gaze through it, sliding over the extremely smooth surface. I caught it kissing the polar ice flows, caressing Europe's shores, visiting Africa's coasts to receive its great rivers. I saw religious India, enigmatic Egypt. I saw hieratic China, the new lands of Oceania and I embraced all of Europe in one thought, with its grandiose and afflicted civilization, fascinating, in spite of judging it hostile. And, after such a long trip, my soul returned to me, verifying that here, as in those places, it was sometimes more and sometimes less. And I began to think that on the free convexity of the planet that created me, there was not one place, not one niche or island where I could live completely, freely. I looked upon the sea again. There was seaweed floating on it, balancing on the waves, from one side to the other, indifferent, at the mercy of the whimsical movements of the abyss. How happy it must be!

Gonzaga de Sá interrupted my roaming thoughts.

"What is the reason for living? Why do you live? You live from your anxieties, your pains, the sparks of happiness that at times burst among them; but this poor devil, whose stock of notions and concepts was too limited to fabricate pains, and therefore, to obtain happiness, why did he live? Do you know?"

"It was apathy."

Soon we took the streetcar and traveled in silence. The vehicle filled with the curious Sunday public. Gonzaga de Sá remained silent and from time to time, looked out on the street; then he rested his hands on his cane and lowered his head to look at the pavement between the gratings on the vehicle. When we got off, I began to say good-bye. He did not allow me.

"I'll have dinner in the city.... Stay!... Let's walk through the streets. For example: let's go to the Passeio Público."

"Let's do that!"

He loved the old garden where we soon sat on a stone bench, in a quiet place, listening to the distant sound of the Sunday band. The calm of the place began to penetrate us. The uneasiness I had felt earlier in the morning was gone, and my companion also seemed more composed, with a quiet look. He was calm although sad. He tipped his hat back, and with the end of his cane began to trace in the sand a large figure ... It seemed to be the outline of a face.... On the other side, by the strip of trees that ran in front of the pub, we saw a multicolored crowd moving with that impulsive energy accumulated during the week; and there, separated from it, silent and apathetic to the forces that moved them, we sat as if outside humanity, like entities of another structure, having nothing in common with them. The large stretch of grass that divided the two rows of trees, with its fountain in the center, marked the boundaries between the two currents, theirs and ours. We looked at them as the passenger looks at the fish from the deck of the ship, across the silver waters. I delayed, watching a couple that embraced in the distance, when Gonzaga de Sá asked me:

"Do you know why the controller on the streetcar inspects the conductor?"

It seemed like a silly question to me, unless it contained an insignificant ridicule. Without trying to answer such an imbecilic question, I said:

"It's difficult to say ... I can't imagine why."

For an instant, he remained silent, contemplating the crowd in front.

I followed his movements. He no longer was tracing figures in the sand and he had rested his cane negligently against his leg. He forced his vision to encompass the greatest possible view of the horizon and without tiring himself, came and went with his eyes from one extreme to the other. He seemed to be a lost navigator searching for faint indications of a coastline.

"I think," he said, after being in that position for a while, "that those unfortunates should be killed in a group at once. Schopenhauer, who proposed the suicide of humanity, went far — it should be only the unfortunate. The content ones should keep their happiness.''

''Propose it, and see if they accept it.''

''Surely not. Their obstinacy is firm, and keeps them alive in spite of everything. I don't understand,'' he added after a pause, ''that a man — an animal gifted with a critical sense, capable of making analogies — can get up at four o'clock in the morning to come to work in the Marine Armory, while the minister sleeps until eleven and on top of that arrives by carriage or car. I don't understand,'' he continued, ''why there exist people who resign themselves to live in that fashion and organize families inside a society whose leaders don't allow those humble homes the same basic rights of those who maintain luxurious homes in Botafogo or Tijuca. I remember one time, for instance, when I entered a magistrate's court and attended a wedding of two poor people ... I think they even were colored.... In view of all the State's theories, it was a just and commendable thing; well anyway, judges, scribes, lawyers without degrees mocked and sneered at that poor couple who believed in what governmental decrees said. I don't know why those people live, or rather, why they insist on living! The best would be to kill themselves, since at least the principal chemicals of their bodies, soon by the tons, would go to fertilize the poor lands. Wouldn't it be better?

''In Europe, the peasants suffer....''

''Oh! There it is another thing! There is a literature, a philosophy, that binds great ideas, that spreads a healthy spirit throughout individual men — a source of sympathy for the weak, worried and anguished over human destinies. Here, what is there?''

''Something.''

''Nothing. Our literary emotions are interested only in the folks from the backlands, only because they are picturesque and perhaps there is no way to verify the truth of their creations. Everything else is a continuation of the Portuguese exam, a rhetoric more difficult to develop since the theme is always the same: Miss Dulce, a young lady from Botafogo in Petrópolis who marries Doctor Frederico. The commentator, her father, is against it because this Dr. Frederico, in spite of being a doctor, has no job. Dulce goes to the mother superior of a religious school. The latter writes to the wife of the minister, a former student, who arranges a job for the boy. The story ends. It's important not to forget that Frederico is a poor boy, that is, his father has money, a plantation or sugar mill, but can't give him a large monthly allowance. This is the great love drama in our literature, and the theme of its literary circle.''

''When will you see in your land a Dostoyevsky, a George Eliot, a Tolstoy — giants like these, in whom the power of vision, the unlimited aspects of creation, don't fall prey to sympathizing with the humble, with the humiliated, or for the pains of those people where at times they haven't come — when?''

''Our people don't suffer. They are insensitive.''

''Are you serious?'' And then he added, ''They suffer. Yes. They suffer their own humanity.''

My friend spoke calmly, but with a bit of irritation in his voice.

"If I could," he adduced, "if I were given the complete gift of being an author, I would be a Rousseau, in my way, preaching to the masses an ideal of strength, of violence, of power of calculated courage that would correct the goodwill and depressing sweetness. I would saturate them with a ferocious individualism, with the desire to be like the climbing vines of Java, loving the sun, winding around the thick trees in the forest and climbing higher than the highest branches finally to show their glory. Do you know whose it is?"

"No."

"It belongs to he who increases the vital force."

During the dialogue, he had risen to his feet. His eyes had lost their softness and shone extraordinarily in their gentle and even socket. He spoke with calmness, and warmth, shaking out his words one by one; the last ones, therefore, being said with intensified passion. Before he sat down, I looked at him for a moment; he answered with a fixed smile full of soul. He seemed as if he heard someone invisible ... the angel Gabriel, perhaps. He was like a Mohammed who was preparing to take his poor people in one hundred years from the Pyrennes to the Sonda Islands! The smile came apart on his lips as he sat down. Seated, he said haphazardly:

"No. The greatest force in the world is mildness. Let's stop all this noise-making...."

Unworried, quiet for hours, we watched the ducks in the lake and talked about unimportant things. The lights were already on when we left for dinner. We had soup in a restaurant on a main street and Gonzaga said to me:

"Don't pay any mind to those words before. They were longings for Ramualdo, sadness for his death. I truly valued him, and in my life I only met him, outside of my circle, to love me and understand me. At my age, you ought to know, a blow of that nature brings indirect manifestations, but violent ones."

He took his handkerchief and wiped his eyes quickly. He then added:

"How life must have been difficult for him! At the age of fourteen, they put him in a school that is more like a prison. From body to military body he drifted in suffering the hardships of discipline and of hierarchy, as well. All of this exacts a toll on life. It takes initiative, the sensation of what he is capable of doing.... One fine day, he is made an attendant and there he is receiving humiliations from all the pretentious officials, from the minister to the office boy. He is married. He, valiant, born in a place where personal bravery is necessary for even daily life, was afraid to go out with his wife, because ... oh! it's not even nice to talk about it."

And he continued to eat the following courses, exchanging one reflection for another, while I reached the limits of my surprise. Gonzaga de Sá never had shown that facet of common sentimentality before. At first I had thought he was a cold being, then spiteful and next, a type of pure intelligence that looked at life and its institutions only to find its contradictory aspects. One day in which I was giving him much thought, I found him to be like André Maltère, of Barrès, who was born to understand and rearrange. How was it that at this moment he was being a sentimentalist, almost whiny?

It's true that on certain occasions I almost felt he was that way. But at these times, it was always something dealing directly with him, and there is no one who isn't that way with himself. During the almost two days in which I saw him in the presence of the death of his friend, he had transformed himself, abruptly, to become a common sentimentalist exactly like any other man. I was desperate to understand him. I formed all sorts of hypotheses and put them in various combinations but I must admit that nothing brought to me the solution I sought; and to this day, when I think about the different ways in which he appeared to act today, yesterday and tomorrow at different moments and hours, I'm flabbergasted at the incoherence and inconsistency of his actions, and I see him in the back of my mind just like I saw him sitting in the cafe, looking all about the room and all of its contents. How enigmatic he is to me!

After leaving the hotel and heading down Avenida Central, we ran into heavy traffic. We went up to the Monroe Pavilion. The Sunday night crowd out in the streets had a distinctive rhythm of its own. There are the same idlers, artists, writers and bohemians, the same street hawkers, beggars and prowlers that add to the picturesque charm of the public avenue. On Sunday, therefore, like any other one, come the girls from the suburbs with their pallid complexions and their typical outfits. The Armenians come from the Rua Larga section and in their eyes, garnished with long lashes with tourmaline reflexes, a flash of Asiatic ferocity can be detected at times. Besides these, there are the workers on their stroll with clothes wrinkled from having been stored in their trunks too long. There are salesmen with eternally new clothes and large, violently clad feet.... We continued walking through these people until we reached the balustrade that leads to the sea, upon which we leaned looking down the length of the illuminated and lively avenue.

"Notice," said Gonzaga de Sá, "how these people move happily. Why should we disturb it with our anxieties and desperations. Wouldn't that be wrong?"

"It's a matter of conscience."

"What is that evidence worth to me? Who is sure of his revelations? Who would believe his conscience? I am for systematic doubt ... I don't feel proof of things. I don't suffer from that which Renan called the horrible mania of certainty.... Everything runs away, escapes from me, and can't be gathered.... What exists are beliefs, creations of our own minds made by it for its own use, alien to the outside world, which is all probability and has no order to be bent to that which we create.... Once conscience is determined, is it worth disturbing the peace of those Panurgian people?"

I didn't know how to answer him, and he also didn't ask for a response. We looked again at the rows of lights that lined the entire public avenue. Soon after, we walked down the street. We went for a beer and sitting on the bar stools, we discussed trivialities. When we parted, he said to me:

"I am going to have Aleixo Manuel, Ramuldo's son, educated. I'll make a Titus Livius de Castro out of him."

I had an inauspicious thought, and asked myself: Will Gonzaga live to accomplish so much? Would it be worth the trouble?

XI
IT WAS A NATIONAL HOLIDAY

I left my house annoyed. A bad night filled with bitter memories put me in an unhappy mood, irritated me, and made me want to flee, cowardly as the thought was, to some distant place. It was a national holiday. The legislature decided to celebrate it with the noise of a parade to be followed by a reception at the palace and a gala celebration at night under a tent in the Old Guard section of town. I walked down to disappear in the crowd, to get drunk in the display of the shiny uniforms, as well as the yellowed ones, to become fragmented by the blasts of salvos, running away from myself, my thoughts and my anxieties. I got off in Campo de Sant'Ana, slipping among the people, entering into the garden so that I could see the battalion, ingenuously, humbly, as if I were a child. The troops were in formation, awaiting the general's visit, later to file through the Catete and in plain view of the president. I saw regiments, I saw battalions, brilliant general staff, heavy gun carriages, Brazilian flags, without emotion, without enthusiasm, placidly looking at it all, as if it were a cinematographic event. It didn't arouse in me patriotism or revolt. It was a show, nothing more. Brilliant, certainly, but not very thrilling nor intelligent. Next to me, two democrats argued when the formidable forces of the nation passed by, their resources of land and sea. They had an almanac in their brain; they knew the names of the officials, the brand names of the cannons, the weight in tons of the battleships. They argued with obvious pride, satisfied, protesting here and there, disgusted that there should be such a small number of cavalry regiments and so few battleships of the high seas. I looked. I looked at their boots, I looked at their hats — suddenly I glanced at the arrogant generals that galloped by the side of the golden admirals.... Oh! Society rests upon the resignation of the humble! A great truth, I thought to myself, remembering Lamennais.

I looked at them again. They continued to argue heatedly. They made comparisons with the armed forces of neighboring nations and a sensation of pride showed on their faces when the comparison was in our favor. Why did those men, mistreated by life, by the social system, with many necessities, excommunicated, speak in such saintly enthusiastic terms about a society in which they suffered? Why did they want it standing, victorious — they who received nothing from it, they who would be scorned by the highest or lowest authority if they ever were to be so foolish as to have business dealings with any one of them? Would it not be fundamental, structured in all of us, in them as in me, that spontaneous separation of our pain, the probable fault of that social body in which we live? Could we live without it, without the laws that crush us? Would not hidden precepts of our nature impose that resigned subordination? Who knows? And as Gonzaga de Sá said so well, what business had I, a man of imagination and education; what business had I in bringing unrest to their souls, those of the poor people, to transmit my nervous imbalance? I looked at them once more.... One of them saw me and smiled at the other. I turned away, looking towards a street in front of me, its entire length in plain view, thanks to a large opening in the crowd. Looking through it, I remembered that only a few days ago in that long furrow that opened through the length of the shaft, filthy men were digging, and that in pouring rain or blazing sun they will continue to dig....

And I hit upon all the injustices of our lives; I brought up at once all the evils that cover our ideas and prejudices, our organizations and studies. I decided to organize my own Republic, right there, in seconds, to build my own Utopia, and for an instant I saw days of Good, Satisfaction and Contentment shine throughout the land. I saw all human faces without anxieties, happy in a dance. As quickly as this dream came to me, it disappeared. I don't know what diabolical logic was overcoming me; I don't know what deep-rooted reflexive habit chased away the dream; I abandoned my thoughts with dismay. All this was without a cure. If one prejudice died, another would be born in its place. Everything on earth aims to create them: Art, Science and Religion are its sources, the shadows from whence they come and only the death of those illusions, only the forgetting of their canons, their deliriums and their biases bring men the happy state of total absence of all notions. Would it be so someday? Would none remain? Wasn't it the essence of human nature to have your way to oppose that of one's neighbor? Didn't the Tupi have theirs against the Tapuias; didn't the Portuguese have them against both of them? What did it matter to me that today I suffered through the notions of some European academics and the nonsense of my fellow citizens, if tomorrow, as a savage with javelin and slingshot, I would suffer in the same manner as my neighboring tribe or even as my own? For minutes on end I had these confusing thoughts. As for me, finally, I was certain that it was wiser not to do anything. To propose ending the present sources of suffering would be to prepare the birth of others; if my actions were to continue the march that humanity has been making to the present, it would be the same as returning it to the days that have already passed. I had the insane thought of ending it all; I wanted those houses down, those gardens, and vehicles; I wanted the earth without man, without humanity, because I wasn't happy and I felt no one was, ... Nothing! Nothing!...

The bugle sounded. One played in the distance, and then the others one by one as if the sound of one made the next vibrate. The troops began to file. They paraded. Before me came smooth, shiny black faces, fair hair that slid from the cork helmets, copper-colored men, with a hard and strong look, various races, a variety and mixture of humans moved in unison and in one voice. Their fathers had come from faraway places and from the most contrary corners of the globe. What strange reasons, given the cruel facts of history, explained that strange impulse and that same obedience to the same ideal and the same command? What nonsense, I suddenly thought, to be thinking of such imbecilic things when next to me stood such boutiques of fashion, the Moorish Pavillion, or the "Pequenos Ecos," so replete with intellectual and important things, where I could distract my attention and studies in a more meaningful and worthwhile manner.... What an idiot I am!...

The troops continued marching in the direction of the Catete. I simply watched them go by, as I had watched them form. After they had passed, I walked down several streets feeling the crowd: in it, I floated pleasantly, enjoying the sensation of my annulment.... I came as a drop of water in the riverbed, and when I became lost in the Largo do Rossio, I was to meet up with Doctor Xisto Beldroegas, a graduate in law and Gonzaga de Sá's colleague in the Department of Religious Affairs. He walked slowly, worried, deeply worried. I had met him through my friend who had described to me his curious mental activity. Beldroegas was the custodian of the contentious traditions in the Department of Religious Affairs. Enthusiastic about the cultural legislation in Brazil, he lived obsessed with the notices, judicial directives, laws, decrees and agreements. At one time he had a minor nervous condition because no matter how many papers he consulted in the archives, there was no way of discovering a document that stated exactly the number of arrows piercing the image of St. Sebastian. Gonzaga de Sá told very funny stories about his law colleague. He always pointed out his spiritual necessity for standardizations, the resolution on official paper of everything. Beldroegas could not understand why the number of rainy days per year could not be fixed, and if it weren't yet in a notice or judicial directive, it was only because the Congress and ministers were no good. If it were he ... Ah! ... The movements of stars, the growth of plants, chemical actions, all nature, to his understanding, was controlled by notices, judicial directives and decrees originated by certain congresses, ministers and other governing agents that had existed long ago. He didn't believe that other wills or forces more powerful than the obvious members of the political powers could govern. They were, alone, the vote ... what foolishness! ...

In spite of being well versed in legislation, he had no idea of its origin or goals and he did not associate it to the totality of life in society. It was a separate thing, and a human communion, an immense flock, whose shepherds had the right to decide, in writing, the manner in which they would poke their sheep with the goad. For Doctor Xisto Beldroegas, law was offensive, an enemy of the past. No one had rights before it, and everything requested should be denied, not immediately, but after a thousand times being informed by twenty or so departments, so that the governmental machinery could more completely crush the daring person. On top of this, he had a strange interpretation of the law. Once I mentioned to him the laws of heredity.

"Law," he exclaimed. "That is law!"

"What?"

"It is not. It is merely a sentence by a doctor there.... Which parliament approved it?"

A law, to the understanding of Gonzaga de Sá's colleague was two or three typed sentences numbered on the side, possibly in paragraphs which should be presented by a deputy or senator to their respective chambers approved by them, and sanctioned by the President of the Republic. What occurred in this manner was a law, all else ... nonsense!

. . . .

Xisto was worried, deeply worried. I hesitated in speaking with him. I didn't have time, therefore, to make a decision. He then looked directly toward me.

"Doctor," I said, pretending surprise and contentment.

He didn't answer me clearly, and he articulated only a piggish grunt, the requirement of his bureaucratic respectability. I am stubborn and I insisted on having him talk. I kindly insisted;

"What are you thinking about, doctor?"

Xisto approved of my dependence, arranged his "pince-nez," fixed his look and said:

"This is going badly . . . I don't know where we will end. . . ."

"Why, doctor?"

"Well, this is all just confusion!"

"There is no doubt," I agreed.

"There isn't even any enjoyment in working. Just imagine the man who more than ten years ago, according to my sources, realized the need to standardize the number of lines in public notices. . . . It's necessary to regulate that exactly. . . . Now, some have five lines, now some have ten, fifteen, thirty. . . . It is hell! . . . Look only to the newspaper 'Pais.' It calls something that is a simple notice, a "message." It is because of the deficiency in doctrine. It is true they will always be ignorant; the matter could be determined and the journalists might not know . . . What! On this earth, to be sure, no one understands each other! The people that are good are all under the ground."

For a few minutes longer he told me other disenchantments in his government officer's soul. I interrupted him, asking:

"And Gonzaga, how is he?"

"It seems to me he is sickly. . . . The other day he suffered a severe fainting spell."

"Did he get through it?"

"Yes, he made it, but at his age, it is bad. . . . They say he will be retired."

"What a shame."

"He has nothing to lose. He is a good companion, but he doesn't understand the job. . . . Even today, with almost forty years of service, he still wasn't accustomed to putting the number of the Republic on the decrees. Imagine! . . . I like him, I admit; in respect to his service however, he was nothing great there. . . . He knew it, that is certain, but anything about novels, philosophy, magazines . . . I feel sorry for him. . . . He had some funny stories to tell. . . . Many people will say that I am happy because his retirement will profit me. I am next in line for a promotion. . . . But no, I feel sorry for him."

The last words were said almost half voiced. He was silent for a while, and then, walking by my side, he began to talk about his department and colleagues. The head didn't understand; the director, even less, the minister. . . . With difficulty, I was able to leave that prodigious man whose hand graduated the force of laws and sustained the majesty of the State. Leaving him, I felt like going to visit my friend. It was a little after two o'clock. It was too early and I didn't want to inconvenience him with a prolonged visit. I remained on the streets until four in the afternoon when I left in the direction of his house, longing to see him, since it had been almost twenty days since I last saw him. It was Gonzaga himself who came to the door.

"They told me you were sick," I said upon entering.

"What! A light infection in the air. Who told you?"

"Xisto Beldroegas."

"I thought so! They are the ones who make me sick ... I can't tolerate them any longer ... What bores! They imitate me... It is incredible that only now, sixty-odd years old, I am beginning to feel incompatible with 'them'..."

"Did you have a fainting spell?"

"Yes, something insignificant.... What I suffer is really boredom, it is tedium; I suffer in feeling alone, I suffer in seeing that I have organized a mind that does not harmonize with any others. My colleagues bore me.... The old ones are ossified, the young ones, graduate students.... I thought that books would be sufficient for me, that I would satisfy myself ... It was a mistake! The ideas I accumulated I didn't know how to use either for my glory or for my fortune.... They didn't leave me ... I am sterile and shall die sterile ... I lack words; the ideas don't find adequate expressions to manifest themselves. Then, I am at the end of life, and only now I feel its emptiness, I notice its lack of objective and utility ... my heart was uncultivated ... I wasted a fortune on futile things ... Life demands other things ... I spent forty-one years circling around myself, living hours surrounded by imbeciles. Imagine that my director, several days ago, organized a strange system to nominate the president of the Republic, and with all seriousness, I assure you."

"What was it?"

"You began as clerk and then promotion by promotion, you arrived at the presidency ..."

"Ingenious!"

"Do you know what advantage he said it had?"

"No."

"Whenever there be the need to draw up a degree in the palace, the president would be able to do it ... Oh! Impossible! Not even the patience of a saint! ..."

We conversed, seated in that den where Gonzaga de Sá had received me the first time. I was surprised by that release, it wasn't his habit; I didn't expect it. From a few days back I had noticed that he was less resigned, irritable, more depressed, without energy to contain himself. He had lost a bit of his sharp irony; he would let himself become easily angered and pitied himself dishearteningly. I didn't try to comfort him; he is not the type to be comforted. I looked for a moment out the window. The heavens were calm, the sky was very blue and clear. The sun shone without violence, softly enveloping the stilled palm tree. The beveled flank of the quarry, on the other side, could be seen in the distance through the open window, brusquely clear, arising between the dark shrubbery and the rock like a wound ... The workers were busy ... Human ferment in indifferent nature. ...

From the street, monotonous chants of the roaming vendors reached us. From the front window, I saw the tips of the palm trees near the palace and the height of the Guaratiba hill, quietly hanging over our noisy banquets. ...

Gonzaga de Sá lifted his eyes from the sheet of paper upon which he had been scribbling, looked at the three walls of the room facing the outside and remained a few minutes with his lost look. Finally, my old friend turned to me and asked once again:

"Who told you I was sick?"

"I already told you . . . Xisto Beldroegas."

"What an idiot! With that castrato voice; with that turtle walk. . . . I am nauseated by him, nauseated by his stupidity. . . . Imagine that to upset me one day he began discussing philosophy with Baltar. . . . Do you know what they discussed?"

"No."

" 'Listen,' Beldroegas said to the other; then looking at me, 'Baltar, let's discuss philosophy.' Baltar became vain, puts his hands back and says with assurance; 'Let's.' Baltar coughs; Beldroegas tries to speak, chuckles and asks, "How did Socrates die? Fortunately I escaped becoming a doctor. . . .'"

I laughed while Gonzaga de Sá lit his cigarette with difficulty. He shook; several matches went out. I got up to discard mine, which was burning out, and caught sight of the paper upon which Gonzaga de Sá had scribbled. They were indefinite strokes of a human figure . . . Always that obsession. I sat down and he continued:

"Before, I felt sorry . . . today hate arises in me. I feel like breaking their faces. . . . The idiots defame me . . . eunuchs, castrated ones! They gathered some opinions, pieces of thoughts from my lips, and with them went to offend and irritate me. Human stupidity is fathomless! I am displeased with myself, my cowardice . . . I am displeased with myself for not having looked for the light, the heavens, for having remained cowardly among these ducks, among such turkeys, burros and evil fellows, braided or not, ignorant and sordid, incapable of kindness, gratitude and respect for the values of others. . . . How did I end up with those idolators of titles and positions, charters, and obsequities, bending to power and money? I don't know. The ones closer to me, I would attempt to improve; I gave them authors, news, different ways of thinking . . . And they? Oh! What idiots! What idiots! What upsets me most is having reached this age completely empty, empty of glory, friendship, alone, and almost isolated from my kin and those that could understand me. I am abandoned, like an old tree uprooted on a beach. . . . I lived long and I expect to live more. . . . I saw thieves, I saw assassins, I saw robbers, I saw prostitutes — all these are good people, very good in comparison to these graduated kibitzers in whose midst I lived. . . . I ran away from positions, love, marriage, to live more independently. . . . I regret it all. . . . Venus is a vengeful goddess!"

Gonzaga was delirious. Never had I seen him in that character, using that violent language. He got up from his chair, his hair was disheveled and in his left hand his cigarette rose like a burning torch.

"Gonzaga, be merciful! Forgive!"

He didn't answer me and sat down. Outside, a slight wind began to stir, and the palm tree leaned over to our side. On the wall, all the figures of the allegory "Spring" seemed to look at my unforgettable friend. The bronze stork seemed to extend its head a bit more, and above the facade the owl moved his eyes in closer, as if he had been frightened with Gonzaga de Sá's attitude. All those companions of many years were surprised at the sudden revolt. They had been surprised like me, in spite of it all. I understood then that Gonzaga's temperament was of violent passions, that the ivory had disguised the bruise of not having found anything to which he could apply them and that a muffled effervescence of rage must be buried within him. With the strong understanding of the dignity within him, and in the conquering pride for his intelligence, atrocious wounds must have opened in him during the entire length of his life; and now with the decadence of energy that old age brings, he could no longer tolerate these cruel pains, and he cried. It was one more interpretation of my friend's soul.... I concluded also that that was a convulsion, an inevitable disturbance provoked by old age in his usual calm and the sad irony that perfumed his lonely life, disturbed even further by the death of his compadre. Annoyed, during a few moments, he was silent, finally saying to me:

"You never saw me like this, did you?"

"?"

"You will have to forgive me.... Never again ... I will not have any reason to be like this again...."

He was breathless and then continued with his usual voice, soft and kind:

"You did well in coming. You will dine with me and then we will go to the Lírico. I want to see those places for the last time; I want to see the present center of all those illusions.... You shall come with me. Your youth will stimulate me to see again my twenty-five promising years...."

I didn't want to go because I felt a hostility in the theater-going crowd. But I ceded and had supper with him, the aunt and the godchild.

The supper was sad. Dona Escolastica, with her green eyes indifferent, always dined ceremoniously, having a fixed, kind smile upon her lips. She never lost that air of tranquility, of placidity. But with such passiveness that I did not guess any contradiction, having discovered the crises her nephew was undergoing. It was like one of those beautiful landscapes we run to when our souls are heavy with displeasure. We contemplate them hours on end, awaiting comfort, a caress, and they say nothing. They continue, as always, pretty in everyone's eyes, but without kind understanding for anyone among all those who search for it. Dona Escolastica continued placid and tranquil but she seemed to be that way with everyone, without choice or preference. Before the recent agitation her nephew had undergone, and in view of her apathetic indifference for everything, from her intellectual nihilism, she was always like the landscape: she remained silent, silent without a word to encourage him or without advice to quiet him. When supper was over, Gonzaga de Sá dressed patiently, with care. We were going to the second class seats as, because of the way I was dressed, I couldn't join him in the first class rows. Meanwhile, he buttoned himself, arranged his pants so that they fell well over his shoes, he knotted his tie very carefully, put on perfume and we then left to buy the tickets beforehand. When we got off at the theatre door, the cars already had begun to arrive. Generally the "coupés" brought three people and the "vitórias," six, not counting the servant next to the coachman. There was only one groom for all the cars. As soon as one came to the corner of the Rua Senador Dantas, the poor man ran and followed parallel to the vehicle up to the exact place to open the door. If one by chance arrived with the exact capacity and with its own coachman's assistant, everyone was surprised. It was as if it were the prince's coach. Most of the people arrived in "ceroulas." And, once I was surprised that some people that sported such expensive dresses and suits could not come in more appropriate and less crowded carriages. At a certain moment, Gonzaga de Sá said to me without any reason:

"I feel pity, not offense at this luxury...."

The bell announced the show. We entered. I had been to the old Pedro II Theatre only a few times and the few shows I did see were from the gallery; thus, the way that the brilliance of that society swarming over seats and boxes, from a distance, seemed to be dressed in a grandeur that intimidated me. Bent over the gallery, the tailored coats and rich outfits the ladies wore were a dazzlement for my poor eyes; and since I did not like to analyze performances I enjoy, I accepted that society as dazzling, grandiose and brilliant. Nevertheless, in a vulgar way and to a great degree, at the door it seemed to me that those ladies wrapped in capes and other coats had the air of someone going to a bath; meanwhile, in the hall with their laps empty, they seemed like marble in a museum.

In the Casino, whenever I would see in the special boxes those well known *grandes dames* from abroad, much like Mexican galleons brimming with jewels and silk, I also felt the same impression of greatness, beauty and majesty. After years of staying away, I finally agreed to enter the Lírico. I now was to see all of that from up close, thanks to Gonzaga de Sá, to his encouragement and to the reinforcement that he gave to my natural humility.

The performance had not yet begun. Ladies talked with gentlemen at the entrance of the boxes. I was very close to the right aisle. I saw some of the seats very closely and the chairs in the boxes seemed quite inferior to those in the dining room of my modest house. I noticed the lining of poor, painted paper, the floor of cheap pine boards; I looked down the corridors and besides being restricting, I judged them to be dirty, common, guiding feet toward useless places. The ceiling always intrigued me. With its cross beams, I always imagined them to be destined for trapeze acts and other acrobatics. Opera, or circus? Meanwhile, I was at the most elegant spot in Brazil, the spot to where the best in my land converge.

It was to shine here that we all fought, killed and stole, all over the eight million square kilometers of Brazil. It is unbelievable! The musicians had completed tuning their instruments; soon the maestro arrived. The president appeared in his box seat and the orchestra played the national anthem. We rose, and when the opera began, we sat down to listen.

"A beautiful house!" I whispered into Gonzaga de Sá's ear.

" 'Chic', rich! Half the people didn't pay admission...."

"It had been a long time since I have seen so many powerful people together...."

"And in any case, curious and representative," he told me.

We appreciated the sweetness of the music for awhile, even further enhanced by the sweet voices of the two singers that reached our ears like an unusual caress. I saw in a box seat a beautiful lady with a high bust and an angular figure who seemed to be alone. I tried to see her face. It was Pilar, a Spanish woman who perhaps had great influence in the country.

Gonzaga de Sá was listening and I disturbed him by mentioning the Spanish woman.

"Do you know her?" I asked, "Who is she?"

"Pilar! The nymph of high politics, high finance, of all swindlers with a title."

"Aha! It is fair that they exist for all classes; moreover, she is envied. Look at how the honest Mme. Aldong is looking at her ... the seventh box in the first row to the right ... See?

"I saw," Gonzaga de Sá answered.

"Do you know who Mme. Aldong is?"

"No, she's the lady over there.... Do you really know who she is?"

"Well, no, nor does anyone else. But she's high society, she's a widow, and without being rich, she spends rivers of money. There is no reason for envy."

"Are you moralizing?"

"No, absolutely not. I am verifying facts. Notice those three girls to the left ... They are pretty, aren't they?"

"Certainly."

"They are the daughters of the moralist of the newspaper 'Vanguarda.' He recently won 200 contos in damages in the lawsuit he pleaded for the construction firm for the port of Tabatinga, for that company which never began the construction of its last piers. It was last month. I'm surprised he still has money...."

"It was useful; they came to brighten our scene. And that lady over there?"

"What do you think about her?"

"Wife of a senator or banker?"

"Exactly, of a gambler. For thirty years he has been one, in spite of all the codes prohibiting this. The uselessness of laws.... A good subject!"

"And that admiral that seems to have seen all the seas on this earth?"

"Since his first apprentice voyage, made on a sailing vessel, he never again sailed, except in Niterói."

"Very practical."

"On land," said Gonzaga de Sá quickly.

"A beautiful house!"

The act was ending. Enthusiastic clapping ensued from the galleries and some in the chairs also clapped. We went out. I began watching the features of those people so unkindly categorized by Gonzaga de Sá. They had something of an unknown restlessness, an unknown uneasiness in their eyes that distressed me. I wanted to question my friend.... I stopped for an instant to see Pilar, who was passing by. She brushed past me and I was able to see her features. They were calm and her look was assured and satisfied. In view of that general uneasiness, her calm seemed to me superior, aristocratic, exercising that special fascination of a human that is competent and sure of herself and has no worries. I observed all this to Gonzaga de Sá; he smiled quickly and responded.

"No wonder! They know how they are here. They know that those who with noisemaking and early rising frequented the Lírico or the Provisório forty years ago, in my time, don't have perhaps one representative among them. Where did they go? No one knows! They fear the future.''

He looked over those elegant gentlemen and those comely ladies and said to me:

"You, the young ones, did badly in dethroning the old. In spite of it all, we would have understood each other in the end. Those of today...."

''Nothing stops us from coming to an understanding with these people, as well.''

"Who! They are strangers, new to the country, hardware dealers and money changers who became rich, new people.... You are separated from them by almost four hundred years of history that they don't know or feel in their bones — which, for them is a shame, because those past years give you power and rights that should be asserted. In short, you will have to use force for them to respect you. Those four hundred years ... summarizing,'' Gonzaga continued, ''you found new rulers with whom you'll never be able to deal, and you oust the elders whom some day you would have come to understand. You erred and greatly.''

The bell rang and we went to our places. Pilar was already in the box seat; from the others, as the ladies respectively entered, their first look was directed to her. The president was already seated in plain view. Pilar looked detainedly at him, gazed throughout the room and turned once again toward him, without envy. It was as if she was saying; ''Here, you and I!'' The orchestra began to play. The curtain rose and I prepared to listen to the sweetness of the Italian music. The show continued past midnight, and we remained to the end. We left saddened. It was the first time I was leaving a theatre that way. When I was a student I would always leave happily.

Surrounded only by friends, among the minimum of comrades, the piece would be like attending a class in which during the interval, an equal to equal, I would argue and talk familiarly with the others. This time, without that favorable atmosphere of colleagues, I collided brusquely with a hostile world. There was not even a single word that hurt me, not even a look; however, merely the contemplation of those grand people that seemed to me so rich and so enormous made me feel inferior. Where did this feeling come from? Was it my culture? No — I received the same education as the most educated ones of my age who were there. Was it my character, or a lack of morality? No, also. I felt I had it; in comparison with the bulk of those neat gentlemen, I was pure, immaculate. There was nothing else left to compare, unless it be that my blood made me perfectly inferior; but the same type, I believe, also ran through those to whom I judged myself inferior. Where, then, did that feeling that saddened me come from? I analyzed in my mind the performance that had hurt me and combined it with what Gonzaga de Sá had said ... I remember that they had come from all of Brazil, from all its points to fight, to rob their relatives, their women and their government, to cheat both the rich and poor, and also to kill groups and groups of immigrants in the arduous farming jobs. That was their prize! ... They had avoided all the social conventions, all the moral precepts — they were courageous while I ... Oh! Sometimes over there, some revelries and a lot of alcohol! Narcotics! That was it.

Realizing the truth, I was outraged at my weakness at my wavering and contemptible soul that made me stop before the ten commandments, before the moral pre-

cepts. I was a coward, a slave; they, princes and kings. I will no longer be like that!...
If it is necessary to fight — we shall fight! They chose war — they shall have it.

We went for a beer at a night-life café. Gonzaga de Sá was wrapped in an overcoat
with the formality of a traveled ''parvenu.'' At first, we drank without talking,
finally Gonzaga de Sá broke the silence.

''I leave these things saddened....''

''Well!''

''No, it's true. Regrettably, I have a remote patriotism and when I see that, the
Lírico, the reappearance of fake society the same as forty years ago, I become
depressed. They are the same plantation masters, human blood suckers; they are the
same politicians without ideas; they are the same wisemen, memorizers of foreign
abstracts without a single thought of their own; they are the same ''literati'' as in the
style of Otaviani, litterateurs of cotillion matters, the same moneylenders.... Forty
years ago it was like that; it didn't change. Will they always be like that?''

Unintentionally, I responded immediately:

''Certainly.''

Then I saw a certain contradiction between what Gonzaga de Sá told me in the
theater and his observations now. However, I didn't mention it.

''I also feel that way,'' he confirmed, ''but now, I must say that the others were
more our relatives.''

And calmly, we sipped long drafts of beer, until we emptied our glasses. Gonzaga
de Sá paid and when I bid him farewell, he asked me:

''Where are you going?''

''Home.''

''Honestly?''

''My word of honor!''

''Come sleep at my house. Tomorrow you can help me arrange my books.''

Together we took the streetcar to his house, on the outskirts of Rua Bento Lisboa,
in Catete, on the Santa Teresa hillside.

In the streetcar there were few passengers. There was a girl with a large hat and a
long and beautiful cape on one of the front seats. Gonzaga de Sá observed her for a
long time and there, by Rua da Lapa, he suddenly said, looking at the woman:

''What I regret is that those women are not different from the society ones. If they
were, perhaps I would try....''

And he didn't say anything of importance until his door, where we entered;
already the roosters were crowing, and we were received by the sleepy greeting of the
old black, Inácio.

XII
LAST ENCOUNTERS

I slept magnificently in a large room, like those in the old Rio de Janeiro houses that give a good image of the opulence and freedom of the bourgeois during the middle of the last century. It was larger than the rooms of our rather paltry houses of today. I woke up late. The room in which I had slept led to the dining room. Walking into it, I met dona Escolastica of the placid green eyes attentively watching little Aleixo Manuel who was having a quick morning snack before going to school. Gonzaga de Sá was not there.

When I entered, the boy lifted his head from the cup and for an instant, rested his large black eyes (alive with silver) upon me, inquisitive as always.

Seeing that child, I don't know what distant memories of my childhood flashed. It was the hope of my initiation into dark matters of the alphabet. It was my teacher's caresses and astonishment. It was also the painful experience of my restless and unsettled youth.... That chlid didn't see what he invoked in me, with his intelligent, rigid forehead and his strong, round head of a man of character! He looked at me, gave me the morning greetings, answered me, and I sat down. The elderly dona Escolastica told me then that her brother had risen early and was working in the room. I remained talking for a while and, in passing, spoke to the child.

"Are you ahead of your class?"

Aleixo Manuel hesitated in responding, the elderly lady therefore obliged him to answer quickly.

"Answer, Aleixo, aren't you listening to what is being asked? Answer: Are you ahead of your class?"

"I'm not, no sir," he finally answered.

"What book are you in?"

"The third."

"With your nine years, you are doing well," I said, encouraging him. "Are you already studying Brazilian history?"

"Yes, sir."

"Who discovered Brazil?"

"Pedro Alvares Cabral."

"And America?"

"Christopher Columbus."

"Which was the first discovery, America or Brazil?"

"America."

"Why?"

"Because Brazil is part of America and whoever discovered America also discovered Brazil, because it is in America."

"Then it was Christopher Columbus who discovered Brazil. What do you say?"

The boy became quiet, wrinkled his forehead for a minute then said with complete firmness:

"No, Columbus was the one that saw for the first time a place in America, that is why it is said he discovered it all, but Cabral saw later, for the first time, places in Brazil, which is why it is said that he discovered Brazil."

With effort, I disguised my surprise at the clarity of the boy's rationalization. I didn't want to sharpen his pride with a warm eulogy; I wanted his intellect to continue growing without his being self-conscious, and then when it was strong, he would become aware of his capacity, as if it were revelation, a surprise. I limited myself to saying that he was right and began asking other things.

Finally having answered my questions with a quickness that surprised me, he put his school-bag strap over his neck, picked up his blackboard, and bid us goodbye. He kissed and hugged dona Escolastica, and he did it in such a way that it made me realize that each wanted something else of the other, and that neither one knew why they didn't have it. He left.

"The boy is intelligent," I told the old woman.

"Quite. What a desire to learn that little one has! You can't imagine! He fools around, it is true, but at night, he grabs his books and his homework, and studies, without anyone forcing him. How I hope he remains like that to the end!"

"Why shouldn't he?"

"Well! There are so many that, like him, are off to a good start...."

"It is true! But, does their lack of will come from within themselves, the fading of love, dedication to their studies — or is it rooted in external reasons, apart from them, that only at a later age do they understand, when their conscience shows them justice and injustice, making their initial impetus deplorably weak?"

I thought dona Escolastica did not understand me, and tried to say the same thing in other words.

"Who knows if at a young age they study because they learn new things that, once known, discourage them and make their studies seem in vain?"

"What, doctor (for that is what she called me)? It is precisely that way!"

And she became silent after her positive affirmation, just like the great and infallible wisemen of our Brazil.

I drank a cup of coffee and then went to meet Gonzaga de Sá in his vast study. He, sitting in the rocking chair, was reading a newspaper attentively. We greeted each other and then I observed:

"I thought you were cleaning up. But I see that you have been carried away in reading the periodicals."

"Some French newspapers I have just received. I have postponed the cleaning up."

"What newspaper is it?"

"The 'Figaro' ... I read one a day as if it were published here and delivered to my door. Because of that, I'm always behind in the world news. At what stage is the Hague Conference?"

"Classification of nations...."

"I didn't get there yet ... I'm behind..."

"Where are you?"

"At the nomination of commissions."

"So you are always 15 days behind the world?"

"Sometimes much more.... Now, take time.... A subjective notion that exists only for us.... A fatality of our cerebral organization, independent of experiences. A criteria, a category for our human interpretation of phenomena.... What is it worth?"

I did not answer because I had nothing to answer. My old friend, after a short pause, asked me:

"Did you see Aleixo Manuel?"

"Yes."

"What did you think?"

"Very studious and intelligent."

"Thank God."

And he again returned to the French newspaper he was reading. I picked up the daily papers on the top of the central table; I read them, and around nine o'clock said good-bye to him. I didn't accept anything to eat, I would arrive too late at the office.

After saying goodbye, Gonzaga asked me:

"Come more often to talk to Aleixo. He is so alone...."

After his compadre's death, his constant preoccupation was the godchild. Without any pretext, without cause or reason in the middle of a conversation on a removed topic, he would begin to talk about Romualdo's son. Once he said: "I have to take him to the museum." Another time he said: "It might be a good idea to put him in a boarding school so he can make acquaintances and gain assurance and sociability. What do you think?"

I had little aptitude for educational matters, almost none, and would respond evasively. I would notice, meanwhile, that the constant presence of the child, the contemplation all day in the familiar intimacy had quickened the change of mood and temperament of my old friend that I have commented on already; and it brought upon him one more load of apprehensions that he was not used to. He would change.... Gonzaga loved the boy tenderly; it was obvious that he loved him as a son; and as he treated him in the smallest of ways and in the simplest words that he spoke to him, he added the affection and sweetness of a father. After this visit, once again I caught him looking at his godson with the look of a brother. There was some unknown great effort of penetration in his look, that I thought he was trying to decipher the little boy's future. Once, after one of those looks, he said to me:

"This life is a swindle...."

His godchild's presence alone was not enough to explain the change in mood Gonzaga de Sá was undergoing, a change which I was witnessing now since I was visiting him more often, as he asked me to do so.

It is true that I always knew him as a sad person, but one of a philosophic and general sadness, so to speak, that sadness of deeply feeling the insignificance of our human condition, always battling with our excessive wishes and dreams. But now his sadness was more present, more commonplace. It was as if the presence of his god-child Aleixo Manuel had lifted from the depth of my friend's being painful memories that he had buried forever, memories that were his secret and of which he had never spoken and I didn't find the minimum hint to discover them in the papers he willed to me, as testimony, together with several hundred books. I recall, upon writing these words, that one day he had said:

"Did you ever have a love?"

"Never."

"Look, I am speaking of love! eh?"

"I understand."

"You should have it.... I have always told you that the old folks confirm that Venus is a vengeful goddess.... She does not forgive and you shall suffer if you don't worship her...."

"There is no Venus," I responded.

"Who knows?"

We exchanged those words on the last few days of his existence, when the change in his temperament had already left its mark on his health; I saw clearly that Gonzaga de Sá was fading, was slowing dissolving in the slow flame of his secret memories, and the displeasure that their presence left upon his soul. His cheeks became hollow, his eyes, his gentle eyes were losing their brilliance, seemed dimmed, and were gaining a strange glow. He didn't have that same determination and his moods continued to be yet more unbalanced. After a time, his conversations were cut short by abrupt explosions of irritability, complaints undeserving of his nobility, in general, childish and without basis, changing frighteningly from the most intense sadness to the most blatant joy.

Aleixo Manuel, the godchild, brought him — who knows? — something to his life that he would never want to see, nor to reappear; and he suffered with this, he became saddened by it, he became dispirited by it in body and soul, without it being possible for me directly to attribute such changes in my friend, to the docile, affectionate, obedient Aleixo Manuel that he had brought to his home — to become his son.

"I shall make him a person," he would say to me at times, full of hope and joy.

He was not able to see it through to the end. When he began his preparatory course, that was when he "picked the flower," "fell" and "died."

The aunt saw the boy through to the end with complete love and renunciation.

Blessings to both, who in their educational mission knew how to be good, without selfishness or calculations of any kind in spite of their both having contributed to expanding the habit of analysis and reflection that studies bring the child's mind, which should have been limited only to the basic information needed for daily life, without having a constant bruise and a fatal, permanent principle of inadaptability to his environment, creating for him an irremediable discomfort and consequently a dissatisfaction with life, crueler than the ever present thought of death!

What does it all matter, then, if the temptations of the old folks were generous, if the suffering of the child externalized by great acts or great works could contribute some day to many of the equals who would follow him? What does it matter!?

Man's final happiness and his mutual understanding have demanded, up to now, greater sacrifices. . . .

Clara dos Anjos

Translated by
Earl Fitz

I

The postman Joaquim dos Anjos was not a man given to serenades and serenading, but he liked the guitar and *modinhas* [simple art song]. He himself played the flute, an instrument that had been held in high esteem during other times but no longer. The elderly people of Rio de Janeiro remember still the famous Calado and his polkas, one of which — *Cruzes, minha prima* [heavens, cousin]! — is still a moving memory to *cariocas* [inhabitants of Rio de Janeiro] about seventy years old. Since that time until our own, however, the flute has declined in importance, and now, only one flautist of our days has succeeded for a brief moment in reinstating the gentle, delicious instrument of our parents and grandparents. I am speaking of Patapio Silva. With his death, the flute again came to occupy a secondary place as a musical instrument, one to which those learned in music — whether they be performers or erudite critics — gave no importance. It became plebeian once again.

In spite of this and because of the humbleness of his birth, origins and class, Joaquim dos Anjos believed himself to be somewhat of a musician since, in addition to playing the flute, he also composed waltzes, tangos and the accompaniment for *modinhas*.

One of his polkas — *Siri sem unha* [Nailless Crab] — and a waltz — *Magoas do Coracao* [Sufferings of Love] — had gained some success so that he sold the copyrights of each one to a music and piano shop on Rua do Ouvidor.

His musical knowledge was minimal and he guessed more than he made use of any theoretical notions he might have studied.

He learned his musical art in the land of his birth, the outskirts of Diamantina, where he had played flute in church festivals and was thought by many people to be the first flautist of the area.

Although he enjoyed and was excited by his fame, he never wished to further his musical knowledge. He retained the art of Francisco Manuel that he knew by heart, but he did not wish to leave it and move on to something else.

As in music, he showed little ambition in other areas of his life. Fed up with the mediocrity of existence in his small home town, he accepted, one fine day when he was about twenty-two, the job offer of an English engineer recently come to those parts to explore the lands and terrain for diamond deposits. Everybody guessed that his interest involved prospecting for diamonds; the truth, however, is that the scholarly Englishman was merely making some disinterested studies. He was undertaking pure geological and mineralogical investigations. Diamonds were not the goal of his study but the people who stubbornly clung to their vision that the guts of the land on the outskirts of the city were full of diamonds could not believe that an Englishman who picked away at rocks from morning until night, busily taking notes and operating some crude instruments, was not doing all of this in order to find diamonds. There was no way of convincing the simple-minded people of the area that he didn't really wish to know anything about diamonds as such. Not a single day passed that His Majesty's subject did not receive some proposition for the sale of land on which, according to the seller of the property, there must surely be an abundance of the precious stones. This was so, they said, for numerous reasons, all of which would be obvious to the eyes of any experienced prospector.

As soon as the geologist arrived, Joaquim was hired as his assistant and was so obedient, and so pleased the learned man that the latter, upon finishing his field research, invited Joaquim to come to Rio de Janeiro and take charge of moving his baggage of rocks until it was stowed away on board his ship. The British man of letters pledged his word to pay for Joaquim's stay in Rio and this he did until he finally embarked for Europe.

He gave Joaquim some money so he could return to his home, in addition to a cork hat, some leggings, a pipe and a tin of Navy Cut smoking tobacco. But Joaquim had already grown accustomed to life in Rio de Janeiro in the month's time that he had been there in the service of Mr. John Herbert Brown of the Royal Society of London, and he resolved never to return to Diamantina. He sold the leggings and the cork hat to a secondhand dealer and took to smoking the aromatic English tobacco in the pipe that had been given him, while he strolled around Rio, as long as he had money. When his funds finally ran out, he looked up some acquaintances who had some money. In a short time, he found a job as an office clerk for a great lawyer, a man who was a fellow countryman, that is, another *Mineiro* [inhabitant of Minas Gerais].

"I won't pay you anything that's worth your trouble," his employer told him immediately, "but you're going to be learning and making contacts here, and you can arrange for something better later on."

Joaquim saw clearly that the *doutor* [bachelor of arts] was indeed telling him the truth so that his entire ambition in life was reduced to obtaining some small, public service employment that would give him the right to a pension and life insurance for the family he was going to establish. At the end of two years' efforts, he succeeded in obtaining the postman's job, — this happened a good twenty years ago — which made him content and satisfied with life so that he received successive promotions.

He married a few months after his appointment to the position, and when his mother died in Diamantina, he, as an only child, inherited the house there and also some land in Inhai, a parish of that Minas Gerais city. He sold the property and tried to acquire the little house in the suburbs in which he had been living, which was really his. Its price was moderate but even so, the money he was to get from the settlement of his mother's estate wasn't enough, and he had to pay the remainder in installments. Now, however, he was in full possession for a few years of his place as he used to call his humble abode. Indeed it was simple! It had two bedrooms. One opened on the living room, and the other on the dining room. Corresponding to a little more than a third of the house's total width, there was, toward the back, a little wing that had a kitchen and a miniscule pantry in it. This wing was connected to the dining room by a door. The pantry, on the left, made the wing narrower because of the short corridor that ran as far as the kitchen where it widened again into its normal width. The door that linked it to the dining room was right next to the one that led from this room to the back yard. Such was the floor plan of Joaquim dos Anjos's house.

Outside the main body of the house, there was a large shack, a bathhouse that also housed a washtub and other laundering items. The back yard was a reasonably sized area in which guava trees were growing as well as two or three orange trees, a Galician lemon tree, a papaya tree and an abundantly fronded tamarind tree well toward the back.

The street on which his house was located became a flat plain and, whenever it rained, it flooded and became like a swamp. Nevertheless, it was heavily peopled and had become the main route running from the Central railroad station to the distant and populous parish of Inhauma. Covered wagons, horse carts and lorries traveled almost daily along this path from beginning to end to supply the retailers with merchandise the wholesalers furnished them, a circumstance indicating that such a heavily used public thoroughfare deserved more attention than it got from the local government and its officials.

It was a tranquil street and all or nearly all of it was built-up in the older style of the suburbs, that of the chalet. It was populated almost entirely from one side of the street to the other. And from this street, a beautiful panorama of mountains and their constantly changing colors opened up. The colors changed in accordance with the time of day and the condition of the atmosphere. These mountains were really quite distant but they seemed to encircle completely the city and its surrounding areas. The street was the axle of that ring of mountains that, during the day, seemed to be lighted by luminous projections, clothing itself in shades of green and blue. By dusk it was draped in shades of purple and gold.

Aside from the classical suburban chalets, other types of houses were found there too. Some were relatively new with a few frills and a certain sense of courtliness that hid their lack of room more effectively and justified their exaggerated rents. There was one house, however, worthy of note. It stood almost in the center of a large farm and was characteristic of the houses on the old estates of earlier times. It had a long frontal façade, did not have much depth, and had a low, squat roof lined with glazed tiles that extended about halfway across the right side. Somewhat ugly, in fact, it really was! It also lacked any sense of smartness. It was perfectly matched with the old mango trees, however, the robust jack trees, the insolent palm trees and with all the other old trees, big and small, that had perhaps been planted by people who never lived to see them bear fruit. Among them, one could see the vestiges of the old garden. There were statuettes made of Portuguese porcelain with blue lettering. One was ''Spring''; another was ''Dawn.'' Nearly all of them were mutilated in one way or another. Some lacked an arm, others had no heads and still others were just lying on the ground, having been knocked off their crude supports.

The walls that, at an appropriate distance, surrounded the house against which the iron grating on the front of the structure was leaning, were covered with ivy. This ivy growth blanketed them totally or in part, not like a shroud but like a rather severely ceremonious but living mantle, one that dated from another time and from other people, thus provoking the sense of *saudade* [nostalgia] and longing that animate these ruins. Today in Rio de Janeiro, it is rare to see a wall covered with ivy. Thirty years ago, however, in Laranjeiras, in Conde de Bonfim, in Rio Comprido, in Andarai, in Engenho Novo, in short, in all of the old neighborhoods — years ago areas of relaxation and pleasure — one could find long, ivy covered walls, walls that emitted at every step an air of melancholy and evoked numerous reminiscences.

Joaquim dos Anjos had become familiar with this old country home and with the people who lived there. Finally, these people moved out and the old place was rented to the "Bible Beaters." On Saturdays — this being the day of the week designated for sacred rest — their canticles were intoned almost continuously and even swelled into the surrounding neighborhoods, burdening their audiences with the gloomy shadows of mysticism. The local people did not view them with hostility, however, and a few humble men and poor girls from the surrounding vicinity even came to visit them, an indication of an intellectual superiority over their peers or at least a hope of discovering in these new religious beliefs as opposed to the more traditional ones some sort of solace for their pathetic and ragged souls, some relief from the pain and sorrow that seems to follow each and every human existence.

Some of these people, among whom was Joao Pintor, could rationalize their frequent visits to the "Bible Beaters" because — as Joao would say — they were not like priests who wanted money for everything.

Joao Pintor worked in the shops in Eugenho de Dentro at a job that related directly to the meaning of his surname [painter]. He had very black skin, thick lips, prominent cheekbones, a short forehead, very fine, brilliantly white teeth, long arms, enormous hands, long legs and feet impossible to shod. He had to have his shoes specially made but even so, they fit so poorly on the first day that on the following day, he had to slit them open with his razor blade if he wanted to be able to take a few hobbling steps, if only to go as far as the amusement park.

The Daredevil, a follower of Father Sodre, the chaplain of the Sanctuary of Our Lady of Lourdes, used to say that Joao Pintor got mixed-up with the "Bible Beaters" because they had given him a room at their country place headquarters where he could live for free except for certain minor duties he was to perform. Joao Pintor would have denied this allegation vehemently but it is certain that he lived on their estate.

The Protestants were led by an American, Mr. Quick Shays, a tenacious man full of biblical eloquence that must have been magnificent in English. In his dubious Portuguese, it became simply picturesque. Mr. Quick Shays (or Shays Quick) was a member of that curious race of Yankees who were the founders of various new Christian sects. From time to time, some Protestant citizen of this curious race that desires the happiness of the others, both in Heaven and on earth, by means of the illumination wrought by some new interpretation of one or more verses from the Bible, founded a completely new and unique Christian sect. Then, dedicating himself to the propagation of this sect, he immediately sought to discover dedicated followers although such people might not fully understand just what the difference was between this new religion and the one from which they had just come.

In their own homelands, as here, these disciples of Luther make proselytes although more so there than here. Mr. Shays obtained, among the neighbors of the postman, Joaquim dos Anjos, not exactly proselytes but many listeners, of whom about a fifth finally became converts. When it was time to begin a new class, the novitiates were found sleeping in the Army tents that had been set up in the empty spaces around the main house and in between the old trees that stood on the mismanaged and abandoned country place.

In Mr. Quick Shays's religion, the ceremonies preparatory to the initiation lasted for a week full of fasting and religious chants full of functions and appeals to God, our Eternal Father. The old playground property, with its military encampment-like atmosphere and its never-ending psalmody, soon acquired an unforeseen and weird aspect, that of an open air convent masked by a crude and bellicose scowl. One might say that it was like the detachment of some soldierly or monastic cavalry batallion preparing for combat against the Turks or the infidel Moors somewhere in Palestine or Morocco.

In that particular area, however, those who were orthodox followers of Mr. Shays's religious doctrines were not numerous. In addition to that species already mentioned, there were those who attended his sermons out of mere curiosity or to delight in the oratory of the American pastor. At any rate, his temple was always full on its solemn days.

Those who participated in one religious disposition or others went there without any feelings of aversion since it is characteristic of our poor people to create an extravagant amalgam of religions and beliefs of all sorts and to help themselves to this one or that one, depending upon the crises or momentary hardships then present in their lives. If religion concerns itself with averting life's setbacks, it appeals to sorcery; if it tries to cure some tenacious and stubborn affliction, then it seeks out the spiritualist. But do not speak to our humble people about not having their children baptized by a Catholic priest because there is not one of them who would not become angry! "You're crazy!" they would say. "My child would end up a pagan! May God help me!"

Joaquim dos Anjos didn't frequent Mr. Shays's place or the Reverend Father Sodre's, the one at the Sanctuary of Our Lady of Lourdes, in spite of having been born in a city embalmed by incense and steeped in the sonorous echo of litanies and constant fervor. He was not inspired by religious fervor. His wife, Dona Engracia, however, was devout and to an extreme degree, although she actually went to church very little because of her domestic obligations. Both were in agreement on one point of Roman Catholic religious doctrine: to get the children baptized as soon as possible in the Roman Catholic Apostolic Church. That was what they did, not only Clara, their only surviving daughter, but also all their others who had died.

They had been married for nearly twenty years and Clara, their daughter, the couple's second child, was nearing her seventeenth year.

She was treated by her parents with great devotion, prudence and tenderness. When Clara wasn't with her mother or father, she only went out with Dona Margarida, a very respectable widow who lived there in the neighborhood, and who was teaching Clara embroidery and sewing.

This, however, was a rare occurrence and only happened on Sundays. Clara would then sometimes leave her house to go to the Meier theatre or to Engenho de Dentro. But she did so only when her sewing teacher was willing and available to accompany her because Joaquim was never able to do so since he didn't like to go out on Sundays, the only day of the week he set aside for playing cards with his habitual companions. His wife not only disliked going out on Sundays but on any other day of the week as well. She was sedentary and a homebody.

Joaquim's habitual companions in this card game were two men: Senhor Antonio da Silva Marramaque, his *compadre* since this gentleman was the godfather of Joaquim's only daughter, and Senhor Eduardo Lafoes. Their playing never varied. Every Sunday about nine o'clock, these two gentlemen came knocking at the postman's front door. They never went into the main body of the house but, by following the path that divided it from the neighboring house, directed themselves toward the great tamarind tree in the back yard. Beneath this tree there was a table with score keeping cards, little red and black pieces made from the seeds of a pepper tree, and a deck of cards lying upon it. Also on the table were some small saucers, three snifters and a litre of rum, all in view in the center of the table and imparting a cynical challenge to the conventions of sober propriety.

Joaquim dos Anjos was already there at the table waiting for his friends and reading his favorite paper. They arrived, informally exchanged a few words of greeting, sat down, wet their whistles on the litre of rum, and then began to play using some old coins as chips.

Hours and hours later, while waiting for the Sunday meal which nearly always arrived at their table at the usual supper hour, they kept playing and tippling the rum. Usually they did not cast a glance towards the ring of naked, rocky mountains scalloping the high and distant horizon.

From time to time and without very great intervals in between, Joaquim shouted out to the kitchen:

"Clara, Engracia! Some coffee!"

They answered him, occasionally with a certain peevishness:

"Coming right up!"

In order to prepare the coffee, the women had to get one of two charcoal braziers and a pot from among those they had already used to make supper, and then brew the coffee. All of this only served to make supper even later.

While they waited for the coffee, the three suspended their game and conversed for a while. Marramaque was and always had been more or less political in nature, in his own way at least.

Although he was really only a simple doorman for one of the ministerial offices and didn't actually perform that job or any other job well because of his condition — that of a semi-crippled invalid partly paralyzed on his left side — he had once belonged to a modest circle of bohemian litterati and poets. In this group, along with poetry and assorted literary matters, they also discussed politics a great deal, a habit old Marra-maque still retained. When the revolution of '93 took place, the circle broke up. Some of its members went with Admiral Custodio and others sided with Marshall Floriano. Marramaque was one of the latter and even attained the rank of lieutenant in the army. That was about the time that he suffered his first attack of congestion, that is, at the end of the Marshall's government in '94.

His group didn't include anyone of real prominence but some of its members were worthy of admiration so that on occasion, more well-known groups sought out its members.

Whenever he told stories about this period of his life, he took great pride recount-ing his acquaintance with Paula Nei and his dealings with Luis Murat. He didn't lie about these things although he never confessed to the others in just what capacity he had been a part of the literary circle. Those who knew him from those times could not dispute the aura of honor and respect that always went along with membership in a poetic cenacle. Having intended to write verse, Marramaque's good sense and the integrity of his character soon showed him that he was not suited to the task. He abandoned it and cultivated charades, puzzles, etc. He ended up as a rather skillful charade player and as such, nearly always served as editor or collaborator for the jour-nals his friends and companions from the world of literary bohemia, poets and men of letters, improvised at a moment's notice, men who almost never had money for a new suit of clothes. Growing older and becoming a semi-invalid after two strokes, he was obliged to accept the humble job of doorman simply to have something to live on. His merits and wisdom, however, were not out of keeping with the position. He had learned many things, but in a second-hand manner, and making use of this infor-mation, he enjoyed talking about these matters. As a boy, he had had a good family life and that, more than anything else, really explained the secret source of his knowl-edge. Marramaque, in spite of everything — the state of his health and the difficulty he had in getting around — never dropped his innocuous mania for politics. He in-sisted upon going out to vote, even at the risk of getting involved in some rumpus about universal suffrage, razor fights, head-butting, gun shots and other eloquent electoral manifestations from which, because of the precarious condition of his legs, he could not safely flee with necessary speed.

Having frequented refined people all his life, not as we have seen, to become rich but to seek education and knowledge, and having always dreamed of a destiny other than the one he actually had, and because of his crippled condition, Marramaque was, naturally enough, a rather sour and contrary man. One Sunday, he had singled out Doctor Saulo de Clapin to criticize.

"You'll see! Clapin has had it! He's already finished in politics. He had the impu-dence to go against the popular will; he's skewered himself! The man who has really won is that bearded Melo Brandao, that mixed-blooded Jew! He's a snake in the grass but he's a master at politics."

Joaquim was only moderately interested in arguing about politics but Lafoes had some strong feelings on the subject and retorted:

"That's not so! Do you really think, Marramaque, that an intelligent man, as superior a fellow as Doctor Clapin, is going to let himself get tangled-up with a sweet-talking swindler or even worse, someone like Melo Brandao?!! I should say not! And besides, what about all the working people...."

"What's he done for the working people?" demanded Marramaque.

"A lot."

Lafoes was not a worker as one might think. He was a guard at some public buildings. A Portuguese by birth, he had come to Brazil as a child more than forty years earlier. He got involved very early in the city's water works department and soon attracted the attention of his superiors because of his rigorous conduct. Little by little, they moved him up in rank until finally, he became the supervisor in charge of the gas and water mains and of the spigots that emptied into the laundry tanks of certain houses in the area. He lived very contentedly with this position and later, with his appointments as the information desk officer at a public building, and his Brazilian citizenship. If he had not been so content, it is possible that he might have become wealthy. Nevertheless, everything he did made one think he was because of the self-important airs of this ingenuous bumpkin who worked at some government job, and the solemnity of his demeanor as he crossed those rutted paths that served as roads in the suburbs.

Lafoes always wore a khaki uniform and a cap that bore the letters of his department. He also carried a parasol that, when not unfurled to protect him from the rays of the sun, he used like the walking stick of a Portuguese village vicar, breaking up the dirt and pushing it along only to smooth it out again in time to his long strides.

Lafoes responded thusly to Marramaque:

"A lot. In all the posts that Doctor Clapin has held, he's always tried to get jobs for the greatest number of workers."

"What a great service! He exceeds his funding limit and at the end of two or three months time he sends more than half of these people away . . . you can't call that protection, you've got to call it finagling!"

"Maybe so, but still he *does* something! What about the others? They don't do anything. Actually, he's a democratic man. For a long time now, he's fought for equality among the nation's workers. He doesn't want any distinctions made among public servants and other workers. He believes that anybody who serves his nation — in whatever capacity — is a public servant."

"Nothing but high sounding words! And they will not fill your belly! Why doesn't he work to reduce the high cost of living around here and do something about the high cost of housing?"

"For Heaven's sake, Marramaque!!! Didn't you read his proposal about the construction of houses for poor and below average income families? You read it, didn't you, Joaquim?"

The postman, who had been listening to the conversation but didn't want to offer any opinion, answered Lafoes' question:

"Yes, I did read it but I also read that he increased the rent on his many houses by some forty per cent."

"That's right," Marramaque quickly interjected. "Clapin is very generous with other people's money or with the government's, but with his own he's as stingy as a Jew and as greedy as a money lender. The hypocrite!"

Happily, Clara arrived then with the coffee, and the impassioned discussion drew to a close. Joaquim's two guests then received the girl's greetings:

Blessings, godfather ... good day, Senhor Lafoes.''

They returned her greetings and began to jest with the girl. Marramaque said:

"Well, goddaughter . . . when are youg going to get married?''

"Oh, I don't even think about that,'' she said, making a face.

"What?!!'' observed Lafoes. "You're already getting to be quite a young lady. Listen, on your next birthday.... Yes, it's true, Joaquim, but one thing, though.''

The postman set his cup down and asked:

"What is it?''

"I just wanted to ask your permission to bring a guitar and *modinha* teacher here for Clara's birthday.''

Clara, without thinking, quickly asked:

"Who?''

Lafoes answered:

"Cassi. You....''

The public works guard was unable to finish his sentence because Marramaque interrupted him furiously:

"Are you mixed-up with scum like that? He's somebody who shouldn't be allowed in anybody's house ... certainly not in mine, at least....''

"Why is that?'' inquired the host.

"I'll tell you why in just a moment ... you bet I'll tell you why,'' said Marramaque, becoming even more upset.

They finished their coffee and Clara removed the tray and the cups.

"I wonder who this Cassi fellow could be?'' she thought to herself, seized by a strong, tenacious and unwholesome curiosity.

II

Who was Cassi Jones?

Cassi Jones de Azevedo was the legitimate son of Manuel Borges de Azevedo and Salustiana Baeta de Azevedo. No one ever knew where he had gotten the name ''Jones'' but he used it from about age twenty on, perhaps, as some people explain it, because he thought the English surname sounded nice. The facts, however, are otherwise. During one of her crises of vanity, his mother used to tell people that she was the descendent of some fantastic Lord Jones who was supposed to have been the British Counsel in Santa Catarina, and that her child had thought it good taste to Anglicize his signature with the name of his spuriously aristocratic grandfather.

Cassi was a young man just under thirty, light skinned and freckled, an unimposing person in physiognomy and build. Although he was well-known as the greatest *modinha* player, in addition to having equal renown for other, more truly ignoble deeds, he did not have the shock of long hair typical of a virtuoso of the Spanish guitar or other features of that calling. He dressed conservatively according to the styles of Ouvidor street but, because of his carefully studied appearance and the ''cool'' manner of the suburbanites, his clothes soon attracted the attention of other people who persisted in trying to discover that perfectionist tailor from the outskirts of the town who made his clothes. In keeping with his activities was the only foppish ostentatiousness that he showed, which consisted of drenching his hair with oil, parting it down the middle, and thus achieving the famous style in which heavily plastered bangs hang down over the forehead. He didn't wear a pompadour or mustache. His shoes were always right in style and they had to have those little details demanded by a dapper young man from the suburbs; one who would enchant and seduce the ladies with his irresistible Spanish guitar.

That guitar was very mysterious indeed; it truly seemed to be some sort of elixir or talisman of love. Whether it was he or his guitar or both, the fact is that Senhor Cassi Jones — even at a relatively tender age — could cite close to ten deflowerings and the seduction of an even greater number of married women!

These deeds were nearly always followed by scandal in the papers, at police headquarters or in some magistrate's courtroom, but Cassi, speaking through his lawyer, slandered his victims, made use of the most ignoble means to prove his ''innocence,'' and always succeeded in escaping a forced marriage or spending time in the reformatory.

Whenever the police or those responsible for his victims — parents, brothers or legal guardians — got him into a position where they could prosecute him effectively, he ran to his mother, Dona Salustiana, crying and swearing his innocence, and alleging that whoever the girl was — and this could be any one of a number of his victims — she had already been ''deflowered'' by some other fellow and that entire affair was merely a trap set for him. They hoped to cover up one evil deed with another. After all, they all knew that he, Cassi, was from such a good family ... etc., etc.

In general, the girls he seduced were of moderate means and varying skin color; he didn't discriminate. The real question was whether there was anybody among these girl's kinsfolk capable of overcoming his father's influence, gained through solicitations from his mother.

Cassi's mother listened to his confession but she did not believe it. Since she did have aristocratic pretentions, however, it was repugnant for her to imagine her son married to some black-skinned servant girl, a poor mulatto seamstress, or an illiterate but white washerwoman.

Thanks to her prejudices based on their supposedly aristocratic origins and lineage, she didn't hesitate to battle with her husband over the question of whether he would act to free their boy from jail or from some police inspired wedding.

"But it's the sixth girl, Salustiana!!!"

"Oh, come now! He gets slandered a lot, that's all...."

"Slander, nothing! That boy is perverse, he's shameless. I know the names of the others! Listen, there's Ines, that little black girl who was our parlormaid, the one we raised; there's Luisa, the one who was hired by doctor Camacho; there's Santinha, the one who helped out her mother by taking in other people's sewing and who used to live over on Valentim street; and then there's Bernarda who worked at the 'Joie de Vivre'...."

"But that's all history, 'Maneco.' Do you want your own child to go to jail? Because if he has to get married to one of those bitches, then he won't *get* married! I won't allow it!"

"It'd be better for everyone if he did go to jail. At least that way he wouldn't be corrupting somebody's household everyday."

"Well, you do what you want. But if you don't take the necessary steps, I will. I'm going to see my brother, doctor Baeta Picanco," the arrogant woman concluded.

Cassi's father was a truly upright man. Though narrow in his ideas and routinized by the civil service job he had held for nearly thirty years, he had certain profound moral sentiments which guided him in his relationship with his children. He was never openly affectionate and he avoided any exhibition of exaggerated sentimentality. He was, however, capable of holding his children in profound esteem and of loving them, but even so, he did not ignore his paternal duty of judging them lucidly and of punishing them in accordance with the nature of their respective wrongdoings.

He was not a tall man but he always held his head erect. He had a high, straight forehead, a strong jaw and a firm gaze framed by the gold wires of his *pincenez*. A bit obese, he was in truth a respectable and likeable old man. In spite of his bureaucratic grandeur and the gruffness and dryness of his manner, everybody thought well of him in the same measure that they hated and despised his son. People even felt sorry for him, facing as he did, a lifetime of acerbity because of Cassi's debaucheries.

His wife wasn't much loved in those parts either, nor was she held in great esteem. She had delusions of being a great lady and felt she was far superior to other people in the area and even to her acquaintances. Her pride stemmed from two sources: the first, a brother who was an Army doctor with the rank of Captain; and the second, having attended the Sisters of Charity School.

When somebody asked her, ''What was your father?'' Dona Salustiana responded, ''He was a Military man,'' subtly distorting the true meaning behind her chatter. Her father wasn't exactly a Military man. He was simply a clerk who worked at the Army Arsenal. Through much sacrifice and thanks to a modest sum of money which had once happened to come into his hands, he had been able to educate his two children.

Dona Salustiana's vanity, however, never allowed her to admit this and was so contagious that her two daughters, Catarina and Irene, now always referred to their grandfather as though he had been a General in the Paraguayan campaign. The girls were less vain than their mother but much more ambitious, especially when it came to marriage. Dona Salustiana had married Manuel when he was still only a trainee who had to do proofreading at night for the local newspapers just so that he could meet the expenses of running his household. Catarina and Irene, however, dreamed of marrying professional men, either those with good positions or rich ones, because they thought they were on the verge of blossoming out, the first in music and piano, as a result of attending the fraudulent National School of Music, and the second, through attendance at the dull and tedious Normal School in the capital city.

Needless to say, both of them had a profound disgust for their brother, not only for his vile moral conduct but also for his equine stupidity and absolute lack of good manners and decent conduct.

In the beginning, their father consented — in spite of everything — to allow Cassi, the illustrious Cassi, to sit at the family supper table. Nobody said a word to him unless it were his mother. The girls talked to their father or their mother or to each other. If Cassi showed signs of wanting to say something, old Manuel would give him a severe look and the girls would hush up.

There was one painful event provoked by Cassi's perversity that made his father take the extreme action of expelling him from their home and table. Thanks to Dona Salustiana's intervention, however, he wasn't wholly expelled ultimately.

Among his sisters' friends, there was an extremely poor girl who lived in the neighboring area. Her mother was the widow of an Army Captain and she, Nair, was their only daughter. With the help of some relatives the widow had been able to put the girl on the right track in life with studies appropriate to young ladies. Nair had a talent for music and approached Catarina hoping to learn music from her. She was about eighteen, cheerful and gay, a dark complected brunette with very black hair, was small and lively and had turbulent, luminescent eyes.

Cassi caught sight of the girl and immediately thought of her as prey in spite of Nair's not being totally devoid of protection. Cassi wanted to seduce the girl in his father's own house whenever Nair came there to receive music lessons from his sister. The latter, however, perceiving the scheme, forbade her brother, under the threat of telling their father, to come into the room when she was giving lessons to Nair. The mere mention of his father's name terrified Cassi who didn't admire him but did indeed respect his father because the old man, strict as he was, was quite capable of throwing him out into the street again. If that were to happen, Cassi would have no place to go and the little money he could earn gambling at cock-fighting and from the commissions he got for arranging loans would be absorbed in paying for housing and food with little or nothing left over for clothing, shoes and neckties. Without these things, Cassi would be lost. Good-bye romance! If he wanted it, he would have to pay for it....

Considering this possibility, Cassi obeyed his sister; and decided to approach Nair on the outside. When she was leaving, he would go out first, stand in the doorway of the bakery and greet her as she passed by. Later on, he was able to strike up a conversation with her and finally he succeeded in declaring his intentions by means of the fateful letter. This letter was usually a reproduction of a model given him by one of his disreputable companions, one Ataliba do Timbo who had obtained it from a drunken poet who lived in Piedade area. That poet whom the meddlesome Ataliba described in such glowing terms as excellent was the celebrated Leonardo Flores, a name known throughout Brazil and a man who lived the pure life, that is, one consisting entirely of dreams.

Finally, however, little Nair, inexperienced and a victim of confused emotions, without anyone to orient her properly, placed her fate and her belief in Cassi's power, and in so doing, took the wrong step. Her mother finally discovered Nair's error because of her belly, and ran to see Senhor Manuel, but he wasn't at home. Because of this, she had to speak to Dona Salustiana who, drawing herself up haughtily, said dryly:

"My dear lady, I am unable to do anything for you. My son is a grown man."

"But if you could only talk to him with the sentiments of a mother, a mother who has daughters of her own, maybe you could get him to do something about this. Dear lady, please take pity on my girl and me!"

She began to sob and cry.

Without showing even the slightest hint of having been touched by that woman's implacable pain, Dona Salustiana responded sourly:

"I can't do a thing about it, my dear lady. I've already told you. You can go to the authorities, to the police if you wish. But that's all you can do."

Nair's mother calmed down a bit and remarked:

"That's just what I wanted to avoid. It would cause a terrible scandal for me and for you and your family."

"We don't have anything to do with what Cassi does. But now let me say that if your girl were *our* daughter...."

She didn't finish the indirect insult but got up and extended her hand to the disconsolate mother to dismiss her.

The widow left downcast. From there she went to see the district police chief and explained everything to him. The chief told her:

"Although I haven't been in this district for six months, I know all about this scoundrel Cassi. My greatest ambition has been to get him on some good, solid charge. But I can't, at least not in your case. You're not destitute. You've got your insurance checks and half your husband's Army pay. I can only take the initiative for prosecution when the victim is the daughter of destitute parents with no resources."

"But isn't there any other way, sir?"

"Not unless you hire a lawyer."

"Dear God! Where am I going to find enough money for that? My poor daughter, disgraced like this! Oh, my God!"

And she began to cry profusely. When she finally quieted down, the chief of police ordered one of his men to accompany the woman to her home. Then he began to ponder all the vile activities, all the pain and misery in people's lives and his everyday duties of investigating them because of the nature of his job.

The next day, Nair's mother committed suicide by taking lysol.

The papers probed into the event and exposed the causes of the suicide with all the details. When he read the paper on the train, Manuel de Azevedo, Cassi's father, jumped off at the first station and returned home bursting in like a hurricane. He had been transformed and his face was distorted by hatred that had changed him into another creature, a man who was no longer the kindly, reserved and amiable bureaucrat he really was.

"Is he still here?"

"Who?" asked his wife.

"Cassi," said the man, with fists tightly clenched and a wild-eyed glare searching out the four corners of the room.

"What's wrong, husband?" said the now frightened woman.

"Here, read this!"

He gave her the newspaper, pointing out the suicide story.

"But what guilt does this...."

Dona Salustiana never finished the sentence; her husband interrupted her immediately:

"Oh, he's guilty!!! That villain has no moral sensibility whatsoever. That murderer...! That wretch...! His only aim is to seduce all the girls and women who pass in front of his eyes. I don't want him around here any longer.... I don't want to see him at my table ever again. Tell him that, Salustiana; Tell him that before I kill him."

The girls had just arrived home and guessed the cause of the explosion of hatred and anger, such a rare occurrence in their father. They tried to calm him.

"Calm down, father, calm down."

Catarina who had already seen the paper, suffered greatly because of Nair's dishonoring. She sincerely lamented the tragic outcome of her student's mother, and said to her father:

"Father; I feel partly responsible for this since I brought Nair here to study music with me."

After a pause, she added:

"What's there to do? That's life."

"I don't ever want him here again," repeated the head of the family.

The newspapers weren't satisfied with simply reporting the facts of the suicide. They revealed Cassi's life and told about his many escapades. Upon his mother's advice he went to spend some time with his uncle, a doctor who had a small farm in Guaratiba. Through the stories in the daily papers, one could easily organize the entire web of deceits, lies, and false promises with which he had enveloped his poor, ingenuous victim whose seduction had caused the suicide of her mother. As usual, he made no mention of his affairs to anyone, especially not to his mother and father. Earlier, in order to win the poor girl's confidence, he wrote in his letter to her that he had told his mother how much he loved her, or, and we quote:

"To mama I confessed that I was madly in love with you, ..." and then he told her, "...let me warn you not to put any stock in what they say about me and I beg you to take into account all my suffering." And, with this spelling and syntax, he ended by saying: "Think carefully and see that you're resolved to do what you said in your note." He claimed to be a poor devil who adored her so much and lamented that this sentiment was not returned by her.

In another note, he indicated he was interested in the state of Nair's health and, after giving some instructions about leaving the window open so he could climb through it, said, "As soon as I found out that you were bedridden, I went to doctor R.S. to find out what you had and he told me that you had done something crazy like soaking your feet in cold water," etc., etc. Then he touched upon the secret details of feminine hygiene and added, "It was a great sadness to learn that doctor R.S. knows about your personal habits." Towards the end of the letter or almost at the end, he said, "Finally, I should know if you don't want to be completely mine, as I am yours."

He didn't stay at his uncle's house for long. The doctor, the pride of his sister Salustiana and the guardian whom she always placed in the middle of his nephew's unsavory adventures, was suspicious that the latter was plotting one of his schemes there around his home so, without further delay, he sent him back to his sister's house, back to Cassi's mother. He told her to keep the boy because, he, Doctor Baeta Picanco, never wanted to have such a nephew in his house again.

Cassi didn't return immediately to his paternal home, which was located near one of the first stations after leaving the downtown area. He stayed around Engenho de Dentro. Through Ataliba do Timbo, he sent a letter to his mother asking for instructions. His mother responded by telling him to come home but to avoid meeting his father at all costs. She had arranged things, and he would always have a place to eat and sleep. The basement was reserved for him, as well as the granary, a place where he could relax and where his father rarely went. He ate breakfast, lunch, and supper in the compartment of the basement where he lived. On the first morning when he woke up in his familial, though humiliating dwelling, he immediately thought about going to see the cages that housed his fighting cocks, the most revolting, unpleasant and repugnantly ferocious bird ever seen. They were fine. His mother had taken care of them just as he had asked her.

His fighting cocks were the only motivating force behind his dubious activities; indeed, they constituted his only business enterprise. At times, he won a great deal of money by betting at the cockpit, something that tended to offset the losses he had perhaps had at dice. That was the way he found the means by which to pay his tailor or buy dapper shoes and eye-catching neckties. He performed every possible type of operation with his roosters, always with the goal of making money; he bartered them — always with strings attached — he sold them, bred hens, for future sale and gifts to important people from whom, he supposed, he might one day need aid and assistance against the police and justice.

Incapable of any continuous work, it was astonishing to see him caring for those horrifying fowl every morning. He looked after all the litters feeding them millet and chaff and examining the baby chicks one by one to see if any had the yaws or distemper.

No matter what time he went to bed, in the morning there he was attending to his Malayan roosters and their progeny of cockerels and chicks.

He had never been able to keep a job and the deficiency of his learning impeded him from getting one equal to the social pretensions he had inherited from his mother. Because of his disconnected education, he was incapable of assiduous work, a condition that became an incapacity was now almost a disease. His mother's morbid fondness for him, in keeping with his personal vanity, together with his father's scornful indifference, in time made of Cassi the worst domestic vagabond one could imagine. He is a very Brazilian type.

If he was already egotistic, his egotism tripled in scope. In life, he pursued only his own pleasure as long as he could gratify it immediately. No consideration of friendship, respect for the suffering of others, empathy for the misfortunes of his fellow man, and no moral dictums ever held him back when he was seeking gratification. He was restrained only by force, by the decisiveness of a revolver wielded with determination. Then, yes....

Sometimes, he got what he deserved. Once while traveling on the trains, he noticed that a young girl carrying books and dressed in the uniform of a normal school student was looking at him a great deal.

He took careful note of her appearance and on the following day and at the same time, positioned himself at the station and waited for her. She didn't come. He waited for another train but she still didn't come. He waited for several trains. On the day after, he was happier; she came. He found a convenient seat and began to give her the eye. The girl paid no attention to him. He persisted for several days. One fine day he was calmly searching for the ungrateful girl when she appeared accompanied by a young man who, by the intimacy with which he was treating her and judging from his age, appeared to be either the girl's brother or husband. Quite accustomed to coping with relations of this sort — though spineless ones — he was not intimidated. Seated across from him, they made the same trip chatting calmly. Cassi watched them insistently. They arrived at the downtown stop and the young man said goodbye to the girl who made her way off to school. The young gentleman turned and let his gaze seek our Senhor Cassi.

"Are you Cassi?"

Cassi Jones responded:

"I am."

"I've been wanting to talk to you very much. Let's go to a cafe. It's a private matter and we'll be more comfortable there having a vermouth."

Cassi was starting to smell a rat but went along with the stranger who, with a smiling and rambling air, continued speaking:

"You may not know me. But I, my dear sir, know you very well. In the suburbs, everyone knows about your accomplishments, Senhor Cassi Jones. And although I've only been living here for a short time, I've already heard about your reputation."

Cassi was growing uneasy with the young man's calm and began to size-up his physique. He hadn't brought a razor because he feared arrest, after that business about Nair and her mother's suicide, but if he were armed, well.... He tried to gauge the muscularity of the stranger. He seemed weak rather than strong but he carried himself well. They arrived at the cafe and sat down. The waiter served their vermouth and when they had drunk about half of it, the other said abruptly to Cassi:

"Do you know who that girl who was with me is?"

Caught off guard, Cassi wasn't able to equivocate and said quickly:

"I don't have any idea."

"She's my sister," confirmed the stranger.

"I didn't know that either," the terrible Cassi responded docilely.

"Naturally you couldn't have known," allowed the young man. "I leave home early to get to the office and I return home late, since I eat lunch and supper in the city. Now, I called you over here to tell you something; if you continue to harrass my sister, I'll put five slugs in your head."

Upon saying this, he pulled out from his inside coat pocket a magnificent Smith and Wesson highly polished and with a luxurious butt made of mother-of-pearl.

Cassi redoubled his efforts not to let his fear show and feigning an air of calm, said:

"But my dear sir, I don't believe that I've ever failed to show your sister her due respect."

"That's true but you must stop bothering her," affirmed the other who then added, putting an end to the conversation:

"Would you like another drink?"

"No. Thank you."

They said good-bye without shaking hands and Cassi went off to his gang, Ataliba do Timbo, Zeze Mateur, Franco Sousa and Arnaldo.

One of them asked him:

"What'd that guy want with you?"

"Nothing. He's my neighbor; knowing that I'm an old resident, he asked me to arrange a horse sale for him. He was going to give me a commission."

That was Cassi and that was the way he maintained his reputation as a tough customer. Do not believe that he held any esteem for the youths who ran around with him, or that he had any sense of friendship for them. He didn't care for them, or anybody other than himself. It was a gang worthy of him, which deceived him about the vacuum around him created by the absence of all the other young men in those parts.

Ataliba do Timbo was a light skinned mulatto, foppish, quite well-groomed but obnoxious because of his false arrogance and his fatuousness. He had been a workman in one of the State shops. He became involved with Cassi and in a short time, abandoned his job and his mother for whom he was the only breadwinner, and decided to imitate his master. But he had not been so lucky. He had gotten involved in a matter with the police and a young girl demanding marriage, habits of Cassi's, but he got caught. They made him get married. He was manly enough to stay with the woman although she resignedly suffered all manner of privation living in the horrible district of Dona Clara while he ran around very elegantly attired. He even had several soccer uniforms.

He could make a little money shooting dice or playing cards and even soccer at which he was considered a good player — a *pleiel,* as they say there.

He had been expelled or had voluntarily resigned from several clubs because his teammates suspected that he had been bribed by their adversaries so that they could score points. Finally, he became an agent for the lottery and his wife began to enjoy a few more comforts.

Poor Ernestina! She used to be so happy, such a chatterbox; she was an attractive little girl with her slender figure and her brown complexion, a little too dark it's true but not to the point of making her ugly, when she met Ataliba. And today? She was skinny, had several children, and showed signs of all manner of suffering; she was always poorly shod although during the time she was single, shoes were her only luxury. To see her then and to see her now!

Zeze Mateus was truly an imbecile! He didn't have two ideas to put together and he never saved a thing from the money he made. His only real interest was drinking and telling everybody how tough he was. He had tried all kinds of jobs: hoer; fish and vegetable seller; hod carrier; and bird catcher. He had other talents along these same lines.

He was white-skinned with a thick, pasty face that was full of premature wrinkles, and toothless. He was flabby and indolent. He had a low forehead and a long, narrow head that people called "donkey head."

Totally inoffensive and almost an invalid because of his native imbecility and his drinking, one family for which he performed minor services — going shopping, going to the butcher shop, housecleaning, etc. — gave him a shack at their country place where he slept and ate if he was there at mealtime. That human ruin was the best one of the bunch and the only one who didn't have evil in his heart. He was sub-human and nothing more.

Franco Sousa on the other hand, was a more refined good-for-nothing who, at some time or another, had joined Cassi's group. He gave himself the title of attorney and made his living by bilking the credulous clients who fell into his clutches. Everyone knew that he didn't really do that kind of work, that he was absolutely incapable of doing it because he did not know any forensic tricks and because he was, in fact, not a lawyer. Nevertheless, ingenuous hicks or simple widows always appeared and sought him out for his services concerning the boundaries of disputed lands or the eviction of backsliding tenants. He received advance payments and a little money ahead, and in accordance with the ingenuousness and lack of experience of his clients, did nothing. Meanwhile, he lived very decently with his wife, sons, and daughters. Cassi had never set foot in his house and after a while, Franco began to keep away from the guitar player, thanks to the advice of his wife who was extremely concerned about the reputation of her daughters, fast becoming young ladies.

If there were candles, however, fruit, cheese, cookies, or berries, he would take them home and tell his wife that the only reason he struggled so hard to make money was so he could buy such tasty morsels for their children. He made use of some of the most startling ruses in order to avoid paying rent for the house in which he lived. In one, eight months late in paying his rent, he was presented with all the bills by the collector. Arnoldo asked to see them and then demanded to keep them for a time alleging that he was going to consult somebody competent in matters concerning the authenticity of their official seals because they did not seem legal and proper to him. He never returned them, and despite all kinds of threats, he continued to live in the house for another four months. His neighbors used to say that he was also in the habit of snatching money out of his children's hands when he found them alone, holding the money in plain view with childish openness as they were on their way to the store where they were supposed to do the shopping for the entire household.

It is useless to repeat that Cassi had no sense of friendship at all for these men, not because of the baseness of their characters and morals, a matter in which he superseded everybody, but for the very simple reason that his moral and emotional nature was sterile, a wasteland. He never showed even the slightest sign of affection for his parents or his sisters. For his mother, who had many times gotten him out of scrapes with the police when they were on the verge of sending him to the reformatory, he only hinted at fondness, and then only when he was mixed-up with the police again or in front of some judge. His background and his beginnings explain in part his moral and emotional sterility.

His upbringing and education were quite neglected. He was the couple's firstborn at a time when the demands of supporting the family obliged his father to work day and night, which meant that he spent very little time at home and was unable to take care properly of such needs. Rebellious at a tender age, Cassi was spoiled by his mother's prejudices and excessive gentleness. He didn't go to school; he played hooky running with other urchins through the woods on the outskirts of his parents' residence located at that time in Itapiru. What they did, one can only guess, but his mother pretended not to notice and ran her hand over her darling child's head saying nothing to his father who slaved away almost twenty-four hours a day. Cassi grew up, therefore, with no moral force to guide him; his father would have been the one to impose it.

When his financial situation improved, thanks to an opportune promotion, and after the purchase of the house near the Rocha station, effected with the proceeds of an inheritance his wife had received, Manuel de Azevedo found his son, age thirteen, completely corrupted. He was smoking in public, read poorly, stuttered and stammered, and wrote worse. He sent him off to the Salesians in Niteroi. The weekly information reports were discouraging and at the end of three or four months at the school — it isn't known just what depravity Cassi committed there — on one fine afternoon and in the company of a thin priest with the sharp, angular features of an ascetic, Cassi was brought home to be turned over to his father. The Reverend Father spoke to him at some length and Manuel de Azevedo, nearly in tears, then said good-bye to the priest. Manuel begged the priest's pardon and then said to the ecclesiastic in this singular fashion:

The last of the *modinha* player's partisans was one Arnaldo. He was even more disgusting than Cassi. His occupation consisted of stealing on the train: parasols, walking sticks, and the packages of passengers who were napping or who were otherwise distracted. In the afternoon, his specialty was packages; sometimes, very late at night, he positioned himself on the edge of some little frequented station and just as the train was starting to pick up a little speed, he reached in through the compartment windows and snatched off the passenger's hats, especially if they were straw hats and new. He would then sell them the next day just as he sold the parasols, the walking sticks and the contents of the packages if they contained anything of value such as woolens or underwear, books, crockery, silverware, etc.

"You are right, completely right. I am sorry to have a child who's so evil and vicious at such a young age. What a chastisement ... my God!"

His wife wanted to know the reason for the expulsion but the father's dignity and sense of shame prevented him from telling his wife what the boy had done.

Several days later, he proposed to his wife that they have the boy learn some trade by means of which they hoped to discipline him. Dona Salustiana got upset and shouted angrily:

"My son learn a trade, become a laborer! I should say not! He's the nephew of a doctor and the grandson of a man who spent many years in the service of his country."

Always aware of the difficulties of their early years when she had helped him so much and given him the strength to carry on, Manuel held a great and sincere affection for his wife and did everything possible to avoid countering her wishes, and consequently, he did not pursue the point any further. Months later, however, just as he was arriving home, his wife and their two daughters, all crying, begged him to go and free Cassi who was a prisoner at the police station. The lad was about sixteen years old and showed signs of being well along in a career of fraud and swindling. He had been apprehended by a guard while inside a vacant house attempting to rip out the lead water mains in order to sell them.

His father returned to the idea of putting him in a shop to see if manual labor, either by dint of exhaustion or by association with honest, hard-working people, could steer him clear of the bad path he had started. His mother consented although it was repugnant to her, and he became a printer's apprentice.

At the end of one month, however, he was let go because, after going to collect on a bill for some visiting cards, an amount of about five *mil-reis,* he returned without the money saying that he had lost it. After a careful search, however, the money was found intact between his stocking and high topped shoe.

His fascination for money and his obsession with it were his weaknesses. He wanted to have money but without working for it, and to have it only for himself. He never repaid even the smallest debt he had and he never gave money to anyone. There were those who, knowing him and knowing about his unwholesome stinginess, explained his endless deflowerings and his constant seduction of young married women as the result of a scarcity of money, a lack that had started him down the path of such wanton love affairs. It was also the result of sexual activity carried to the extreme, further explained by his stupidity.

Whether it was because of this or that cause, this or that motive, the fact is that he was not a neurotic or a psychopath. He never succumbed to the impulses of a sick man; he did everything in a calculating fashion with complete deliberation. Quite stupid in general, he nevertheless mapped out his plans for seduction and debasement with the consummate skill of the intelligence of other natures. He outlined everything lucidly and showing great forethought, removed any obstacles.

He carefully sought out his victim, feigned love for her, wrote abominable, languorous letters, acted as if he were suffering for her, and employed the entire arsenal of old-fashioned art of seduction. It was an arsenal that had a great effect upon the weak hearts of the poor girls of the area. They were girls in whom poverty, limited intelligence and educations combined to make them concentrate their hopes for happiness in the powers of Love, in great and eternal Love, and in requited Passion.

Without being a psychologist or anything like one, Cassi Jones knew unconsciously how to take advantage of the propitious ground of his victims' morbid psychological condition in order to consummate his horrifying and cowardly crimes. And, nearly always, the Spanish guitar and the *modinha* were his accomplices....

III

In spite of Marramaque's lack of formal education, even rudimentary education, he had lived around learned and well-educated people and had mingled with people of different social classes. He was from a small city in the state of Rio de Janeiro, near the "Royal Court" [Rio de Janeiro] as they used to say. When his primary school studies were finished, his parents sent him to work in a general store in the city. We still had slavery then although it was beginning to come to an end, and the old province of Rio de Janeiro was rich and prosperous with its highly controversial coffee plantations populated by black slaves who suffered from whippings and the torture of the stocks.

The store where Marramaque was an employee carried a little of everything: hardware, ready-made clothes, shirts, pants, coarsely woven long-johns for working men, firearms, crockery, etc., etc. Its owner bought directly from the Court's own wholesalers. In addition to this commerce, the owner was the intermediary between the farm workers and the giant commercial establishments in the capital city, that is, he bought merchandise there while representing accounts for the farmers, a service for which he received a commission.

Marramaque was contemplative and melancholy and spent his time resting his elbows on the counter of the store listening to the drovers and farm hands tell all kinds of stories — deeds of bravery, ill-fated encounters on deserted roads, musical improvisation duels on guitars and of rustic love affairs.

In temperament, he did not take after his father who was a very active fellow from the north of Portugal, a hard-working man, reserved and frugal. After a few years in Brazil, he succeeded in saving some money and buying some land on which he cultivated the so-called minimum tillage crops, cassavas, sweet potatoes, squash, tomatoes, okra, oranges, cashews and melons, the latter item, providing him with quite a reasonable profit towards the end of one year and the beginning of the next. With the passage of time, he bought a small boat and twice a week, accompanied by a companion whom he paid, he transported the products of his labor, navigating a small, more or less canalized river and crossing Guanabara to the market. He went down the river with the land breeze and returned with the sea breeze.

His son, however, was not capable of such endeavor. Rather, he was more like his mother who, although nearly white, still retained certain traces of her Indian blood and sang languid, melancholy *modinhas* all day long.

As an overgrown boy, there were great mists within his soul, a diffuse desire to pour out his grief and dreams on to sheets of paper in verse or whatever form he could manage. He also possessed a strong sense of justice. The spectre of slavery with its retinue of infamy caused him a great and secret revulsion.

One day, a traveler who had stopped at the store to rest left on the table in the room where he had been staying, a volume of Casimiro de Abreu's *Primaveras*.

Marramaque had never read any verse regularly. Only in the journals and magazines that happened to fall into his hands, on scraps of paper and on the loose pages of newspapers that ended up at the warehouse as packing material was he able to read any poetry at all. Consequently, in his melancholy nature full of a sweet sadness were found an obscure sentiment concerning the shabbiness of his destiny and a propitious terrain so that Casimiro de Abreu's book fell upon his soul like a revelation of new lands and new heavens. Marramaque shed tears over it and dreamed of the sorrowful grieving of the *sabia* [Brazilian bird] of Sao Joao da Barra and did not fail to note that between the poet of the *Primaveras* and himself, there was something in common — both had begun their careers as sales clerks at a country store. Reading the verses of the fluminense tanager caused a crystallization of his most profound emotions. Marramaque resolved to act, that is, to acquire some education ... and to write verse too. But in order to accomplish this, he had to leave, he had to go to the Royal Court.

From time to time, there at the store where he slept, travelling salesmen stopped, men who worked for the great commercial houses of the Court and who had business with Senhor Vicente Aires, Marramaque's boss. Marramaque's natural goodness, his helpfulness and his amiable radiance, an effect of his vague and accumulated daydreams, made him much esteemed by everyone. There was one fellow, however, whom Marramaque liked even more than the others. He was a young Portuguese gentleman, one Senhor Mendonca, Henrique de Mendonca Souto. He was in all things just the opposite of poor Marramaque; he was cheerful, fun-loving, garrulous and could drink his full share, but he was always honest, loyal and straight-forward.

One particular evening while staying in one of the backrooms of Senhor Vicente Aires' store, and having returned from a game of cards at the house of the sacristan of the church, this cheerful salesman came upon the clerk Marramaque reading Casimiro de Abreu's book of poems. It was very late at night, well past midnight, and since the clerk had to get up at five o'clock in the morning in order to open up the store and attend to the drovers and travelers who would be getting ready to leave, such late night activity caused *Seu* [Mister] Mendonca much astonishment:

"Still reading, boy?!! Don't you remember that you'll have to be on your feet in just a little while from now? Good Lord!!!"

"I was waiting for you," said Marramaque.

"Oh really! Then do you think that I don't know enough to get undressed and into bed? What are you reading, anyhow...?"

"*Primaveras,* by Casimiro de Abreu!"

The travelling salesman finished undressing and lay down. After pulling up the covers, he asked Marramaque:

"Do you like poetry, boy?"

Marramaque hesitated in answering and Mendonca said gruffly:

"Go ahead and say so if you do, boy! It's no crime. Anybody can see that you do. Go ahead and say so!"

"Yes sir, I do," said the sales clerk timidly.

"Then you ought to go to Rio," added Mendonca quickly. "You ought to go to Rio and study and . . . well, who knows what might happen there." Mendonca then thought for a moment and said, ''Commerce doesn't seem to suit you. There's a lot of work to do and you're not cut out for it . . . you're an apprentice poet! You've got an inclination for things like poetry and you're bored here. The thing for you to do is to work in some pharmacy. Why don't you tell your father that I can arrange everything for you. I'll write you about it just as soon as I get to Rio.''

Mendonca kept his word and the father consented that Marramaque go to Rio de Janeiro. He went to work in a pharmacy and at night went about completing his formal education as best he could in the philanthropic institutions that existed at the time.

Later on, he tried to write verse. Once he was surprised by one of the habitues of the pharmacy while composing some poetry. The pharmacies of that time were the meeting places for the grave and serious people of the neighborhood, people who went late in the afternoon or during the evening after dining to such places to amuse themselves and to chat. The person who surprised the young Marramaque while he was writing some verse was Senhor Jose Brito Condeixa, second officer of the Foreign Ministry and a poet but, for some time now, a poet only for festive and commemorative occasions. In addition to publishing sonnets and other forms of poetry that alluded to the festivities on days of celebration, he never forgot to commemorate the important household dates of the Imperial Family and he did so in verses that had a distinctly Chinese flavor to them. He was awaiting nomination to the Order of the Rose but he received it only toward the end of the Empire when the third volume of *A Synopsis of National Legislation Concerning Those Laws that Refer to the Foreign Ministry* came off the national press.

Reading the adolescent's poems, Brito Condeixa decided that he liked them and swore that he would champion the clerk's cause. He spoke to the boy's boss and got him a job in a book and stationery shop on the Rua Quitanda. It was frequented by poets and men of letters who had been preparing for their first serious steps during the last fifteen years of the Empire. He got to know them well and was always selected to be secretary, manager or treasurer of their often ephemeral publications. He happily let his job at the stationery shop go and threw himself into the literary skirmishes and disappointments involved in publishing their papers and in running their small press with ardor and enthusiasm and with abolitionist and republican fervor, especially abolitionist fervor.

Such a contrary and uncertain journalistic enterprise provided little or nothing in terms of income for Marramaque, however, and he lived a life of privation and pressing need. Without taking leave of his poet, writer, parodist and artist companions, he finally had to take a second job as a kind of travelling bookkeeper writing financial reports here and there so that he could earn enough money to maintain his house, food supply and clothing needs and at times, enough to help out his comrades. He always remained very much a bachelor.

Marramaque retained from his acolytic life in literary bohemia many lively remembrances that he later liked to talk about, imbuing these tales with a deeply moving sense of *saudade*. He had anecdotes about one person, told the circumstances of another, then recounted somebody else's life story and narrated everything with flashes of wit and sureness of memory. The figure of his own time who most impressed him was a minor poet who never gained a nickel's worth of fame and notoriety and who is today almost completely forgotten. In everything concerning this poet, Marramaque resorted to the profound sentiment employed when speaking of a dearly beloved brother:

"Ah! Aquiles! What a soul! What a poet!" Turning to an occasional interlocutor, he might then say, "You, sir . . . don't know him?"

"No. I don't remember him."

"Not even his name? He left many works."

Whoever he was conversing with would respond, sensitively:

"The name. . . ? Oh, why yes . . . of course. . . ."

And then Marramaque would forge ahead.

"What a great spirit Aquiles Varejao was! He died just a short time ago, in '94 or '95, and if my memory doesn't fail me, in the Santa Casa Hospital. He died in the worst kind of misery. Even so, everything he ever earned — he was a typographer by trade — was always available for distribution among his friends. I was unable to go and see him at the end . . . I'd had my first heart attack and was undergoing treatments but I remember his last sonnet. It was published in the *Gazette.* What a thing of beauty! Aquiles was a poet who didn't have to strain for effect; he didn't need a compass or a straight edge to make his point! Just listen to this:"

And, struggling because of the semi-paralyzed condition of the left side of his mouth and with his eyes bulging out because of the strain of his struggle to pronounce the words well, he would recite:

"Prostrate upon this pallet, I feel life
Passing by, bit by bit, seeking out the nothingness;
For me there shall never be another morning sun,
But only the tremor of the dying day's light.

Pleasures, where can you be? The long avenue of
Loves upon which I have trod on this long journey?
All is finished. This oasis just precedes
the tolling of the departure bell.

Happy is he who has a family! He has the love
Of his mother and his wife near his bed and he
Does not suffer the horror of discovering himself lonely.

But to my fate I am submissive;
I ought, beating my wings, without a snug retreat,
To seek what? A more perfect world?"

Nearly without exception, Marramaque finished his recitation of his friend's verses with moist eyes. The listener was moved not only because of the pain expressed by the declaimer but also because of the elegiac tone of the sonnet, and, before anything else, commented:

"It's pretty . . . yes, it's really lovely!"

Marramaque, a frustrated poet, had one great virtue, such as it was: he never denigrated those companions of his who moved up in life or who gained fame and fortune. He always praised everyone without ever taking note of any flaws in their characters.

Having lived his life in this fashion, in such varied and distinct manners, gaining experience with and knowledge of men and life, he was well suited to judge just what sort of man Cassi Jones was. Furthermore, because of his intimacy with men of letters, poets and writers, Marramaque had acquired the tyrannical habit of reading daily all of the journals and papers he could lay his hands on in the government bureau where he worked. Indeed, because of his health, he did little else.

From time to time, Marramaque encountered certain news items that were more than merely scabrous; at times they were truly gory stories in which the name of the notorious guitar player was often involved. He remembered some of them perfectly well because they had caused in his soul, the backward soul of an idealist and a dreamer, the soul of a poet who wished only to be loving and chivalrous in his dealing with people, the greatest sense of revulsion and an irrepressible sense of nausea. Joaquim dos Anjos was not aware of such things since he didn't read the papers closely and neither did he gossip very much with people from the suburbs, men and women who would have known these things. Marramaque had to rely upon his skillful ability as a storyteller when relating the facts of these stories to Joaquim.

A couple once came to live in one of the suburbs near Cassi's home. The wife was a young woman rather generously endowed, fleshy, tall, robust, and had large, black eyes; she was a southern type such as one might see around Rio Grande. The husband, an officer in the Navy, a machinist, was dark complected and close to being a mulatto, short, always sad looking, stooped and pensive. In spite of the difference in their appearances, which was obvious, and their ages, also apparent, they seemed to get along well together. They almost always went out in the late afternoon to go to parties or the theater and on Sundays they tried to visit the picturesque districts of the city and then return home at night. They often dined out and had only one maid, a black girl of about sixteen, for the minor household chores. No one knows exactly how, but Cassi was able to get to know the southern woman and seduce her. The husband had barely left home in the morning when Cassi would get in their house with his guitar. But the neighbors started to talk about their shameful little episode. From one mouth or another, the husband came to learn about it and one day, revolver in hand, furious, and beside himself with rage — crazy, really insane — he burst into his house and fired two shots at his wife who died from her wounds a few hours later. Then, after having wounded his wife mortally, the husband took off in pursuit of Cassi who, without his shoes, in trousers and shirtsleeves, was already jumping over walls and fences desperately trying to put himself out of the indignant husband's range.

Handing himself over to police officials, the machinist told all about his misfortunes and about their cause. The police then ordered that Cassi be picked up and succeeded in catching him unaware one evening. The authorities had to beat the bushes for him but the Don Juan was finally captured and taken away to a dark, dank cell.

It was, by chance, in this prison that he came to make the acquaintance of Lafoes. The latter had been detained and then taken off to jail for having caused some disturbance in a saloon where he had been on a bender in commemoration of winning about one hundred dollars in the lottery. When they caught Cassi, Lafoes had already been in prison for about four hours.

Cassi, who had fled from the machinist's revolver without his jacket or his vest, the pockets of which contained his money, was unable to buy cigarettes, but Lafoes had some. The professional seducer asked him for one and received it. He then said to Lafoes:

"I'm going to get you out of here, old man. You seem like a good sort."

"Why are you a prisoner, my good man?" asked Lafoes.

Cassi responded calmly and with great indifference, as if he were dealing with an everyday matter:

"For no reason, really ... just a little matter of the ladies, old man. It's my weakness."

Through the bars of their cell he caught the attention of a guard that he knew and whispered something to him. In a short time, another soldier then came up and took the first one's place. Seeing this, Cassi said to Lafoes, the old man:

"You'll be out on the street in a minute. I told the guard to speak to my political boss; he'll intervene so you can be let loose."

"And what about you?"

"Don't worry about me. I'll just have to testify...."

Lafoes was, in fact, set free. It did not, however, involve any intervention by Cassi's political boss. The person who liberated him was the same police commissioner who had locked him up but who knew him to be an upright and basically good man who had probably learned his lesson.

The public works guard, however, always supposed that his liberation had been the work of Cassi, and that's why he was so grateful to him and why he defended Cassi with such ardor.

Lafoes was really a simpleton who was perceptive only about his financial affairs. Always running in small, restricted circles, habitually judging the worth of men by the cut of their clothes or by their connections, he could not even imagine what an appalling character Cassi was, that his soul was too evil and corrupted for him to intercede generously on behalf of anybody.

Very different from the guard was Marramaque, a man whose social circle had always been more ample and varied in scope. He embraced a greater span of human existence. . . .

When Lafoes suggested that the celebrated Spanish guitar player be invited to the party, the old doorman saw immediately all the dangers the presence of that professional dishonorer of families could bring to the peace and tranquility that reigned supreme in the home of Joaquim dos Anjos.

Besides being his compadre, Marramaque was a close personal friend of the postman. Joaquim had helped Marramaque through his various crises, crises that had originated somewhat out of the bohemian habits he had not entirely abandoned and somewhat out of the exiguity of his salary, which also sustained a widowed sister of his who had two small children and with whom he lived not far from Joaquim.

In his varied and hectic life, Marramaque had always taken note of the atmosphere of corruption surrounding girls with the birthright of poverty and brown skin like his goddaughter. He had also noticed the generally low opinion which people held regarding the virtuousness of these girls. They were assumed to be morally lax *a priori* and everything and everybody seemed to condemn their efforts and those of their people to elevate their social and moral condition.

If such was the case for honest women, what would happen when a scoundrel, a good-for-nothing, a heartless cad or some vagabond loafer — all of which Marramaque knew Cassi to be — was involved?

During supper there was a great deal of discussion about this topic, but it was a very reserved conversation because the presence of a young girl required that it be so.

"We'll give it a try, my dear Marramaque. "He knows who he's dealing with. . . ."

"Well, for my part, I don't have anything more to tell you. He's always treated me well and I'm grateful to him," said Lafoes.

"The fact is, Lafoes, that you don't read the papers."

"What do you mean, the papers! Nonsense! Anyway, everything you read in them is a pack of lies!"

Clara was listening to this dialogue with strict attention and great curiosity. At one point, she couldn't restrain herself any longer and asked:

"What does this Cassi fellow do, godfather?"

Her mother replied harsly, saying:

"It's none of your business!"

Clara, the postman's only child, had been reared with such care and delicacy that, given her situation and class, perhaps she had actually been harmed by such strict supervision. She took after both her parents. The postman had light brown skin but, as they say, "bad" hair; his wife, although darker complected, had fine, straight hair.

The girl took after her father in color, her mother, in hair.

Joaquim was tall, quite tall, much more than average, with square shoulders and a muscular build. The girl's mother, not short herself, did not possess the modest stature which, in general, is characteristic of our women. She had a measured physiognomy with small but regular features, which wasn't the same in the case of her husband who had a large, flat nose and very prominent cheekbones. The girl, Clara, was halfway between them; thus situated and reflecting the perfect balance of her parents' features, she was truly the daughter of both.

Used to the musical soirees of her father and his friend, Clara had grown up enveloped in the strains of *modinhas,* all of which had clouded her soul with the affectations and the simpleminded, amorous sentimentalism of the singers and popular crooners.

Clara rarely went out of the house unless it was to go somewhere very near such as to Dona Margarida's house, the place where she learned to embroider and sew, or unless she was accompanied by this woman to the movies or shopping for dry goods or shoes. This lady's house was only about four steps away from the postman's. In spite of the suburban custom for the girls and the women to go to the stores to do the shopping, Dona Engracia, Clara's mother, never consented that she do so although their house was within view of everything that went on in *Seu* Nascimento's general store, the business concern that furnished most of the family's needs.

Such cloistering caused Clara's soul to be immersed in daydreams and vagrant thoughts. This condition was made even worse because of the influence of the *modinhas* and because of certain poems then popular.

In that state of mind, Clara's greatest wish was that her father consent to the visit of the famous guitar player whose infamy she knew nothing of nor even suspected as a result of the zealous efforts of her mother to shield her from the facts of life. Clara imagined that Cassi must be able to draw truly magical sounds from out of the Spanish guitar and that he must surely sing of celestial things. . . .

Joaquim dos Anjos, finally gaining his wife's assent and curious to learn of Cassi's skills on the guitar with popular tunes, finally consented that Lafoes bring Cassi to their house on Clara's birthday. He would come just that one time and never again. . . .

Lafoes received that decision with obvious pleasure and immediately set about trying to contact the ill-famed musician. He succeeded.

When Cassi's comrades in vagrancy learned of the news, they made cynical comments about the invitation:

"I know who that postman is. He doesn't work around here. He works in the city, in the bank district. I'll bet he's really got a pile of money, too. He's also got a daughter who's really something. . . ! My God, she's something!"

"Well, then . . . that's that, right Cassi?" Zeze Mateus added doltishly to Atalibo do Timbo's comment.

Cassi, the suburb's master guitarist, the real ace, pretended to be upset with all this and retorted with feigned displeasure:

"You're the ones who discredit me all the time. You talk about things I never did and don't do now; everybody's disgusted with me . . . if they don't actually hate me! I'm not all those things you say I am!"

Timbo felt an urge to laugh out loud and although he was stronger than Cassi, the latter held some strange and dominant force over him. Timbo couldn't explain it but it was true. Zeze Mateus, however, with his odd, imbecilic half-laugh, said:

"Aww, I'm just joshing, man. I'm your pal . . . you know that."

They always talked standing up, loitering around some street corner. They rarely sat down at a table in a cafe. And Ataliba's untimely observation, followed by Zeze Mateus's comment, had cooled off the little society's discussion for that day. They said good-bye to each other and each went his own way.

Cassi, after Timbo's tendentious words and Zeze's comment, pretended to be annoyed, but was, on the contrary, very pleased. He had decided earlier not to go to the party but now, because of what Ataliba had told him, perhaps he had nothing to lose. He would give it a try.

Cassi smacked his lips and headed off to his club, lighthearted and with a clear conscience. . . .

IV

The day of the celebration arrived and the little house was bursting at the seams. There was one curious thing, however; there were more middle-aged guests than there were young men and women. This fact can be explained by the limited number of personal relationships enjoyed by Clara and her parents, a condition which came about as a result of the type of life they led. Among the young women, there were two or three of Clara's schoolmates, Lafoes's daughter, an unmarried niece of Dona Engracia, one Hermengarda, and a few others. Among the men, there were two young colleagues of Joaquim, Sabino and Honorio, a brother of Hermengarda and a godson of Lafoes who was a watchman at the docks. On the other hand, the older women, mothers of families, were numerous. One of these, Dona Margarida Weber Pestana, seemed to stand out because of her virile manner. She kept her only son, about fourteen years old and dressed in his school uniform, close to her side all evening. That lady had the temperament of a true domestic heroine. She had come to Brazil as a child with her father who was German. She, however, was born in Riga and was therefore Russian as her mother had been. She was orphaned of her mother before her sixteenth year and her father then emigrated to Brazil finding work in the construction of buildings in Candelaria. He was a plasterer, a marbler, and something of a sculptor. He was, all in all, a fine workman, especially on those jobs requiring revetments and the interior decorating of luxury buildings.

She quickly showed a strong interest in a typographer who used to eat his meals at the pension that they erected on Rua Alfandega and that they ran energetically. They married, but he died two years after the ceremony of pulmonary tuberculosis and left her and their son, Ezequiel, who never left her side. A year and a half later, her father died of yellow fever. She carried on with the boarding house for a while but soon sold it and bought the little house in the suburbs in which she now lived, the one next door to Joaquim. She took in sewing, did embroidery, raised chickens, ducks and turkeys and maintained herself serenely, honest and upright. Senhor Ataliba do Timbo had, on one occasion, pursued her intending to enjoy a sordid little affair with her. One fine day, however, she had had enough and vigorously whacked him with her umbrella. At night, with the intention of defending her chickens from thieves by scaring them away, she opened a peephole which she had made in her kitchen window and fired her revolver through it from time to time. She was respected because of her courage, her goodness and because of the strict propriety of her widowhood.

Ezequiel, her son, took largely after his father, Florencio Pestana who was a mulatto, but he had the glaucous, translucent eyes of his half-Slavic, half-German mother, such strange eyes, so foreign to our own people and especially, to the dominant bloodlines of the little boy.

Next to Dona Margarida Pestana was Dona Laurentina Jacome. She was an old woman, excessively devout, who was a pensioner from the time of the previous emperor and was now a maid in one of the neighborhood chapels, the cleaning of which she was responsible for, even the washing of the altar cloths. She was unable to talk about anything that wasn't ecclesiastical in nature and, nearly always, she talked about her church.

"Dona Engracia, do you know something?" she inquired.

"What's that?"

"Father Santos said more than twenty masses this month and received money for only five. Poor Father Santos! He's such a saint!"

And then she contracted her wrinkled countenance and, sitting up a little, would arrange her hands in the manner of one who is praying.

Among the other guests, there was only one other woman worthy of note; that was Dona Vicencia. She, too, lived there in the neighborhood and made her living by telling people's fortunes with cards and by undoing the workings of Fate. Her behavior was above reproach and she exercised her profession as a fortune teller with complete seriousness and conviction.

There were other ladies present but none was so outstanding as these three. Among the gentlemen, only one man stood out. Lafoes and Marramaque were there next to each other. The gentleman worthy of particular note was a short black man, was a little hunchbacked, had his right shoulder a bit elevated, and had an enormous head with a prominent and convex forehead. He possessed a narrow face, which down to his chin, gave a monstrous V-shaped appearance to the front of his head. At the rear of his head, his huge occipital bones drew his monstrous profile to an end. His name was Praxedes Maria dos Santos but he preferred to be addressed as *doutor* Praxedes.

The abnormal size of his head had begun to cloud his reason. He thought he was a great intellect, a great lawyer, and subsequently began to frequent notary offices serving as a witness when it was necessary, going out to buy revenue stamps, in short, involving himself all he could in the affairs of the legal profession.

In time, however, he gained more useful knowledge and began to handle wedding documents. He also organized a particular type of library, one dealing with juridical manuals and indices of legislation.

He always dressed in a cutaway coat, high button shoes made of patent leather with vamps, and he was never without the type of folders lawyers carry. When it became the style to carry papers rolled up, that's what he did; later, when the style was to carry them in a sack, he bought a bag made of luxurious Moroccan leather with gold latches.

He could only talk about laws and decrees:

"... Because," he would say, "Law number 1.857, of the fourteenth of October, 1879, says that the married woman, by the laws of marriage, may not avail herself of her possessions, have money in commercial banks or savings banks; on the other hand, Decree number 4.572, of the twenty-fourth of July, 1889, determines that. . . ."

Aside from this legislative hocus-pocus, he enjoyed poetry; but not the *modinha.*

This was the most noteworthy gentleman who came to Clara's birthday party. The fact is that up until that moment and much to the dismay of the girls, Cassi the troubador had not yet appeared.

Clara couldn't hide her disappointment at this, and one of her schoolmates told her in confidence:

"Clara, be careful. That man is no good."

The girl did not respond but walked off toward the dining room in order to disguise her emotions as she pretended to get a drink of water.

Clara was very nicely dressed. Her dress was made of crepon with a matronly though pretty and well-made lace trim. Her neck was uncovered and the collar of the jacket ended in a yoke hemmed in lace. She wore highly polished shoes, and stockings. On her ears were large, golden earrings and she had parted her long hair in the middle sweeping the ends back around to the upper part of her neck where she arranged it in a bun held in place by means of a large comb made of turtle shell or some similar material.

As she went to get a drink of water, she was followed by her friend, Etelvina, a lively black girl who had been a good friend at school. This girl dressed in terrible taste. Her dress was sky-blue and edged with black lace; her shoes were yellow and her stockings the color of squash. Around her head, dividing her forehead in two, was a red ribbon, a very garrish red ribbon. The Greeks called this type of feminine adornment a *stephane;* and, it seems that the girls who wore these were not considered particularly virtuous.

Etelvina was, however, the party's best dancer and until then, she had not missed a single square dance.

The orchestra was composed of a flute, a ukelele and a guitar, a trio as the serenaders would describe it.

The dance was just getting underway when Lafoes's daughter came running in from the large iron gate in the well-kept garden at the front of the house and announced happily:

"*Seu* Cassi's coming!"

He came in. A shudder ran through the guests like an electric shock. All the girls, of different colors attenuated and harmonized by the poverty and humbleness of their condition, began to admire him immediately despite his general insignificance; how powerful is the fascination of perversity within the feminine mind! Not even Caesar Borgia, entering in disguise a fancy dress ball given by his father, Alexander VI, would have caused so much excitement. If they didn't actually shout, "It's Caesar! It's Caesar!" women then must surely have said to themselves, "It's he! It's he!"

The young men at Clara's party, however, were not so pleased at his arrival sensing as they did the women's pleasure at it. Among themselves, they began to retell the *modinha* player's scabrous personal history.

As Cassi was presented by Lafoes to the hosts and to their daughter, nobody noticed his lascivious stare as he lowered his eyes to gaze upon Clara's proud young breasts.

The dance continued lively and gay. Cassi, however, wasn't dancing but was reinforcing the trio of flute, ukelele and guitar with his own instrument.

Dona Margarida, severe of demeanor and watching the other ladies, was seated on the Austrian sofa with her son at her side. The polka was the favorite dance and everybody danced it with the voluptuous movements of the samba. Those guests who weren't dancing had scattered all over the house. Joaquim, Lafoes and Marramaque were listening to *doutor* Praxedes explain what a preventive *habeas corpus* was.

"Let me give an example," *doutor* Praxedes was saying, raising his right hand in an authoritative manner and pointing his index finger toward the ceiling, "It is a perfectly legal prophylactic exercise, because. . . ."

On this point he was challenged by *doutor* Meneses, a dropsical old man with a mania for the physical sciences. He was a man who lived in abject poverty in spite of clandestinely practicing the profession of dentist.

"*Doutor* Praxedes," interjected *doutor* Meneses, "I don't mean to sit in judgment of your comparison but each science has its own area. . . ."

The discussion soon became ponderous and Joaquim got up to leave. As he did so, Meneses followed the postman with his eyes to see if he was going to the kitchen to order supper. The wily old dentist had come at the last moment in hope that there would be something to eat. He hadn't made enough money recently to buy even a cup of broth. Joaquim, however, bored by the discussion, had simply gone to the visiting room to announce supper:

"Whoever would like a bite to eat and drink . . . some cookies or something, just come on in here. Don't stand on ceremony."

While the host was saying this, Meneses was gobbling down a couple of little meat balls and four sandwiches as he took large swigs of rum from a bottle that was there.

The master of the house made a special point of offering a drink to Cassi who answered that he wouldn't have one, that he didn't care for liquor . . . it wasn't to his liking. . . .

As he went into the parlor, Joaquim made him a request:

"Why don't you sing for us, *Seu* Cassi?"

Until then, nothing had been said about this. Strumming the guitar chords, the master guitarist never ceased letting his lascivious gaze fall upon Clara's swaying hips as she danced to the trio's music.

No one so far had dared to invite him to sing but waited for the head of the house to do so. Once the invitation was made, Cassi responded full of ceremonious affectation:

"My voice really isn't up to par; I wore myself out quite a bit last evening at doctor Raposo's and. . . ."

But seeing that her father had invited him, Clara then grew bold:

"Why don't you sing, *Seu* Cassi? Everybody says that you sing so well. . . ."

This "so well" was softly prolonged and Cassi smoothed his hair, greased down as usual, with his hands and then wiped them on his handkerchief. Acting coy, he slyly and willingly let himself be persuaded.

"Really, dear lady! My songs are just for entertainment among friends. . . ."

But Clara insisted:

"Sing, *Seu* Cassi! Go ahead!"

Then, bowing his head down to the left and raising up his open palmed hand and pretending that he had been forced, he responded:

"Since you insist, I will sing."

Marramaque, who had overheard all this, was fearful at his goddaughter's lack of restraint. "Damn," he said to himself.

The guitarist, with great affectation, took hold of the instrument, strummed the chords and announced:

"I'm going to sing an old *modinha,* but one that's very genteel and literary. It's called "In the Country.""

Many people were disappointed because they already knew it but others liked that particular *modinha* very much and approved of his selection:

"One day I saw / dancing in the country / a lovely *mulata* [mulatto girl] / with a lively spark in her eye. . . .""

This was sung almost in a single breath but with no vocal modulation at all while the guitar twanged away on the same notes with indolence, such monotony of sound that it made one drowsy to hear it. Then he got to the refrain:

"The *mulata* was smiling / for one whom the foreman / said had died / perished from love."

At that point, he began to make use of his irresistible specialty, his unmatched guitarist's and *modinha* singer's tic. While still singing, he began to roll his eyes around like a moribund person. The Cardinal of Retz, in one of his famous *Memoirs,* says that Madame de Montayon or some other duchess was loveliest just as her eyes were fluttering shut. Cassi might likewise have appeared more attractive had he possessed any type of appeal at all, but as it was. . . . Nevertheless, his tic deeply impressed the ladies.

Clara, whom the *modinha* always transfigured by carrying her off to regions of perpetual happiness and of visions of Love, satisfaction, and joy, transporting her, whenever she heard such music, to the vegetative life and leaving her in mystical ecstasy, totally absorbed by the sonorous lyrics of the tune, was profoundly moved by the fluttering of his eyes, the final touch with which Cassi completed the verses of the *modinha.* "He's really suffering; if not, he wouldn't put so much heartache into it when he sings," she thought.

She was so enraptured, her thoughts soared so wildly that when Cassi had finished, she forgot to applaud the artistic troubador who had aroused in Clara such basic pleasure and powerful emotions.

People were still talking about master Cassi's musical talent; he heard praise and criticism from all sides. Just at that moment, however, like an apparition arising from some magician's trap door, *doutor* Praxedes suddenly appeared in the center of the room, the celebrated lawyer of the suburban lecture halls. He began to speak:

"Ladies and gentlemen. May I have your worthy attention so that I might recite a lovely poem composed by one of our own compatriots. The poem is a masterpiece of style and morality. Its author is Major Urbano Duarte who died, if my memory is correct, a brigadier general. If you will permit me, I shall recite it for you. It is called, "The Tear."

Upon saying this, his general grotesqueness became even more so with the disorderly gesticulations of his rigid arms which flew stiffly up and down and all around his head and shoulders. They seemed like the wings of an old fashioned windmill. Praxedes began to shout out the first stanza and to froth at the corners of his purplish lips.

"Upon the seacoast the lovely Marieta brooded,
Watching sadly the wake of the ship,
Which, moving away, was absorbed in the horizon,
Carrying, to distant lands, her first true love."

His shouting, his slobbering and his gesticulations were all increasing. When he got to the sonnet's first tercet, he had almost lost his voice. Those present were seized by a crazy urge to laugh out loud; many were able to contain themselves but others had to move away so they could guffaw more privately. *Doutor* Praxedes saw none of this, however, and continued unperturbed. Finally, he finished:

"Later, when the moon was bathing the seascape
In the pale flow of mysterious light,
I saw in the breaking surf of the raging sea,
the tear, buoyed up upon the petal of the rose."

After he finished, he received applause and sitting down, worn-out from such rigorous muscular effort, he said:

"The tear is Marieta's, the one the poem speaks of in the beginning. You ladies and gentlemen should not forget that detail."

Marramaque, unobserved up to that moment, had been watching the insistence with which Cassi the troubador was staring at Clara and the older man decided to have a little fun with him. Leaning upon his walking stick, his left leg shrunken as a result of his heart attacks and his left arm fixed at a right angle because of the attacks, he moved or hobbled toward the center of the room to take his turn at some recitation. The left side of his mouth was also defective and this caused him a great deal of difficulty in pronouncing the words well.

He paid no attention to any of these difficulties, however, and stood up straight to recite.

This was what he intended to do: he gave the title of the poem, "Perseverance," and began to recite it very naturally in the manner of one who, when hale and hearty, could recite the poem to perfection. While reciting the verse, he looked squarely at Cassi who, now quiet and apparently reserved as a well-mannered young man, was standing, leaning against the bay window at the front of the room.

Eyes darting around the room, Marramaque attacked the verses:

''If, at times, I come up against you
And shout, howl and complain
That for a long time you have brought me much pain
Because of the passion I have for you.

You run away and I cling to you,
Brooding (and in this I don't err),
That if I have a soul of mud
You show you have one of iron.

And if I never pursue you again
That is to say, if I don't run after you anymore,
It's because the whole affair already smells and I'm angry.

What is it you want of me? I myself have begun to take
a Powerful dislike to this love for which I'm withering away;
But I cannot help it; the truth is, I'm really just a jackass.''

The final line caused a wave of frank hilarity to sweep over those present and even Clara broke out laughing. But nobody asked who the author was; and even if they had asked, Marramaque wouldn't have known his name. It was an anonymous poem from some journal that the old man had liked and memorized.

People are averse to remembering the names of authors, even the authors of novels or serials that require days and days of reading. The work itself is everything for the typical reader, the author nothing. . . .

Cassi, who had almost immediately felt hostile toward Marramaque, understood that the point of the poem was directed at him. Even somebody more stupid than the much praised *modinha* artist would have perceived that in view of the persistence with which the old cripple looked at him. Cassi thought to himself, ''I'll get even with this old devil.''

What he feared in regard to Marramaque's action was his courage. Marramaque, old, poor and a semi-invalid, had solemnly challenged the strong, healthy vagrant, a young man quite accustomed to strife and conflict.

Cassi didn't stay around much longer. He asked for his hat, bade good-evening to the heads of the household and to their daughter, and moved through the other guests saying good-bye. When he got to Marramaque whose partly open mouth, left arm fixed at its right angle and gaze fixed strangely upon him, Cassi cringed. The old cripple seemed like some strange specter. . . . He had ceased to be the crippled door-man Cassi had seen earlier; now he was something else, something more than the simple Marramaque . . . something that made Cassi afraid and made him tremble.

Because of the fearless attitude of the crippled old man who now stood face to face with him and who had guessed the evil nature of his intentions toward Clara — Cassi didn't understand how he could have guessed — Cassi suddenly sensed, in spite of his almost innate moral sterility, that there is in this life or in the next one, some silent or secret guide that weighs upon our acts and demands in order to support them and to orient us toward inner peace and contentment with ourselves. We must practice, in all of our actions, the virtues of Justice, Loyalty, Truth and Generosity. That moral guide, as he now saw it in Marramaque, would give strength to the weak, courage to the timid, and a seraphic, intimate satisfaction to anybody who did his duty with honor and dignity. This guide was Conscience.

Cassi pondered these thoughts confusedly. With the passing of terror and fear that old Marramaque's rigid, vitrified, supernatural gaze caused in him — a gaze which, for an instant, made the suburban Don Juan withdraw within himself and examine what he found there, however, he suddenly returned to his usual attitude, and uttering a disdainful, "Well, now," he repeated to himself his previous threat: "I'll get even with that old puppet!"

After Cassi left, people continued to dance until the first light of dawn. Meneses, who had had a good nap, was, around daybreak, still able to eat a little of the roast pork and chicken leftover from supper. He couldn't spark any more discussions with *doutor* Praxedes because the latter had already departed explaining that he had to appear very early the next morning in the office of a Justice of the Peace to inquire about a testimony in an important case for which he was acting attorney.

When everybody had gone and after Clara had retired to her room opposite the dining room, Joaquim and his wife remained there nibbling on the few remaining morsels. It was then that Engracia said to her husband:

"Everything went very well. Everybody conducted himself decently and respectfully . . . but there's one thing I want no more of."

"What's that?" her husband asked.

"Cassi must never come here again. Dona Margarida told me that he's a . . . a libertine. Didn't you see him . . . with his indecent songs and rolling his eyes. . . . I don't want him here ever again . . . if he should come and. . . ."

"Don't get upset, Engracia. I didn't like him either and he'll never set foot in my house again."

Clara, in bed in her room, overheard this conversation and silently began to cry.

V

Anybody who knew Engracia intimately would be astonished at the decisive attitude she took toward Cassi's visit. Her temperament was completely passive and inert. Very good, honest, a good housekeeper she was, however, utterly incapable of taking the initiative in any kind of emergency. She handed everything over to her husband who really was in charge. It was the husband who organized the shopping list for things to be bought in *Seu* Nascimento's store daily, and also the list for the beans and other vegetables. He specified everything in writing and left the necessary amount of money with the greengrocer each morning as he went off to work and on the way, he left another list with *Seu* Nascimento whom he paid once each month.

Whenever anything unexpected happened in her home, Engracia became wild and frantic. While they still retained Baba, the old black woman who had raised her in the home of the male off-spring of Engracia's grandmother, among whom was probably her father, Engracia almost went crazy one day when Baba suddenly suffered a seizure. Engracia didn't know what to do and Dona Margarida had to intervene; she called for a doctor, arranged for the prescription to be filled and did everything else that the situation demanded. The old woman, however, died a short time later of a cerebral embolism. Engracia suffered a great deal because of Baba's death since she never knew her real mother who died when she was about seven, and the old woman raised her. Engracia's protectors had been rather well-off. They were descendants of a second lieutenant in the Militia who owned some land in and around Sao Goncalo in Cubande. Shortly after reaching legal age, and coincidental with the death of the head of the household, the boys and girls moved to the vicinity of the Royal Court where they hoped to secure employment in some of the government bureaus. One of the brothers already lived in the capital city and had attained the position of major-surgeon and enjoyed quite a bit of fame. They brought no slaves to the city. They had sold most of them, except for those they liked whom they set free. Only those who had been liberated and were like members of the family came with them. Since the time of Engracia's birth, there had been very few slaves around the house or grounds. Only Baba, Engracia's mother and a black manservant still lived under the patriarchal roof of the Teles de Carvalho family.

Engracia was reared as if she had been a daughter as were all the other boys and girls, children of the former slaves who had been born into the Teles household.

Because of this, word travelled from mouth to mouth that they were all the children of the men of the house. Such rumors were not without foundation because in that family composed of brothers and sisters, still wealthy, they took pleasure in treating these children as their own, the children who had been born in their household. The ladies of the family showed them the tenderness and affection of true mothers.

Engracia had received a good education considering her class and sex. However, as soon as she got married — as is normal among our girls — she tried to forget everything she had studied. She married Joaquim when she reached her eighteenth birthday.

Whether it was the spoiled upbringing she received or some fatalistic flaw in her psychological make-up, it was certain that except for her domestic chores, Engracia avoided all forms of effort.

She almost never left the house. As a rule, she only did so twice a year: on the fifteenth of August, when she ascended Mount Gloria to offer alms to her favorite Saint; and on the day of Our Lady of the Immaculate Conception, when she went to confession. She always took her daughter with her when she did these things but she never let the girl out of her sight. Engracia had an enormous fear that her daughter would go astray, that she would fall prey to some vice. . . . In addition to going out with her, Clara, much to her mother's dismay, occasionally wanted to leave the house to go to the movies, to Meier's, or to Engenho de Dentro, or very rarely, to go shopping for shoes and material at one of the respectable local fabric shops.

Such seclusion and the constant vigilance with which her mother followed her every step, far from causing Clara to flee from the dangers to which her maiden's purity was exposed, tortured the girl with curiosity and made her yearn to discover the reasons behind her mother's strange oppressiveness.

Clara saw all the other girls going out with their parents or with their mothers or with their friends; she saw them going out for walks and having a good time and she wondered why she was not allowed to do so.

That question always remained unanswered because, living as they did, isolated from everybody and everything, there was nothing they could point to as objectionable.

Engracia, whose maternal considerations were laudable and meritorious, was incapable of providing any truly educational influence for Clara. She did not know how to point things out or to comment on various examples and facts that might illuminate the girl's mind and reinforce her character so that she could better resist the dangers and temptations she would later encounter in life.

Joaquim dos Anjos's wife was superstitious and believed in the idea of a mechanical and fatalistic universe and it was from this belief that her monastic treatment of Clara arose.

She was deceiving herself about the efficacy of such treatment because the girl, already a recluse with no social contacts or human relationships, would never be able to acquire even the slightest, most insignificant experience of life and benefit from it. Nor would she ever be able to learn anything about the abjections of which life is so full. Consequently, with her soul contracted even more by the nature of her existence, Clara was forced to escape that limiting world through her dreams — dreams of Love, unrealistic, illusory Love, and dreams which provoked strange physical and psychic reactions in her.

There was also present, moreover, a general preference for the *modinha* in Clara's household. Her mother and father liked them and so did her godfather. There were almost always guitar-playing and *modinha*-singing sessions at their house. Such taste in music is contagious and, in view of Clara's sentimentality and moral condition, such music discovered a propitious soil in which to take root and propagate itself. The *modinha* speaks of Love and is sometimes even lewd about it. In a short time, Clara began organizing some thoughts of her own about Love, which were largely based upon the melodies and lyrics entoned by her father and his friends. According to the *modinha* love can do anything and there are no obstacles such as race, wealth or social standing which can impede its course; Love would conquer with or without the sanctions of the Law, and would mock both the Church and Fate. The amorous state, in this view, is the greatest delight of human existence, one we should strive for and enjoy and for which we should suffer come what may. In fact, suffering gives it more refinement. . . .

The torpid *modinhas* and the corresponding mental debilitation which they induce, especially when viewed in the light of the mother's repressive treatment of the girl, actually drove Clara even farther from the firmness of character and strength of will she might have otherwise attained. Her soul became so enervated that she was rendered weak and susceptible to surrendering herself to any sweet talk or anybody who was more or less bold, perverse, waggish, or even just plain stupid and in whom she might inspire the same ideas the whoremongers have about other girls of her color.

Cassi was of this sort. Clara, however, in her somewhat understandable ignorance of our social life, judged that her parents were being unjust and cruel toward him.

One Sunday, fifteen or twenty days after her birthday party, Cassi came knocking at her parents' front door. Engracia was busy tidying-up the living room; she greeted Cassi with visible displeasure and shouted out to the kitchen where Clara was:

"Clara! Go tell your father that *Seu* Cassi is here."

The girl had already come running, hoping to be able to talk to the *modinha* player when her mother quickly said to her:

"Go call your father! Go on, now."

Joaquim didn't waste any time in coming either, and after greeting him, he addressed himself directly to the young man:

"Well, what is it that brings you to my house, my dear sir?"

"Nothing, really. I went to visit a friend of mine and, passing by your door, I decided to drop by and say hello."

"Thank you very much . . . but right at this moment my card game's really starting to come alive and I can't chat right now."

With an evil expression, Cassi looked at the old mulatto for a moment but didn't try anything. They stood there silently, face to face, for two or three minutes until the famous guitarist took the hint and said good-bye. Clara found out about this little scene only by eavesdropping on her father's explanation of it to her mother. When the girl finally did learn of it, she became greatly upset, angry and displeased at her parents and at the domestic circumstances in which she lived, all of which Clara supposed had been imposed upon her by her parents only to cause her unhappiness and distress.

She rather rebelliously considered her parents' actions. What did they want her to become? Did they want her to end up an old maid or to become a nun? And would she have to get married? It seemed so and in the natural course of things, her mother and father would have to die before she did. When they did, she would be left all alone in the world. Rumors were flying around that Cassi was this and that. . . . Dona Margarida and her godfather said the worst things about him — that he was a lecher, a wicked man who was a corrupter of young girls and married women. How could he be so terrible if he frequented the homes of doctors, Army officers and political leaders as he said he did? It must be that they were all simply very envious of the young man's attributes, among which Clara saw only his modesty and refinement and also his sighings and the flashiness of his excellent guitar playing.

Then suddenly a doubt overcame her; his skin was white and she was a mulatto. But what of it? There were so many cases in which. . . . Clara could even remember some. . . . The postman's daughter soon became so convinced that she indeed had a sincere passion for the rake that, regretting she had ever doubted him, she began to yearn for him even more, sobbing and sighing all the time. Her firm, young breasts were virtually bursting as a result of their virginal yearnings and their desire for Love.

Moreover, Clara's so-called "love" for Cassi was also an escape from the kind of life she was leading, a desire to get out, to learn more about the city, its theaters and movies. . . . Clara knew nothing of all this. She couldn't even get permission to go to *Seu* Nascimento's store, only a few yards away from their house. One day, as it happened, they ran out of salt which was needed to prepare supper, but not even under those circumstances did Clara receive permission to go to the store. Because her mother wouldn't go either, not wanting to leave her daughter home alone, they had to wait an hour until *Seu* Nascimento's store was not frequented by people of questionable repute; indeed, everybody who stopped there was of a certain caliber and devoid of opporbrious reputations. And this last observation of Clara's was entirely correct.

Even Rosalina, better known by her pejorative surname, Madame Bacamarte, despite the unfortunate and difficult life she had led, always conducted herself in a manner above reproach. This poor girl was truly an unfortunate person. Because she was seduced at an early age, the police forced the man to marry her. During the first three years of their marriage, things went along more or less regularly. At the end of that time, however, and because of reverses in his life, the husband began to take a strong dislike to her. He blamed all his problems on his wife and took to beating her. Nevertheless, he still provided her with enough money so that she could support herself and their children. Her husband was already drinking quite a lot even then but later on, he began drinking regularly and immoderately. He drank at every opportunity, at home, in the bars . . . everywhere. He didn't go to work so that he could go out and drink. Rosalina caught her husband's vice and from the little money he gave her or that she earned, she bought rum.

Her husband owed six months rent on their house, a modest little wooden bungalow with a living room, bedroom and a tiny addition which served as a kitchen. The landlord pursued him and he ran off, leaving his wife with the task of explaining his overdue payments. One day, she saw the owner come in with two men. They said nothing. They leaned a ladder up against the little hut's roof and began removing its tiles. Now everything she owned had fallen into the hands of those inhuman beings. She quickly asked one neighbor to look after one of her children and another neighbor to take care of the youngest boy. Then she ran off and threw herself beneath the wheels of the first train that came along. She suffered abrasions and fractures of an arm and a leg, but the doctors in Santa Rosa succeeded in saving her life. She finally left the hospital, completely recovered with her girlish and coquettish face having gained a bit of the exuberance and sauciness which puberty had given it.

Her mother, a poor washer woman, had collected the children. She never saw her husband again.

In the beginning, she behaved well but very soon she began passing around from one person to another until venereal disease began to eat her up and she was obliged to make steady visits to the Santa Rosa hospital to receive shots and to endure operations. Forbidden to drink, she did not obey the doctor's instructions. When she had no money, something she usually managed to secure in one way or another, she would wait patiently until her hens or those of her mother with whom she was living, were laying eggs. When they were laying, she would take the eggs, quickly run down to the store and exchange them for two or three hundred *reis* worth of rum.

Rosalina, however, never caused any kind of disturbance in *Seu* Nascimento's store.

Reared and educated in the country and having run a business in the interior of the state of Rio de Janeiro where he still had a ranch, *Seu* Nascimento liked to have people of a certain type and caliber come into his business establishment to read the papers and journals and to chat, a custom, as we all know, peculiar to people from the interior of our country. His little general store even had the traditional taborets that were used to open and close the doors of older stores and are still used in certain shops in the backlands. Moreover, his place of business was located in a picturesque, tranquil and infrequently travelled location, just in front of the old trees belonging to Mr. Quick Shays's country house and facing the capricious summits of the distant mountains. Many people shopped there and he had a steady supply of customers.

One of these was Alipio, an odd lad who, although poor and addicted to rum, was usually refined and respectful in his manners, gestures, and speech. He looked a bit like a fighting cock. However, far from possessing the repugnant ferocity of the Malayan roosters of the cockfighting rings, he did not, it should be said, have any of their other nasty characteristics. Although he had not received any formal education, he was not an ignorant man; he was, on the contrary, quite intelligent and very curious about mechanical inventions and improvements.

Old Valentim, another strange and picturesque fellow, frequented the store as well. A Portuguese well beyond sixty years of age, he never stopped working, rain or shine. He was the foreman of a grange and perhaps because of the nature of his job which he had performed for close to forty years, his body was bent in an interesting way. It wasn't certain that it was bent backwards or forwards but it did form a kind of "S" shaped figure, without the extremities.

There were some who could tell lengthy tales of adventure that never seemed to end and, among these, Joao de Calais stood out. How he could tell a story! He punctuated his long and complex tales with Portuguese adages that had a delicious charm and presented a rustic philosophy. This was what his listeners enjoyed most in his stories.

On certain occasions, there also appeared one Leonardo Flores. Flores was a poet, a true poet who had had his moment of celebrity throughout the length and breadth of Brazil and had exerted a great influence upon the generation of poets that followed him. At that time, however, because of alcohol and certain sorrows of a more personal and intimate nature, among which the incurable insanity of one of his brothers predominated, he became nothing more than the pathetic ruin of a man; he was amnesiac and occasionally imbecilic to the point of not being able to follow the line of even the simplest conversation. He had published almost ten volumes of poetry — ten successful volumes — from which nearly everybody made money, everybody except him that is. Now very poor, he, his wife, and their children all lived on the income generated by a miserly pension he received monthly from the federal government.

It was rare for Flores even to go out. His wife expended great effort in preventing him from doing so. She ordered somebody to go get rum for him and to buy the papers and journals that he liked so that he would remain at home. Most of the time he obeyed her. But on rare occasions, he stubbornly resisted her wishes and went out with five-hundred copper *reis* or so in his coat pocket. He drank here and there and then fell asleep beneath the trees along one of the less travelled streets or roads. Later, when his alcoholic delirium returned, as powerful as ever, he undressed completely and shouted heroically in a morbid and vainglorious manifestation of personality:

"I am Leonardo Flores!"

People passing by knew vaguely that he was famous for something and they referred to him as "the poet." At first, these people jeered Flores but later, upon learning of his fame they approached him with a more sympathetic curiosity.

"Imagine . . . ending up like this. What a chastisement!" said one fellow.

"That's his fate! It was because he was so smart!" an old black woman said. "Black folks aren't supposed to have brains. The evil eye will put some hex or something on him to do away with this man," concluded the elderly black woman.

Then, there usually appeared some on-looker who was more practical in his pity for Flores and who dressed the poet again and led him away to his home.

Doutor Meneses was looking precisely for him, Leonardo Flores when, on that particular holy day in the morning — it was not really a holiday — he went into *Seu* Nascimento's store. He was limping because of the swelling in his legs. His abundant, white beard, an untrimmed beard was shaped and cut in imitation of our late Emperor's.

Doutor Meneses struggled to reach the threshold of the door. He stopped for a moment as soon as he had gotten inside the shop, put his hands on his hips and stood there breathing hard. Then, after some initial pleasantries, he asked:

"Has Flores been around?"

"He hasn't been around for a long time," said *Seu* Nascimento from half-way down the store's counter.

"I went to his house and his wife told me that he'd gone out. I've really got to get hold of him. . . ."

Upon saying this, he sat down on the stool that the salesclerk had unfolded near the old dentist.

Meneses rested there for a little while and then gasped a huge breath of air and, facing Alipio, asked:

"How've you been, Alipio?"

Only Alipio and old Valentim were in the store; the former seated reading a journal, and the latter on his feet leaning up against the door jam of one of the side doors.

Alipio responded:

"I've been fine . . . not as good as you, though, now that you're running around in the company of dandies and wastrels."

"What?!!" the startled dentist exclaimed.

"That's what they say. The gossip is that you spend just about every night with that guitar player, Cassi Jones, and his friends at some bar in Engenho Novo."

"That's true, yes, but they're all decent young men who. . . ."

"Oh, really? Isn't this Cassi the one who goes around wearing a vest?"

"You know, they say," interrupted *Seu* Nascimento, "that this boy. . . ."

"He's no good!" interjected Alipio. "He deserves a punishment worse than prison; he ought to be roasted alive! He's disgraced more than ten girls and I don't know how many married women he's seduced."

"This is calumny!" protested Meneses. "It's just a lot of idle talk that's going around!"

"Nonsense! The legal proceedings have run their course and the papers have reported on them but he still finds ways and means of escaping any kind of penalty or punishment and then simply sets out to disgrace still more girls and women," confirmed Alipio.

"How could this Cassi fellow manage to do all that?" *Seu* Nascimento inquired.

"Well, in the beginning it was with his father's protection but after the second or third case that came to light, his father threw him out, never spoke to him again and never again interested himself in getting him out of his scrapes. Later, there were a lot of other cases but, thanks to the intervention of his mother and a brother of hers, an Army doctor, Cassi was able to arrange for some unscrupulous types to help him, men who used the most sickening ploys but succeeded in getting him released from jail. They slandered his victims with so-called 'evidence' and called upon people like Timbo and Arnaldo to act as witnesses. Vicencia told me all about it. Don't you know who Vicencia is, *Seu* Nascimento?" inquired Alipio.

"No, who is she?" answered the store keeper.

"Vicencia is that old black woman who comes around here sometimes to do the shopping for Major Carvalho's household. She was employed at Cassi's father's house for a long time. One day — she said she never really knew why — Cassi's father expelled him from their house. His mother then sent him off to her brother's place in Guaratiba. Once there, Cassi actually did or, at least, intended to pull off another one of his escapades but his uncle got angry about it and sent him packing back to his sister's house. Then, after a lot of trouble, Cassi's mother arranged for him to move into the back part of their basement, the ceiling of which was too low for him. Cassi eats and sleeps in that little hideaway and never goes up to the upstairs part of the house because he is afraid of his father. If his father finds out about his daring plans, he'll certainly throw Cassi out into the street for good.''

"And what do you have to say about all this now, 'doutor' Meneses?'' jeered Nascimento.

"I . . . I don't know because I've never been much concerned with the private lives of others,'' stammered Meneses.

"Well, this has nothing to do with the 'private lives of others,' '' Alipio said imperiously. "It has to do with a reprobate like Cassi who has no respect for families, friendships, misery or poverty when he's doing his filthy deeds! This is why I. . . .''

Just then *Seu* Nascimento persuasively intervened and asked for more calm. Nascimento was a tall, light skinned, slightly obese man, a fellow who looked like an old-time farmer and patriarch from one of our old-fashioned plantations. Then he added:

"You don't have to become indignant, Alipio, calm down. This monster doesn't have any more people who'll protect him . . . it's just as you've already said.''

"Oh, but he does, *Seu* Nascimento!'' affirmed Alipio; "he's tricky, a real shrewd operator.''

"Well, who is this new protector, Alipio?'' asked Nascimento who had moved off to sell a piece of candy to a little boy who had come into the store.

Customers continued to appear; in general, they were of two types: children and women. They didn't spend much money usually, two coins on this, four hundred *reis* for that; they bought the kinds of things poor people buy and it was a rare sight when one would see a half kilo of dried beef or black beans among their purchases. All they bought never exceeded a few coins in total. Although he was waiting on these customers alone because his clerks had already gone off to check on the needs of the regular customers, *Seu* Nascimento hadn't lost the line of conversation and continued on naturally.

Alipio, quite accustomed to this kind of conversation, didn't suspend his narration and answered the question.

"His protector now is a certain Captain Barcelos, a political boss in ****. He wields quite a lot of influence and that is why Cassi wanted to get close to him. Even in this last election when they were trying to fill some vacant councilman's post, Cassi and his gang operated on Barcelos's side. There weren't any disturbances because there weren't any other candidates, but Cassi wanted to start some trouble anyway just to win some notoriety. This is how, after just a little while, he managed to win Barcelos's confidence to the extent that Freitas, who was his right hand man, came to feel threatened and supplanted by Cassi.''

"Tell me more about this Barcelos fellow,'' said Nascimento.

"He's a Portuguese, about fifty years old and a good sort really. But having gone to jail once some twenty years ago because they say he fired a few shots at some scoundrel, who had insulted his wife, and succeeded in wounding the rascal seriously, he got to like politics and that's where he picked-up his first notions about this difficult science, in jail. So it was in prison that. . . ."

"Well, I'll be . . ." exclaimed Nascimento.

"You, too, Alipio," said a dubious Meneses.

But Alipio continued:

"So it was in prison that he met a political big wig from the capital who was there to stand trial for masterminding some murder. The man came up to Barcelos and the two of them got to talking. They weren't in their cell; they were in the infirmary, the free-room or some other special place. Barcelos began to tell the other man the story of his life, an existence which, despite his little mishap, had not been bad. Barcelos had a store in **** where he sold things for cash and extended credit to the factory owners of the area. He was happy because, in spite of dealing mostly in credit accounts, he very seldom lost any of the money he loaned out. He was even well thought of because of his cheerfulness and helpfulness. The politician, who had a rival in that same area, saw clearly how he could undermine the rival by making use of Barcelos's talents. 'Why haven't you ever gotten into politics?'' he said to Barcelos one day. The small businessman from **** responded, 'But I'm not a Brazilian citizen, *doutor.*' His prison companion then said to him sharply, 'I'll make you a naturalized Brazilian citizen and a captain in the National Guard if you'll work for me and my people in the elections. I want you to sign up the greatest number of people you can for my side.' Barcelos agreed to this and from then on always worked for one political boss or another. It was through these men that he was able to arrange for improvements in his hometown and for increasing the value of his own lands and buildings.''

"Then it was well worth his trouble to go to jail!''

"That's right, ''Seu Nascimento. And that's the point from which you can measure Barcelos's modest prosperity. He's got close to two hundred *contos* in houses, land and bonds, and that's in addition to the income he gets from his business operations.''

"Alipio, you call yourself an anarchist but what you really are is a novelist. This story of yours is like some novel!'' commented Meneses.

"Oh, come now, *Doutor!* You're the one here who doesn't know the way things really are. I know. Do you know for example that Timbo got a beating from a woman who lives near here?''

"No, I didn't know that.''

Almost at the same moment, Nascimento asked:

"Who's Timbo?''

"He's a clownish mulatto who's a football player and one of Cassi's pals, one of those always selected to testify in his behalf and to slander the victims in his dirty lawsuits.''

"Was he the one who got the beating?" inquired Nascimento.

"Yes, he was. It happened in the Todos os Santos station after a shameful solicitation of Dona Margarida. . . ."

"What Dona Margarida? The one from over there at number seventy-four?" said Nascimento with surprise.

"That's the one. She really gave it to him with her umbrella; and just when he wanted to disarm her a policeman happened by who grabbed Timbo by the ears and hauled him off the platform and down to the ground where he ran away under a hail of hoots and jeers. Among all of Cassi's companions, only Zeze Mateus can be excused. He doesn't mess around with any young girls or with anybody's wife or family, and he doesn't gamble or cause anybody any trouble. He likes to drink, but he pays for his own because when he wants to work he abandons drinking completely and settles up all his debts. But the rest of them are nothing but a bunch of scoundrels."

Alipio fell silent at that point and his interlocutors, with the exception of old Valentim, didn't dare make any further observation. Valentim, who had heard all of their conversation, was calmly smoking his "Sao Lourenco" cigarette and leaning up against the stone door jam. Full of the ingenuousness of the bumpkin who is eternally involved in his first romantic adventure, Valentim first wanted to know about the kinds of girls Cassi preferred and then said:

"But, 'Seu' Alipio, do you really believe that there actually are people as wicked as you make this Cassi fellow out to be?"

"Yes, and not just a few of them either. I know that everything I've told you comes from a very reliable source of information. It's all the pure truth."

Doutor Meneses had become disturbed by the tone of the conversation. He had come to the store looking for Leonardo Flores wanting to talk to him about a business matter but had discovered instead that Alipio knew all about his relationship with Cassi and that he also knew all about Cassi's life. Damn! Would this put him in a compromising situation? He'd already had four glasses of rum but as he was saying good-bye to everyone, he had another drink. Then, walking off, he began to think:

"What should I do now?"

He considered several hypotheses and then concluded:

"I'll see it through to the end."

After all, he continued to muse, there was no danger for him. . . .

But this thought didn't set him completely at ease, and old Menseses yearned to find some way of alleviating his conscience.

VI

The reception Cassi had received on his second visit, dry, hostile, and virtually dismissing him from the family's front door step, a circumstance quite contrary to his first visit to Joaquim dos Anjos's house, caused him to reflect upon all that had happened. But his desire to remove all the obstacles that might impede his pursuit of Clara only increased. Through a process of elimination, he envisioned only two people capable of getting in the way of his plan, an undertaking he had begun so rapidly and effortlessly. Who were they? They could only be Dona Margarida because of her dealings with Timbo and the old crippled fellow who had indirectly insulted Cassi in his poem by referring to the younger man as a jackass.

Strictly speaking, he did not use force in his seductions, a point that made him different from the other suburban seducers about whom the papers, from time to time, published stories reporting the desperation of their victims, women who became murderesses while defending themselves from such filthy characters. It was true, however, that Cassi immediately made use of violence to remove any obstacle to his conquests, even if it happened to be a brother of his intended victim, from his path.

It is important to see that he knew very well with whom he was getting involved. But in this case, dealing with a semi-invalid, he would only have to resort to a minimum of force. And as far as Dona Margarida was concerned, he knew how to deceive and hoodwink that lady.

The power he exercised over people was based upon his reputation as a tough guy and razor blade artist but it was based more on rumor than reality. Even so, he enjoyed a certain notoriety and many people were intimidated by him. This fact gave him a degree of dominance over those who, honest people of good faith, could have cautioned the young women he victimized and exposed Cassi for what he really was. Fearful, they left the *modinha* guitarist a free and open path.

Cassi was opportunistic about this situation and so demonstrated a hardened cynicism which he had condensed into a single sentence: ''Two hearts that love one another with a sincere passion cannot be set against each other.''

Ranking next to this theory — so appropriately his — was the consideration that he had never employed any violence in his seductions, no act of force whatsoever. Cassi, armed with his singular sense of morality — that of the *modinha* playing guitarist/libertine — never felt the least guilt or criminality for his activities although he had seduced close to ten girls and an even greater number of married women. The suicides, the murders and the populating of many different brothels — all of which were the direct results of his lascivious activities — were, in his view, events unrelated to his own deeds and would have probably taken place anyway. Cassi felt absolutely no guilt for any of this.

In order to find out for certain who at the postman's house was vilifying his character, Cassi resolved to go to Lafoes's house and sound him out.

Lafoes lived quite near the Engenho de Dentro reservoir. One afternoon, Cassi took the Piedade streetcar which, in order to get to his destination immediately after the Meier station, had to burrow along the sides of the mountains and then run along through sparsely populated streets until finally getting onto the track that went to Engenho de Dentro. This roadway was picturesque even then not only because of the crudely constructed poultry sheds that were still standing, but also because of the old country houses with verandas and little windows from an earlier era. Perhaps because it had been a cattle drive trail once, the Light and Power Company's engineers only performed summary efforts to level out its high and low points. The hills, valleys, and marshy places with their mud flats made more solid by the addition of wood chips and trash from the weeded fields all transformed the roadway of the streetcar into a kind of natural roller coaster. It was a scene that, on both sides, evoked a memory of the spectacle of what the roads in the interior of the country were like once, or what they are like now, and it was along these roads that the grains and meats we eat pass and ultimately arrive at our tables.

Sometimes the streetcar crossed the path of a train of coal carts from Jacarepagua, the Mateus mountains or some other locality with its natural forestation, and this would produce quite a colorful scene. The drovers of the region were people of greatly mixed bloodlines; they were large boned, high strung and shrewd, had flat feet, and sometimes they had rather regular features and faces covered by poorly kept beards, and they had expressions of unfathomable melancholy. Such groups were not only composed of grown men, however; there were girls too who guided the burros along in a line.

When the iron fittings of the streetcar started to rattle, whirring like some giant beetle and warning people of its iminent presence thanks to the humming noise in their ears or its whistle like the scream of a locomotive, the men, living as they did so close to the earth and to the spontaneousness of Nature, failed to be frightened by such sounds and to take the necessary precautions for their own safety and that of their animals. These people, standing around in groups, leaned close to the steep slopes that rose along the tracks parallel to the roadway when and where they were able to lean against them, or they spread out along the side of the tracks if the land there was unploughed and had no hedge rows on it when they were on more level ground. These people were always astonished by the buzzing monster that moved along by means of a thick wire thread overhead. The burros, however, in each and every case remained indifferent to the mechanical monstrosity and began to graze upon the foliage that provided them with shade and grew on the higher parts of the chambers of the nearby government buildings.

Cassi Jones arrived at Lafoes's house almost at nightfall. It was a small but well-built and clean house. The little garden in the front needed a bit of tending and in the backyard, there were kale and cabbages growing, both of which were reminiscent of a good, hearty Portuguese soup.

Lafoes, at that time of day, just after his evening meal, usually dressed in shirt sleeves, trousers, and wooden clogs, had finished his reading of the papers he had begun earlier that morning. He sat down at his Austrian rocking chair positioned close to the window and had on his left a little box in which his lighter — he didn't use matches — and his Fusilier cigarettes rested.

He was in that posture, patiently rolling a cigarette when suddenly there came a knocking on his door. He raised up a bit and, twisting his neck around to see better, almost getting his face even with the window pane, asked:

"Who is it?"

But just then he recognized his caller:

"Why, it's Senhor Cassi!"

He got up and went to open the door to greet him. He took his visitor's scruffy but still pretentious hat and his impeccable walking stick and welcomed him joyfully:

"You coming by here? Sit down, please! Make yourself right at home!"

The young man sat down saying:

"Thank you very much, my dear Lafoes."

"And why haven't you come by more often, Senhor Cassi?" Lafoes continued in a friendly fashion.

"I just haven't had the time. During the weekdays there's business and on Sundays there are so many invitations. I came here. . . ."

"For what, Senhor Cassi?"

"To ask you for some information."

"What is it, Senhor Cassi?"

"They tell me that in your office the inspector is going to be hiring some clerks soon for some kind or another of extraordinary jobs. . . . Would you find out if this is true?"

"By all means. I'll ask Braga. He's the errand boy, a very impish sort but he doesn't bother anyone, and he knows everything that goes on there," explained Lafoes.

"When can I return to get an answer?"

"Well, Senhor Cassi, tomorrow afternoon . . . no, because I have to go to my club's meeting . . . but if you're in a hurry you could come back the day after tomorrow about seven or eight o'clock."

"Fine," said Cassi, feigning contentment. "I'm deeply indebted to you. By the way, how are your wife and children getting along?"

"Fine. My wife went out with the youngest boy; they went to some affair or other around here. It's really hell! These priests have invaded the suburbs faster than the street peddlers. It's money for this saint, money for the church's activities. . . . I've just about had it. But Edmeia's out in the backyard. Would you like some coffee, Senhor Cassi?"

"Oh, I don't want to be any trouble . . . well, if your wife has some already made, yes, but. . . ."

"It's no trouble at all. Edmeia can heat it up. Unless Senhor Cassi doesn't care to have his coffee reheated?"

"I'd like that very much."

"Well, fine. We'll see to it," and he shouted to his daughter with the strong voice of a hale and hearty man:

"Edmeia! Edmeia!"

The girl wasn't long in appearing. She was a genteel girl of about twelve, smiling and the possessor of a round face, fine, firm features, and blondish hair cut in the English style.

Coming in, she exclaimed:

"Oh! Senhor Cassi's here. What a surprise! I didn't know. . . ."

She spoke to the young man who then answered her casually:

"I haven't seen you for a long time."

"That's true. Not since the day of Clarinha's birthday party. . . . Haven't you gone back there since?"

"I haven't been able to."

"Why? Oh, there are people there who don't care for you. . . . Especially the old one they call 'pe-pe'. . . ."

"Hush, girl!" scolded her father. "Don't meddle in other people's affairs. . . . Go warm up the coffee and bring us two cups. Go on, now. . . ."

As the girl was leaving the room, Cassi decided that he now had a good opportunity to get to the real reason for his visit and he said:

"It may be that they don't like me, but their prejudices have no basis in fact. I've never. . . ."

"Come now, Senhor Cassi. You're surely not going to listen to a silly child! They don't know what they're talking about."

"Now my dear Lafoes, I noted that on the day of the party Senhor Joaquim dos Anjos's compadre did not accept me."

"That can be easily explained; he was or is a poet and he doesn't think much at all of *modinha* singers. Now, in my own land, the poets of the noblemen and noble-women do not accept the fado singers from the country. They call them yokels — sometimes even worse names. . . . In every walk of life it's the same thing. . . . Haven't you noticed how coachmen scorn barbers? A coachman who isn't worth his salt is called a barber. Marramaque is a sick old man who doesn't know how to disguise his dislike for people who like the Spanish guitar and who play it and sing *modinhas*.

"But . . . what about 'Seu' Joaquim?"

"It's just that they're compadres and close friends, my dear Senhor Cassi . . . that's all."

The coffee was served and the conversation took another direction. They talked about the forthcoming Independence Day celebrations and about the financial crisis, but Cassi didn't have his mind on any of this. He was thinking about Marramaque, the audacious old cripple who apparently intended to interfere with his seduction of Clara. Well he would pay dearly for that! Cassi said good-bye and slowly wandered down to the suburbs below Lafoes's house. Such hatred and obstinance were strange emotions for him. Cassi was not a real "lover," not even in the most elementary sense. His attraction to a woman — any woman — never developed into any sentiment other than lust. He never felt anything else, no confusing or contradictory emotions, no dreams, no vague yearnings, and no anxious, perplexing sensations.

His sentiments regarding women were always reduced to the simplest element of Love — possession. Once he had obtained this, he immediately packed up and moved on, heaping scorn upon his victim for whom he never felt any further attachment. Then he would look around for another victim.

His formal learning was less than rudimentary but even so, perhaps through some intimate necessity to excuse or justify what he did, he liked to read lyric poetry, principally love poetry. He didn't read papers or magazines but here and there, on a scrap of paper, in an almanac or in some book which had fallen into his hands, Cassi, without really understanding how, was able to read a few poems and even understand about half of them. It was from these sonnets and the other snatches of poetry that accidentally happened to fall into his hands that he concluded, with his congenital stupidity and his innate perversity, that he had the right to do the things he did. The poets proclaimed that one has an obligation to Love and tended to grant all kinds of rights and privileges to the Lover, finally arguing that Passion ranks above everything. It is easy to see that Cassi had no real feeling for what those mediocre poets, guides to his lascivious activities were saying. One can also clearly perceive that there was no sense of true Love in his heart, not the slightest bit. What there was in Cassi Jones was concupiscence tied to a history of niggardliness and including a complete lack of any moral sense, even that of a born criminal.

The true condition of Love and the State of Loving presupposes a corresponding condition of semi-madness, an obsessiveness that determines an emotional disturbance that varies from the most intense happiness to the most excruciating pain, produces enthusiasm and despondency, encourages and debilitates and gives a person hope and reason to grow desperate.

None of this applied to Cassi, however. Once the victim of his concupiscence was selected, he attempted to learn all there was to know about her parents, how much money they had and all about the relatives if he hadn't known these things beforehand. Then he began to meet her at dances or at some evening party to try to impress her with his highly affected guitar playing. If he sensed that he had enjoyed some success through these efforts, he redoubled his attempts to meet her again ''accidently'' at the movies, on streetcars, in train stations, etc. At the most propitious moment, he slipped her the fatal letter. All of this would be done with complete calm and premeditation, patiently and without his being disturbed in the least by any sign or impatience or emotion. If the girl or the married woman accepted any of his advances, he was assured of final victory, of getting what he wanted. If she did not, he wasted no time in abandoning any further preliminary efforts and merely waited until another more easily persuaded victim happened to come along.

In Clara's case, he was not prepared to believe the first hypothesis since he was certain that he had seen the rapture his singing and playing had effected in her on the evening of Clara's birthday party. Cassi also remembered the insistence the girl had shown in running up to speak to him when he had gone to her father's house for the second and to date, final time. What seemed obvious to him, for various reasons, was that somebody had intervened between them, ''two hearts in love,'' somebody who was denouncing him to her parents because of his past deeds and because of his reputation as a seducer so that they barred the door of their house to him . . . to him, Cassi! ! !

A moment ago, he had received confirmation of his suspicion, thanks to the ingenuous accusation of Lafoes and his daughter, Edmeia, that it was Marramaque, Clara's godfather, who didn't like him. It was necessary, therefore, to take precautions against the old cripple's intrigues and to get rid of him once and for all. Cassi knew that Marramaque almost always stopped off at Seu Nascimento's store as he made his way home after work. He would sit around the store with the other men tippling away until the place finally closed for the night. But Cassi couldn't go there for all sorts of reasons and Timbo couldn't go either since he was quite well known in that neighborhood thanks to the beating he had received there. Zeze Mateus was an idiot. . . . Who, then, could go and scout around the place? Arnaldo. . . ! No one knew Arnaldo in those parts and neither did anybody know that he went around with Cassi and his gang. Rather reluctantly, Cassi set off toward his parent's home. He didn't yet have enough money to perfect his scheme.

Cassi's domestic lair was located right below the dining room window of his parents' house. The dining room was the room that formed the end part of the main body of the house. The remaining rooms filled-up another long wing. When Cassi was coming in through the door to his room, he perceived that there was somebody other than his mother, father and sisters in the dining room who wasn't usually there. This person said upon hearing Cassi's footsteps:

''Is someone here?''

''Yes, it's Cassi,'' said the mother.

''Doesn't he come up here?'' asked the visitor.

Everybody fell silent and looked at each other while old Manuel de Azevedo explained the situation with a minimum of words:

''Augusto, would you want me, the head of my family, a man who prizes the honor of other people's daughters and of my own, to allow such a miserable scoundrel as Cassi to sit at my side? If I didn't throw him out in the street for good before, it was only because of his mother.''

''You're right, 'Mano,' but all that people say about him might be just more calumny.''

''That's what I think too, Augusto,'' said Dona Salustiana.

The girls remained quiet thanks to their sense of modesty but old Azevedo cut short the argument of his wife and his brother:

''Didn't you read those printed pages that they sent to you two days after you arrived at the hotel?''

''I did.''

''Did you read all the dates, the narration of the facts, all the letters. . . ?''

''Yes, I read them too, but the time. . . .''

''Well, it's all true. Unfortunately nobody knows that better than I. In less than ten years, this. . . , this. . . , my despicable son did all these things. I can't deny any of it, not in good conscience. If I'm not able to. . . .''

As he came in, Cassi, perceiving that the conversation was about him, positioned himself right underneath the window so that he could hear better. He listened attentively and without missing any of it, overheard that part of the conversation in which his uncle had taken part. For a long time, his uncle had been a customs house official up in the North. When old Manuel de Azevedo talked about printed papers that enumerated dates and narrated facts, and about his son's problems with the police and the halls of justice, Cassi became frightened. Who could be exposing him? This wasn't the first time he had noticed the existence of these clandestine printed pages mysteriously distributed to the newspapers. An investigator for one of the suburban police stations had once told him that just as soon as there was a change in one of the captains or commissioners of the station, the new officer would receive a similar notebook. This mysterious persecution was disturbing to Cassi and he was certain that within a short time, it could effectively undermine him. So indifferent was he to the fate of his victims and so devoid of any compassion for them that he was unable to string together a solid line of reasoning pointing to the origin or authorship of the notebooks. He had to run away — he concluded, he felt threatened not by goblins but by traps — masked men, private jails, punishments — the whole fantastic array out of the movies.

Cassi still wanted to resolve the matter concerning Clara first, however, a matter still unfinished.

He got into bed and slept regally until daybreak. As soon as the sunlight reached a certain degree of brightness, he got up and went out to inspect his fighting cocks' cages. Everything was in order and he began tossing them some ground-up corn he took from a tin bucket he carried in his hand. He looked at each of the revolting beasts with the fondness of an honest breeder who fretfully reviews and inspects the fruits of his labor with careful scrutiny and the gentleness of one gazing at new born lambs. He gave ground corn and chaff to his hens and he didn't give ground eggs yet because it wasn't the right day. His delight in and affection for those horrendous birds was sincere — they made money for him! Cassi looked at his birds and asked himself:

"I wonder how much they'd be worth altogether?"

Certain people had already offered him five-hundred milreis for the lot of them and he was prepared to sell the entire flock for that price, but only after his other affair was finished. . . .

He went back into his lair where he had breakfast, a meal brought down to him every morning by Romualda. She was an old woman and it was her age that gave her the one, perfect defense against Cassi's libidinous assaults. Cassi asked her:

"Is my uncle still here?"

"Who's your uncle?"

"That fellow who was here last night."

"Oh! No, he left right after having tea."

They exchanged no further words. After she had served breakfast and Cassi had eaten his buttered bread, old Romualda carried away the tray with the dishes on it, and he got dressed and went out.

Cassi almost never stayed home. He was afraid of meeting his father who, on this day, had decided to stay home for some reason or another. He couldn't tolerate his sister's contempt for him either. To be in the house was more of a punishment for Cassi than the dozens of times he had been in the local jails.

He went looking for Arnaldo who, because he lived in Estrada Real, took the Cascadura streetcar in order to get the train at the Meier station. Arnaldo never failed a single day to go down to that neighborhood. He was always hoping to get some odd job to do or when he couldn't do that, make arrangements for picking up a small job or something from the train.

Cassi hadn't been mistaken. A little after nine o'clock, Arnaldo, marked by a long, anteater-like nose and wandering, searching eyes, arrived. Cassi told him that he needed him and would meet him there at five o'clock. Then Cassi bought Arnaldo a cup of coffee. Arnaldo spoke:

"Sure, Cassi. It's in deals like this that you can see who your friends really are. Sure, I'll be there."

After making the sacrifice of an afternoon's harvest, Arnaldo arrived at the appointed place and time.

Cassi met him there and explained that later on that afternoon, he was to go to Seu Nascimento's store and gave him the address. Arriving there, Arnaldo was to pretend that he had come looking for Seu Meneses, a man he knew.

"And what if he isn't there?" asked Arnaldo.

"Then you say you'll wait for him and you listen to what's being said. With the others there should be an old cripple who's always dressed in his work uniform. But he doesn't know who you are and neither do the others . . . at least I hope not. I want you to remember everything you hear so that you can tell me about it later. If Meneses should appear, you tell him that I want to speak to him about some business matters that might interest him."

Cassi gave Arnaldo two mil-reis notes and he set off down the road on foot so that he wouldn't have to spend the coin on a streetcar. When he got to Seu Nascimento's store, Arnaldo had two disappointments: first, he saw an English engineer, a Mr. Persons from whom he had stolen a rubber cape; second, he saw Alipio who knew that he went around with Cassi.

Not letting himself be discouraged by this turn of events, and walking between Alipio and old Marramaque who were talking, he went directly up to the counter and asked as naturally as he could:

"Do you know an old dentist by the name of Meneses?"

And he added:

"Has he been around?"

The storekeeper responded:

"No, not for several days now," and turning to the others present, he asked, "Have any of you seen Doctor Meneses?"

Everyone responded that they hadn't.

Arnaldo was about to thank them all and leave when Mr. Persons asked him:

" 'Sinhor'! Come over here!"

Arnaldo tried to put on a cheerful expression:

"Oh! *Seu* Mister . . . how's it going?"

"Don't say *Seu* Mister, it's an error. Anyway . . . where's my cape?"

"I've been carrying it around with me for several days now but today I've forgotten it."

"That makes two times you've said that. I need that cape!"

"I won't forget it the next time."

He left in a hurry. The matter of the cape was quite simple. Persons hadn't had his wits about him when he was returning from the city once and had left his rubber cape on the bench next to him while he leaned back on the wall for a nap. Just before the train was due to arrive at a station, Arnaldo sat down beside him with the intention of stealing the cape. Just as he was putting his plan into effect, Persons woke up, but he was only aware of the theft as Arnaldo was running out of the coach. "My cape," he shouted. A conductor was able to grab Arnaldo who was still clutching his prize, but by the time Persons was able to get to the spot where the two men were struggling, his helper had let Arnaldo get away and the train had begun to move. Nevertheless, he did get a good look at the thief's face. Later, accidentally meeting up with Arnaldo, Persons asked him where his cape was and Arnaldo told him he had picked it up by mistake.

Arnaldo left quite shame-facedly but seeing that no one had come out of the shop's doorway, he came back close enough so that he could overhear what they were saying.

The English "Mister" had just finished telling the story about the cape when Alipio said in a gossipy tone of voice:

"That guy who just left is really a menace. I didn't know about his stealing on trains but it's enough to know that he's one of Cassi's bunch for him to be no good. . . ."

Marramaque quickly added:

"I didn't know him, but now I'm going to point him out to my 'compadre.' It's Trembo . . . or Tipo, or something like that, isn't it?"

"Timbo," said Alipio.

"I know this Timbo and I've taken note of him for my compadre. Speaking of this, do you *Seu* Nascimento, and you gentlemen know what I received a few days ago in my mail at the office?"

"No, what?" everybody asked, by gesture or word.

"Cassi's life story."

"Printed?"

"No, type-written with pictures of him, copies of newspaper stories about him, listings of the dates of his trials, and of the policemen and judges involved . . . everything!"

"Who sent it to you?" asked Alipio.

"I don't know. I received the thing in my office. I read it there and then gave it to my compadre so that he could take the appropriate measures."

"He should get out a blunderbuss," observed Nascimento.

"Or a revolver," agreed Marramaque.

Overhearing all of this and seeing that somebody was approaching the store whose closing time was not far off, Arnaldo left the spot where he had been listening to the conversation and ran to meet Cassi who was waiting for him in Engenho Novo.

They met, and Arnaldo, as was not his habit, told Cassi the whole truth about what he had seen and heard.

Neither Cassi nor Arnaldo were particularly given to drinking, but this particular situation seemed to call for a drink. Cassi invited his dedicated cohort to have a bottle of beer with him. They consumed their drinks almost without speaking to each other.

After they had finished, they paid and got up to go. Arnaldo set out in one direction and Cassi moved off in the other, into the shadows of Rua Barao de Bom Retiro.

Although it was not yet late at night, the sounds of gun shots could be heard. The gunfire was coming from the weapons of the suburbanites who, from time to time, fired their arms in order to drive away people who were hoping to steal chickens from their hen houses. One of these guns happened to go off quite close to Cassi who, pretending that he was calm and not frightened, said in a low voice:

"You didn't get me this time either."

VII

The suburbs, strictly speaking, are located on a long strip of land that stretches out from Rocha or Sao Francisco to Sapopemba and has the Central railroad tracks as its axis. This land doesn't spread out much laterally, especially where the flatlands meet the hills and mountain sides that restrict its expansion. But the suburbs continue to extend into small hills and tracts of waste land. Passing through territory that appears to be deserted, one might see down at the bottom of some deep, dark valley where only underbrush grows, an old, tumbledown shack that can be reached only by making a virtually perpendicular descent of the steep hillsides. Walking along a bit further, one can lift his eyes to a level of the horizon and see, there on top of the mountains, a few huts and cottages that wouldn't ordinarily be noticed because of the steepness of the access.

There are houses, tiny buildings, cottages, shacks and hovels built anywhere four wooden stakes could be set down and connected with something that serves as a wall. Anything is used as building material for these structures: unfolded matchbook covers, old tiles, sheets of corrugated steel and sticks of bamboo to serve as ribbing for the mud walls. The bamboo is not cheaply acquired.

There are actual villages and settlements formed among these huts found on the tops of the hillsides which the trees and the bamboo grass hide from the eyes of the passers-by. Among these villages there is always one public water fountain but no sewer system. The entire population, extremely poor, lives under the constant threat of smallpox epidemics and when this disease does break out in such areas, it is truly a curse.

Moving away from the axis of the suburban zone, the state of the streets changes immediately. There are no more railroads or business establishments; there are only the shacks, hovels and other similar buildings. Although these are often perched all alone or have a great deal of open space between them, there is often an entire stretch of tiny houses each having two windows and a door in the middle arranged so as to form an avenue.

The streets, distant from the Central railroad line, are full of grass and hay trays which are used by the families who live there as places to spread out recently washed clothes to dry. From morning to night, these streets are populated with all kinds of small domestic animals: chickens, ducks, geese, goats, sheep and pigs, to say nothing of the dogs that fraternize with all the other animals.

When evening begins to fall, one hears, "Time to come home," ringing out from every doorway; "Come, sweety," and it will be a billy-goat that the lady of the house is calling home, or "Come, my little beauty," and it will be a suckling piglet that some girl is herding into the house. And so it goes. . . .

The sheep, goats, ducks, chickens, turkeys all come right in through the front door, walk through the house and then gather together again in the backyard.

If one of her ''animals'' should be missing, the woman of the house really raises a rumpus; she lambastes her children and then blames the loss on one of her neighbors. When the neighbor comes to learn of this accusation a squabble usually results, a dispute that sometimes degenerates into a full-fledged fistfight between the two husbands.

Poor people find it difficult to get along together. Discovering a point of honor in any and every kind of nonsense, they often end up fighting. This is especially true of the women.

Their state of irritability — an effect of the constant poverty and tribulation with which they are forced to live and their inability to find beyond their immediate and limited field of vision any reason that could explain their sorry plight — makes them vent their wrath in veiled accusations and mistrust of their neighbors, people whom they may dislike merely because they appear to be happier than somebody else. Each woman there believes herself to be of the highest personal worth and a descendant of the finest ancestry but in reality, each one is extremely poor and lives in terrible poverty. An accidental difference in skin color is reason enough for someone to judge herself superior to her neighbor; the fact that one's husband earns more money than another's is also a reason. The paltry ware of some junkdealer or peddler always incites the vanity of these people and feeds their personal resentments.

In general, however, these quarrels last only a short time. Along comes some disease and one of the women's children falls ill; her neighbor then immediately comes over to help with viles full of homeopathic cures.

It is within this intricate labyrinth of streets and shacks that a great portion of the city's population lives, a population whose existence and needs the city government chooses to ignore, although it imposes inordinate taxes upon this same population and spends the money on useless and ostentatious works in other parts of Rio de Janeiro.

Not even death makes things easier for them; that is to say, it is of no help to these people in getting to the cemetery.

In order to get to the one at Inhauma for example, a cemetery arrived at only by travelling through the entire vast suburban district, one has to travel along some very bad roads that make a lot of useless twists and turns, most of which could have been eliminated without very much cost. The burial processions of poor people are made on foot and it is easy to imagine in what condition those who carry the dead person finally arrive at the municipal holy ground. Anybody passing along those roads would almost certainly meet such a procession. The processions for dead children are made up of girls whose own funeral processions would probably be made up of other girls their age. For them, there is no special ''dress.'' They wear the same clothes they would wear to dances and amusement parks. Their clothes are usually pink, sky-blue, or white. They move along carrying their poor, departed friend beneath an inclement sun as they breathe in a suffocating dust. Whenever it rains or when it has just recently rained, they have to bear the casket so that they are able to lift it up high quickly whenever necessary to avoid the splashing muck of the quagmire and water puddles beneath their feet.

The caskets of adults are borne by adults. In these processions, however, there is always some modification in the raiment of those who accompany the deceased to his final resting place. The gentlemen always try to wear clothing dark in color if not actually black. Once in a while, a scandal will develop because somebody wears white trousers. They move along in a not very sad or lamenting state of mind and at each roadside inn they pass, they "salute the deceased," that is, they all go inside to have a good, stiff swig of rum. By the time they arrive at the burial site, their brains don't function too well but the cadaver is still buried.

There was one occasion, however, when the body did not arrive at its destination. Its bearers had drunk so much liquor that they forgot about the deceased and left him out on the road. Upon leaving the bar each man looked at the casket and said, "Oh hell...the guys who are still inside will pick him up," and he went on his way. Finally they all arrived at the cemetery and only then realized that the deceased was not among them. "But . . . weren't you supposed to bring him along?" one of them would ask another. "No, you were supposed to," retorted the other. Each of them passed off the guilt and responsibility to somebody else. They were all very tired and half-drunk but they decided to rent a cart and go back to look for their fallen comrade who had two holy candles burning for him upon the high altar. The poor man deserving a more touching homage from his friends than the one he got from his comrades who were bearing him off to the cemetery on foot, only received a fraction of the tribute properly owed him since he was forced to make the rest of the trip to his final resting place by means of the efforts of two donkeys, beasts more accustomed to hauling quite a different and much less respectable cargo than the one they bore that day.

This is more or less the way life is in the suburbs, with the poverty and virtual abandonment in which the public authority leaves the people who reside there. From the earliest hours of the morning, people came out from all the huts, pockets, and caves to cross the trails, hills, streets and by-ways and walk off toward the nearest railroad station. Some, living farther away in Inhauma, for example, or in Caxambi or Jacarepagua became less attached to their nickels and took the streetcars, always fully loaded, that ran to the railroad stations. This movement of people lasted until ten o'clock in the morning and up to a certain point, people from all walks of life in the population of the city took part in it. There were workers, household maids and servants, all ranks of military personnel, distinguished non-commissioned officers in the Militia, civil servants, and others who, although basically honest, made their livings by means of small, day-to-day dealings in questionable business that usually netted them pitifully few *mil-reis.* The suburbs are the last refuge of all the dispossessed people. Those who have lost their jobs or their fortunes, those people who have failed at business or, in short, all the poor souls who have lost their normal stations in life finally end up there seeking the suburbs as a refuge and a place of shelter for themselves. Every day quite early, they go down the hillsides to look for loyal friends who will help them, friends who will give them money or something to sustain themselves and their children.

During these hours of the day, the stations fill up and the trains descend packed with passengers. Even fuller, however, are those which come from the area bordering on the Federal District and the State of Rio de Janeiro. These are the express trains and there are people everywhere. The interiors as well as the spaces between the cars are jammed with people. The spaces seem to be carrying almost half the total capacity of the cars. Many of these people travel along with one foot in one car and the other foot on the following car clutching the platform handrails with their hands. Other men and women come down the hillsides to the city seated on the access steps leading to the interiors of the coaches while others, more daring, hang on to the iron handrailing with their hands and with only a single foot on the coach's running boards.

All the people who live in the area of Maxambomba and its adjacent lands are actually forced to do so because of the relative cheapness of the housing there. That particular zone offers them no other advantage; everything else is as expensive as in the suburbs proper. There is no water system but where there is one, it is located in the hamlets in and around the Federal District. Therefore, it is a water supply the federal government kindly supplies only to certain public fountains. There are no sewage systems, doctors, or pharmacies. In Rio de Janeiro there are still some highways built by City Hall that might be in about the same condition but as soon as one gets to the border with the State of Rio, everything stops; beyond that point there is nothing even under construction.

The traveler who stops to gaze upon those fields of sparse and yellowish vegetation upon those scarred and battered hillsides covered with entangled thickets of scrub land shrubs, and where raw-boned, skinny cattle graze, becomes distressed and saddened. dened. There are no crops there; green trees are rarely seen and, close around people's homes, it is rare to see even a flourishing orange tree or a wild papaya tree bending down over the entrance.

The streams are, in general, merely channels of putrid muck and mire that, when the big rains come, transform themselves into torrents that carry the most nauseating kind of debris. The impermeable ''clay,'' the dense, clayish soil, and the lack of water do not facilitate the growing of vegetable gardens. To have even a cabbage growing there is considered a rarer occurrence than if it were to grow on the Avenida Central.

Rio de Janeiro has on its anterior side a very lovely diadem of mountains and trees, but this chain does not encircle the city completely as a true crown would. As is obvious from looking at it, the posterior side does not complete the sequence that would fully form the crown resting upon the city's Olympic brow. . . .

Standing in the Meier station, Cassi Jones was watching all those trains full of working people pass by, but he was not considering that, at the age of almost thirty, he had, to date, never worked a single day in his life. His thoughts were of other things.

Ever since Arnaldo had brought him news of what he had overheard in the store, Cassi had been a little bit disheartened about his scheme in regard to the postman's daughter. At the same time, however, he perceived that all those precautions taken against him were because the girl was obviously not indifferent to him. The situation, he concluded, was such that he would have to learn what Clara's feelings were so that he could act accordingly. He knew now that he had to speak to her . . . but how? It would not do for him to lurk around their house because he was so well-known around those parts and would surely be denounced by Clara's father who naturally enough, would demand satisfaction from him. And whatever the outcome of the fight, Cassi would lose. His reputation, his heinous reputation, had now been made vivid by the notebook that was floating around from hand to hand. His reputation no longer had consisted of mere whisperings here and there about vague, nameless deeds; now it had all been documented, including the exact names, dates and places.

There was enough information contained in it for one to condemn a saint and if he were to attack Joaquim the postman, everybody's sympathy would lie with the father who would be viewed as the defender of his daughter's honor to his final breath and there would be none for him, a contumacious and cynical seducer. Until this point, Cassi had been able to count upon the secret benevolence of certain judges and police officials who intimately believed that a marriage between Cassi and any one of his victims would be absurd because of the differences in upbringing, birth, skin color and education. As far as the second and third reasons are concerned — although the second might not be always verifiable — one could admit to their validity. As for the other two considerations, they were erroneous because Cassi was as stupid and poorly educated as any of the humble girls he so irremediably disgraced.

As far as other people were concerned, Cassi could no longer count on having help with anything.

In the beginning, he had had his father and later on, the help of his uncle, the Army Captain and doctor although both had been solicited by his mother! But now. . . ? Now, he was certain that none of them could be moved to spend a red cent on his behalf. There was only Captain Barcelos and Cassi didn't have great confidence in him. The Captain would not make a single move to help him unless it involved some minor matter which would cost him nothing and involve no risk. Under any other circumstances, however, Barcelos would just avoid Cassi. Cassi knew that now he had to be cautious or else. . . .

Cassi continued to consider the various ways and means he might use in order to come to an understanding with Clara. He could no longer count on Lafoes, either. He had seen in his last visit that the old Portuguese fellow was wily. He could no longer be counted upon as an asset. What could he do?

People continued to come down the hillsides in the crowded streetcars and then get out and join the huge crowd that was steadily moving toward the railroad station platform. Some people were going to have a cup of coffee before actually making their way toward their places of work and the daily grind. Others headed to the "lottery" houses and would place a few bets there but ultimately, everybody either went to work or to do something else to earn money. Only Senhor Cassi Jones de Azevedo was left behind. . . .

"Oh, Seu Cassi . . . How goes it?"

The suburban minstrel and master of the languid *modinha* and its lewd accompaniment, the rolling, wandering eyes, turned around and recognized the speaker immediately:

"How are you, Praxedes?"

"I, *Seu* Cassi, am very well, thank you. But this business of jurisdiction. . . . Yesterday, I presented an exception of disability request to the Court and I thought it would be ruled upon immediately. . . . But now the picture's become blurred for me and . . . well, today I'm going to see if some attachments of mine have been ruled upon and received. I've got to go down below. . . . Sometimes a person gets one set-back and then twenty, thirty . . . even fifty things seem to go wrong for him as well."

But seeing that this topic held no interest for Cassi, he changed the subject and asked:

"Have you been back to the postman's house on Teresina street?"

"Not for a long time I haven't, no. How about you?"

"I went there only at the invitation of one of the musicians. I don't really have anything to do with the family. Say, speaking of that, do you know who I just saw coming through here?"

"No, who?"

"Doutor Meneses, that old bearded fellow, the one who seemed to know so much. Don't you remember him?"

Something ran through Cassi's mind that made him ask before thinking:

"Where did he go?"

"He was going to the mailman's house. He's working on the daughter's teeth and he almost always eats there too. He has to. Poor *Doutor* Meneses! Such a learned man but so old and sick . . . he almost never eats anything anymore . . . he just drinks! And that's really doing him damage! He's burning himself up from the inside out. You can drink but you've got to eat, too . . . don't you think so?"

During the entire conversation, Praxedes never ceased to wave his arms about with neither rhyme nor reason and to wag his dreadful head, an appendage that looked as if it were going to become buried between his shoulders.

"It's a godsend for him," said Cassi repressing his joy. "I've got some business for Meneses too. If you should see him, tell him that I want to talk to him."

"I won't forget. But if you're in a hurry, you can find him down at the Fagundes bar at night, the place that's quite close to the fire station. Well, I'll see you later . . . I've got to get down to the city right away."

Cassi said good-bye. Suddenly, because of Meneses's visits to Clara's house, all of Cassi's hopes of having a face to face confrontation with her seemed now to have been put onto the right track. Cassi knew all about Meneses; old, decrepit, needy, vitiated from drink and virtually penniless. It would be easy to overcome his opposition to getting involved in such a plan. But for this first time, the *modinha* guitarist thought, it was going to cost him something to get what he wanted. . . .

In part, he was deceiving himself because although Meneses had fallen onto extremely hard times, he had, until now, never in his lifetime done a single thing that was not legitimate and moral. One could describe him as a completely pure man, one who walked life's straight and narrow path.

Meneses, Jose Castanho de Meneses, was the son of Portuguese parents born in a city on the coast, a little south of the state of Rio de Janeiro. During those early years, such cities were prosperous but in more recent days, an indication of their irremediable decline is that there has been no news of the construction of a single house in the entire area for over forty years, not a single one.

His father had a shop there, a bazaar, that was doing quite well. With the decline of the area, brought about in part by the construction of the Central railroad, his commercial establishment began to fail. His father was obliged to cut back on expenses among which were the education and instruction of his children. Jose, who was then seventeen, came to the shop to work and the others were placed here and there, in their father's weirs and in the fishing factory, an operation also owned by the elder Meneses and carried on at a very rudimentary level.

At twenty-two, Jose, bored with his life there, set out on foot into the world and for about the next thirty-odd years, travelled around the interior of the old provinces of Rio, Minas and Sao Paulo. He did a little of everything and he suffered every trial and tribulation but he always maintained his integrity and unflagging honesty. Here he was a bookkeeper for a general store, later, on a ranch, he was a foreman. In a tiny hamlet he was a school teacher and in one city, he came across a kindly pharmacist who became his friend and taught him to prepare and handle various kinds of drugs, to clean and fill teeth, to prescribe minor remedies and fill prescriptions. That was the place he stayed the longest but it came to pass, toward the end of his vagabond career, that he could no longer change his vocation so easily. On the outskirts of the city, they constructed a depot and some modest machine shops to make minor repairs on the equipment of the railroad branch line which they were going to install there. Jose closely followed the construction of the works, saw all the equipment and was astounded by those marvelous boilers, fireboxes, piston rods, cranks and levers, all of which had to be perfectly coordinated to stop and start those hideous iron monsters, the locomotives. He wanted to know the secret of all that machinery and asked question after question. At first, the men who worked them patiently answered his questions but the questions became so numerous and varied that the men got bored with and angry at their interrogator. Meneses, however, did not get bored, since he was developing a real vocation for engineering and wanted to become an engineer. There was, however, no place there to study for it. He would have to go off to Rio de Janeiro, attend classes on theory and perfect his skills in an appropriate place. His money was very scant but the pharmacy always earned him a little and his income had even grown a bit thanks to the working men's affluence which came from their completion of the local roadbed. Moreover, he was still prescribing medicine. He made money but needed to save it. This is what he did and after one year, he had saved up enough money to go to Rio, establish himself and look for some kind of employment.

His friend the pharmacist didn't want to dissuade him from going but said to him:

"If you were younger, I'd give you some advice because big things are being planned in Rio. But, since you are over fifty, you should do whatever seems best to you. In any case, I'm going to ask Coronel Carvalho to write you a letter of recommendation."

During the long period of time he had lived away from his family, he had received only vague news about his parents and siblings. He knew that his parents had died and that almost all of his brothers had too. The only remaining one was an oarsman in the Captaincy of Porto who took care of an unmarried sister, the only one he had. They lived near Saude.

Meneses left contentedly; he was finally going to realize his true vocation. Up until that moment, he had not discovered what it was but ever since he had seen the machines and mechanisms, he had thought about nothing else. He did not, however, fail to pack his bag with his dentist's tools and his letter of recommendation.

After spending a monotonous night in a hotel, he left on the following day for the Captaincy of Porto, asking questions and checking into things here and there.

Arriving at Porto, he asked for his brother the oarsman. He encountered no difficulties and was informed that the latter would be coming by shortly. Meneses didn't have long to wait; a huge, powerful-looking man with brown, weather-beaten skin and dressed like a sea-faring man came up to the innkeeper and asked:

"Who's looking for me?"

The caretaker pointed at Meneses, who was seated on a bench, and said:

"That gentleman there."

Meneses' brother did not take many steps in his direction, but the older brother stood up immediately, ran over to meet his sibling and cried:

"Don't you remember me?"

"No sir, I don't."

"I'm your brother, 'Juca!' "

They then embraced for a long time. Meneses' brother, Leopoldo, went to the innkeeper and told him who the other fellow was.

"Thirty years ago!" exclaimed the caretaker. "You must have been just a baby then, eh, Leopoldo?"

The seaman responded:

"I must've been about five."

"That's right," Meneses informed him.

Leopoldo went to get permission to leave work with his brother whom he had not seen in nearly thirty years, while Meneses began to chat with the caretaker about things in the back country.

"Oh, you're an engineer?"

"Well, sort of . . . yes. More of a mechanic, really. I also work with instruments and traffic control."

"They must have a lot of work around here for engineers. They're doing big things . . . take advantage of them, *doutor*!"

"I have a letter for the Deputy, Sehnor Sepulveda. Does he have any influence in these parts?"

"Yes, a lot. He's the brains behind politics in Minas . . . but don't let your coat tails get caught on anything, *doutor*."

The conversation was interrupted by the return of Leopoldo who had just gotten permission to leave. After they began to travel down the road, he told Meneses that all the others died, that he had gotten a job in the Captaincy and that he succeeded in marrying off their sister to a colleague of his, one Pedro Rocha, a good, well-mannered man. The couple had given them a nephew, Edmundo, who was about six now and Leopoldo lived with them on Rua Livramento.

Arriving at the house of his brother and brother-in-law, his sister, Etelvina, whom he had left when she was seven or eight, did not recognize him immediately. A short time later, when her husband arrived, she did and there was a celebration held in which only the six-year-old nephew did not participate. This child always had a dirty nose and wore tattered clothes. He was somewhat standoffish and was forever clutching at his mother's skirts without ever wanting to receive his uncle's blessing.

The sister soon invited her older brother to stay with them; there was a cottage in the backyard which when properly repaired would be adequate for Leopoldo's room. His room could be given to Juca. Until the cottage was ready, he would have to sleep with Leopoldo. Meneses accepted the invitation saying:

"That's fine, provided you let me contribute to help out. . . ."

But he was interrupted immediately by everyone:

"Oh . . . no, no, Juca!"

"There's no reason to do that," said the brother-in-law.

"There's no question of that, mano 'Juca,' " said his brother.

Meneses was deeply grateful but added:

"Well, it's just that I would like one of you to find some way for me to speak with Doutor Sarmento Sepulveda, the gentleman in the Legislative Chambers. I've got a letter for him."

His brother-in-law, upon hearing this, suddenly exclaimed:

"What? He's a real shark!"

But it was all arranged and Meneses installed himself in his relative's house with his suitcase and his iron dental tools. He took Colonel Carvalho's letter to the Deputy who studied it carefully, asked him about the important people in the district he had come from and gave him another letter for the Chief of the road building and construction work crew. On the following day, he was admitted to this work. He made good money but he wasn't able to save any of it. Although that was the way things were, he was not squandering or wasting any of his income. His brother had suddenly fallen ill and was dying and his brother-in-law soon did the same. Meneses paid for their medical bills and, when he was discharged from the road construction commission, an occurrence which took place after the deaths of both men, Meneses had little or nothing left for himself. His sister had a small monthly pension of close to thirty mil-reis and a child but Meneses was left with only his dental tools. It is true that he had created a small library on subjects pertaining to mechanical engineering: *The Great Inventors* by Luis Figuier; *The Marvels of Science* by Tirrandier, manuals concerning all kinds of jobs, clippings from journals of scientific or related subjects. All the material was organized and bound into notebooks. He never lost sight of his library. Although he was drinking quite a bit, in time, his unhappiness and misery came to addict him even more to alcohol and eventually, the furor of drink took him over completely. Minute by minute, there in that little suburban house where he lived with his sister and his slothful nephew, Meneses anticipated, divined and even outlined the catastrophe he was certain was about to crash down upon him. This vision of some impending disaster in his immediate future, tended to weaken his will; it made him lose heart and ultimately drove him to the most complete form of escapism, alcoholism. On the street, if alone, it was the same thing; he could only keep this sense of impending disaster from before his eyes if he were in a large crowd of people.

Nevertheless, in spite of all the harsh privations he endured largely for the sake of his sister and her child, his life never included a single action that bothered his conscience. The meagre amount of money that dentistry tools could earn him or that his friends might give him went toward providing sustenance for himself, his sister and her child. Their house, fortunately, was already paid for with the pension that Etelvina, his sister, received.

In order to conquer him — he would attempt this by flanking him — Cassi had conceived of a plan that in a short time would put Meneses completely within his power, a plan that would bind him hand and foot as they say, and without his even knowing it.

He knew where to find him now that it was evening, having been given this information that same day. He found Meneses alone sitting at a table in a corner of the bar reading a newspaper with a sad expression. There was an empty glass near his hand.

The *modinha* player walked up and, without saying a word, sat down:

"Good evening, *doutor*."

"Good evening, *Seu* Cassi," said Meneses, lifting his head up from the paper.

"What's new around these parts? Getting a lot of work?"

"A few things. Right now, things are getting better for me. Joaquim dos Anjos asked me to work on his daughter's teeth and he always pays me promptly even if it's only a small amount. It all helps."

"The good doutor is a dreamer . . . I think you're being exploited. . . ."

"Not really. When I did that work for one of your sisters I was paid quite well. My problem is that I don't have a degree; besides, I don't have the proper clothes. . . . Sometimes, *Seu* Cassi, just to get hold of a pair of the shoes I wear because I can't wear any others, I really have to sweat blood and grit my teeth. . . ."

"That's too bad, *doutor*. Here, have some more of this," said Cassi, in an amiable tone of voice.

Meneses accepted the drink and said bitterly:

"I'm seventy years old and I don't know what I've done with my life."

Cassi was secretly rejoicing and thought to himself, "This old man really has problems." Then he said to Meneses:

"Well, don't lose heart. Captain Sebastiao, that fellow from City Hall, told me a few days ago that he was going to need the services of a modestly priced dentist who can straighten out a boy's teeth. They grew in crooked. It's not a big thing but, even so, it's still worth. . . ."

"I'll do the job," Meneses broke in.

"Oh, yes, *doutor* Meneses . . . one other thing."

"What's that?"

"You are a friend of Leonardo Flores, the poet, aren't you?"

"Yes, why?"

"Well, it's just that I'd like to have a few lines of verse. . . ."

Meneses wasn't able to conceal his alarm at hearing this. Cassi saw this and without pretending, attempted to explain himself better:

"It's for a serious matter, *doutor.* You gentlemen wouldn't have to compromise yourselves at all. . . . I'll even pay you something for doing it."

"I don't think you understand just how proud Flores is. At the bottom of all his low behavior, and inside that wispy-haired, water-logged head of his, he is a god! Nobody should mention poetry to him unless. . . ."

"I'm quite aware of all that. But I also know that you exercise a great influence over him. See if you can arrange it for me, won't you? Look, *doutor,* it's nothing for you to feel offended about. Here, here's a ten *mil-reis* note for the initial expenses . . . five for you and five for him."

"You don't have to do that," said Meneses already giving in somewhat.

But when Meneses' misery began speaking to him; after all, it wasn't really something to compromise his sense of honesty and justice . . . and it certainly didn't involve injuring or insulting anybody. . . .

"No, *doutor,* take it! Everything should be paid for. It doesn't have to be anything great . . . just a few amorous verses . . . but delicate and fine, of course . . . and moral. . . . Do you understand me, *doutor?*"

Cassi left after Meneses promised to arrange for the verse. It was past seven o'clock and, as soon as the guitar player disappeared, the dentist got up, went over to a corner of the bar and said to the bartender, handing him the ten *mil-reis* note:

"Here! I'm going to pay up for six hundred *reis* I owe you. Now you can bring me another round."

He drank it down and returned to his table. Then he bought the evening papers from a newsboy and returned to sit down at his table. But he got up from time to time to go to the bar and imbibe more of his favorite "drink." Then, about ten o'clock, carrying a stack of papers and magazines under his arm, Meneses headed toward home, firm in his intention to keep the promise he had made to Cassi. His house was rather far away if one took the good roads, but by cutting through deserted roadways and by walking up and down some hills, one could get there more quickly.

He did not hesitate to take the short cuts he knew quite well, and following them almost as if by instinct, the old man was able to walk straight to his residence.

It was located on a barren field and was crudely fenced only in front and on the right side, thanks to his neighbor. His residence had a sickly-looking cashew tree growing in the front. This tree shielded the front of the house and also provided a thin shade for the area of the water spigot where Meneses's sister washed clothes, not only their own but other people's as well. From time to time, Meneses thought about planting some fast-growing trees so that they could have more shade but whenever he got around to doing so, the neighbor's goats came along and destroyed all the sprouts. At great cost, Meneses had been able to put up a crudely constructed little pergola next to their house. This provided a little more shade for the dining room which was where Meneses slept and which normally served as kitchen as well. The house had only two, equal sized rooms. These were connected by a single door. Were it not for the street, the residence would not have appeared to have either a front or a back so similar were these two sides. His sister inhabited the front room, divided by a curtain running from the portal of the interior door to where it faced the street. The curtain was made of a flat, smooth, wool cloth.

Meneses arrived home from the tavern and ate the rice and beans and manioc and corn meal mush that his sister always kept ready for him. He did this by the light of a cheap kerosene lantern that had almost burned down as far as it could go. He drank two or three more glasses of run, a bottle of which he always kept at home, and then stretched out on an old couch padded with journals and papers, and which had boxes and plants for a bottom. He carefully removed his clothes and laid them out on the edge of a wooden chair, the only one in the house. The pine table, an old worn out kitchen table, took up the rest of the space. Inside the room, he could also hear the snoring of his doltish nephew. Meneses covered himself up with a blanket made of scraps from other blankets that had been pieced together and slept serenely.

As soon as it was morning, his sister woke him up excitedly the next day:

"'Juca'! 'Juca'!"

"What is it, woman? Can't a person even sleep around here anymore. . . . ?"

Later, changing his tone, he asked:

"What is it, Etelvina?"

"We need sugar and coffee and we owe the baker six-hundred *reis.*"

"Go to my vest pocket and take out all the nickels and silver coins you can find. Leave me four hundred *reis.* I think that you'll still have three to four thousand *mil-reis.* Keep it all but bring me a glass of rum, will you?"

His sister didn't appear to be fifteen years younger than he was. She was old look-ing with wrinkled skin, skinny, almost toothless and had nearly all white hair. Her entire being exuded an air of weariness and dejection.

She called to her son, Edmundo, who appeared immediately. Listless and lax, he had had trouble in learning how to read and how to make his scrawl, both of which he accomplished only because of his uncle's exhortations. He was so indolent and sluggish that he was almost always dismissed from schools he attended. His job was to hunt cavies and frogs to sell to foreigners from the factory, to trap little birds and from time to time, to help on the fishing trips in the port at Inhauma.

With the paltry income she received for taking in washing his mother kept him in clothes because the boy drank up everything he earned although he rarely touched the bottle that his uncle kept in the house. He never brought any liquor home with him.

When Etelvina served her brother his rum, he noticed that the bottle had very little left in it and thinking of the shopping trip that had to be made, ordered her to get another half bottle of liquor. He then poured what was left into a pharmaceutical jar.

His sister couldn't contain herself any longer and exclaimed:

"Juca, for heaven's sake! All this run all the time . . . it's a disgrace!"

''There's no doubt about that, sister, but the way things are now I can't quit or I'd die. . . . Edmundo! Go get the papers!'' he then shouted at his nephew.

''Yes, uncle,'' responded the boy who was half way out into the streets.

Edmundo did the shopping as quickly as possible so that he could return home to eat his breakfast. Their coffee, warming on a wood chip fire, was soon ready and Meneses, his sister and nephew all sat down around the table and had breakfast. Etelvina was seated on the chair and Meneses and Edmundo sat on the couch.

As he drank coffee and read the papers, the old dentist allowed himself to stretch out. It was a holy day, a kind of holiday; that is, an optional work day. What would he do with all his free time that day? He remembered that he had to look up Leonardo Flores. That was what he had to do. He would eat lunch and then go to his house. And that is what he did. Right after lunch, Meneses started walking to Leonardo Flores's house, which was not very far away from his own. It was located on Rua Estrada Real in the same neighborhood in which he, Etelvina and her son lived.

When he got there, he was received by the poet's wife, Dona Castorina, who asked him to come in. She was very old-looking and worn out but not because of her age, for she was not even yet fifty years old, but because of all the travail she had had to undergo with her husband, more than with her own children. Even so, no one had ever heard a single word of complaint from her about it nor any sign of reproach against her husband, Leonardo Flores. She suffered through all his demands with much tolerance and a sense of resignation. Her nature, her sweet temperament and her ability to forgive — even in the face of her husband's almost delirious excitations and exacerbations — allowed him to produce what work he did produce. Were it not for that small mulatto woman standing there in front of Meneses, thin and the possessor of dark, sad eyes, always laughing though with a profound expression of melancholy about her, it is quite possible that Flores would have produced nothing. He was aware of this and he loved her, in spite of everything people could say against them. And she, in the depths of her soul and despite her husband' dissipations, was very proud of his past glories.

Dona Castorina informed Meneses that Leonardo had left their house earlier with one of the children intending to visit a friend and that he might spend the whole day there. Meneses chatted with the woman for a short time and had a couple of drinks of Mangaratiba rum from a bottle that one of Leonardo's children, the one who was a railroad clerk, had brought home for his father.

On the hunch — very plausible and consonant with Leonardo's temperament — that his friend might have stopped off at *Seu* Nascimento's store, Meneses went there. He did not find the poet, but he left with his conscience pained by what he heard from Marramaque, Alipio and the others about Cassi.

Was Meneses remorseful or ashamed of what he was doing? To what scheme was he contributing by agreeing to arrange for the writing of the love poetry? He headed off toward Engenho de Dentro to see if he might find someone to whom he could talk and to see if he might discover some way of dissembling the nascent pangs of doubt and reproach that were beginning to make themselves felt in his conscience. He happened to run into a bunch of young lads from the railroad who had always been kind and generous to him. They were a boisterous and high spirited lot and Meneses sat down at the bar among them. But he couldn't bring himself to talk.

"What's this, Meneses? Dry? Here, have a drink!" said one of them.

He sipped his drink but his thorny problems didn't go away. Finally he was able to chat a bit with the boys but, after a few minutes, seeing that his anxieties and his sadness were beginning to depress their conversation, he got up to go. At that moment, one of the boys asked him:

"Are you going home? Have you any money?"

Meneses responded:

"Yes, I am going home but I have no money."

The boys then apportioned him a sum of cash nearly amounting to a thousand *mil-reis* and just as he was leaving, another one of them, raising up his arms dangling an old, cherry wood walking stick from his hand shouted to the barkeeper:

"Antunes! Give a bottle of 'rum' ... 'rum' ... can't you hear, 'rum!' Give a bottle of 'rum' to our dear old friend, Meneses, so he can get rid of his troubles."

But when Meneses finally arrived home, his sister came running up to him saying:

"Oh, Juca, I'm glad you're home. I haven't got any money for charcoal, kerosene or manioc meal. What you gave me didn't go very far. . . . I went to buy some dried meat and that used up all the money. . . ."

Old Meneses, half drunk and unable to think very clearly, took out the five *mil-reis* note hidden in his pocket, the one destined for Flores, together with about ten "coins" in change and said to his sister:

"Sister, here you've got almost six *mil-reis* and that'll have to last you until Monday. Until then, don't ask me for more money. Today's Friday so we've got Saturday and Sunday taken care of."

Then he had a glass of "rum" from the bottle he brought with him and lay down, intending to read the magazines the boys had given him; but he couldn't. Sleep overcame him until mealtime. When he opened his eyes again and remembered giving away Flores' five *mil-reis* note, his share of the payment for writing the poetry, Meneses became a little disturbed. But he thought about it some and said to himself, "I'll work it out." He ate well and while there was still some sunlight left, he continued to read and reread the journals and papers he had. When night came, he continued to read them sipping on his bottle of rum all the while.

On the following morning as soon as it was daybreak but before it was fully light out, Meneses got up and went out to the water spigot and washed himself all over in the dark. Then he prepared his morning coffee, drank a cup, followed by several stiff shots of rum, and set off down the street before seven o'clock. It was still too early to drop by Leonardo Flores' house so he went to the train station, bought a magazine, read it, and continued on his way towards his friend's house. Flores, as well as nearly everyone else in his household, was up. He received his guest dressed in old trousers and a short sleeved shirt; he had been writing. Upon discovering his friend there, Flores gave him a lingering look and then, making an utterly theatrical gesture with his arms and tipping his head back while puffing out his chest like some actor of great renown standing in the footlights of a luridly dramatic production, he said in a deep and solemn voice:

"You, Meneses! You . . . Pythias of my soul! It has been such a long time since my weary eyes last beheld you. Enter, stellar friend, enter and repose the fatigue of your journey upon this Cordovan credenza that Abd-El-Malek, fallen from the graces of Atlas, sent me from Morocco, Boabdil, a monarch from the line of the last King of Granada, who shed tears. . . ."

"Flores," Meneses interrupted him, "you're being too high flown! Then he sat down on the "Cordovan credenza," which was nothing more than a common Austrian split-cane chair.

"Now drink from this, the liquor of good friendship. It is a genuine product of my ancestral manor lands in Mangaratiba!"

They drank their "liquor of good friendship" and, afterwards, speaking in his natural tone of voice, Flores asked his friend:

"How's it going, Meneses?"

"All right, And you?"

"Sometimes good . . . sometimes bad. It depends on the moon. . . . have you had coffee yet?"

Although Meneses said that he had, Flores insisted upon getting his friend another cup and went into the kitchen to get it. The living room was just the same as it had been twenty years before; it had successfully resisted all aging and change. It had an old Austrian sofa full of holes and two arm chairs in doubtful condition. On the wall hanging among other pictures, there was a magnificent oil painting, one done by a now celebrated artist when the fellow was just beginning his career. There was also an iron bookcase covered with tattered paperback books and a multi-colored woolen cloth. There was an inkwell, pen holders, tips, and other assorted writing materials.

Flores returned with full cups of coffee, bread and butter. He put everything down on the table and then sat down. Meneses noted with surprise that his friend showed no sign of any imbalance or inebriation. This pleased him, and beginning to sip his coffee, he asked:

"Do you still write poetry these days, Flores?"

"What a barbarian you are! How can you even consider that I, Leonardo Flores, would cease writing verse? I live by poetry and for poetry. My mind is an interminable poem, rhyming sublimely in my soul. I know no other language except that of the Divine Muse. . . . I betray myself when I speak as I am forced to speak now. . . ."

He fell silent for a moment and both men began to drink down their coffee in great gulps and to chew large chunks of buttered bread. Then, suddenly, Flores stopped chewing and asked his friend:

"Why did you ask me if I still write poetry?"

Ingenuously, Meneses responded:

"Because I've got a commission for someone for you to write some."

"What? ! !" cried the indignant Flores jumping up from his chair in a single, quick movement and dropping his cup onto the table. "Don't you know who I am

. . . who Leonardo Flores is. . . ? Don't you know that for me poetry is both pain and pleasure, that for me it's life itself? Do you realize that I have suffered through every torment imaginable, through pain, humiliation, vexations of the spirit . . . through everything just to attain my one ideal? Don't you know that I've abandoned all of life's pleasures and distinctions, that I haven't given my wife all the comforts she deserves, that I haven't properly educated my children . . . all this just so I would not have to deviate from my artistic goals? I was born poor and I was born a mulatto . . . and I had only a rudimentary education, one I completed only as best I could. Day and night I read and reread authors and their verses . . . day and night I searched the crude, superficial appearance of things from the hidden order that linked them all together, for the thought that united them. I sought the mysterious perfume and its colors, I sought the sound of my own soul's muted longings, I sought the twilight of a cigarette's melancholy hissing . . . I did all this at the sacrifice of more profitable things, never thinking about fortune, position or respectability. People humiliated me, they ridiculed me . . . while I — I, a fighter — I suffered through it all, resignedly. But my name finally soared . . . it soared to the most distant corners of our miserly and ungrateful country, our Brazil. But now I grow steadily poorer, forced to subsist on this miserable pension when my head is filled with golden images and visions and my soul illuminated by the immaterial light of the celestial spaces. The brilliance of my ideal has blinded me. Life, when it is not transformed into Poetry, bores me. I've always soared in the realm of the Ideal and if this has demeaned me in the eyes of other men — men who are incapable of comprehending certain acts of my existence — it nevertheless elevated my own eyes in the presence of my conscience. It did so because I complied with my duty, my destiny . . . I executed my mission — I was a poet! ! And to elevate myself like this I made every sacrifice! Art loves only those who love it completely, who love it exclusively. . . . And I had to love it because it represented not only my own redemption but the redemption of all my brothers, redeeming us even while it causes us pain. Insane? Could there ever be a mind whose impugnable machinery would be able to resist such unexpected reverses of fortune, such powerful conflicts as I have endured . . . such collisions with such a harsh and unforeseen reality? Could there be?''

Up to this point, Flores had been standing on his feet in the middle of the room speaking his mind and emphasizing everything with great, sweeping gestures and modulating his voice according to the degree of passion sweeping over him. Soon, though, he became worn out; he fell silent for a moment, folded his arms across his body, buried his pointed, bearded chin in his chest and for a few seconds, slowly shook his head. Then, leaning a bit to the left, he looked disconsolately at his old friend.

Flores had a light brown complexion, smooth, flat black hair with an abundance of white strands in it, healthy looking teeth and a well-formed mouth. He was of medium height. In the face of his friend's explosion, Meneses could find nothing to say so he prudently remained silent and tried to avoid Flores' gaze. Flores was censuring his comrade but at the same time, he also felt pity for him because of his lack of understanding of his true nature, the power of his ardor, and his artistic frenzy. He felt that such a lack of understanding ought not exist in an old friend like Meneses.

With less passion and enthusiasm, Leonardo continued:

"Yes, my dear old Meneses . . . I was a poet . . . a consummate poet! and because of this I have nothing now . . . and people will give me nothing! If I had written more refined verse like silken crazy-quilts from China or Japan, they might have made me a Minister or an Ambassador. But I did what my private pain forced me to do . . . I did what my heartbreak dictated to me. Camoes said, 'Sorrow writes it / and I transform it;' I, in my poetry, I transform the pain, the sorrows and the dreams of the endless generations of humanity into new and vital forms. I condense what they suffered until it becomes the blood that courses through my own veins . . . I distill into pure poetry all they etched out with their own tears and blood. . . . My dear Meneses, could the person who feels this way ever sell his poems? Tell me, Meneses, could he?"

"No. He should always keep them for his own."

"Well, I'll not sell any . . . come what may. People can suffer, dream or drink 'rum' all they wish . . . but it won't be enough." After a moment's pause, the poet went on speaking with an even greater melancholy, "One has to have been born as I was . . . I who have lost all my brothers to poverty except for one, a boy who for more than twenty years now, has been ravaged by a most pathetic form of insanity . . . yes, one has to have suffered all this in order to be able to write such poetry. And God be praised that no human being is able to achieve this condition by dint of his own free will!"

Flores sat down, his eyes moist, and took a swig of his Mangaratiba rum. Then he began to write again recommending to his friend:

"Meneses, while I'm writing why don't you stretch out on the sofa and read the journals until it's time to eat?"

And Meneses did. But he soon fell asleep. Later when he awoke, he was amazed to be in the still spacious room with his legs unencumbered. He had dreamed that he had been made a prisoner and put in chains. . . .

VIII

One of the most appealing of Joaquim dos Anjos's character traits was the confidence and good faith he always placed in other people. He did not, as people say, have any malice in his heart. He was not particularly intelligent but neither was he mentally blighted; he was not clever but neither was he simple-minded. Hence, he was unable to suspect anyone of anything because to do so pained his conscience. This is not to say, however, that he did not, from time to time receive certain people with reserve and caution. And while such an occurrence was rare, he was more at ease when he had been alerted beforehand. In general, no matter who it was, he greeted the person warmly and with open arms. In his simplicity, evil, bad faith, perversity, and the duplicity of mankind seemed such rare things so unlikely to be thriving in any of God's creatures that he believed only those people who go out actively seeking such features ever encounter them.

Up until this time his life had been played out in the highest measure of good faith, and from his point of view, since his had been an essentially happy life, with his fifty years of experience, he judged the rest of the world to be a kingdom of peace, harmony, honesty and fidelity. And he believed this in spite of what was printed in the papers.

He had never been a habitual reader of the papers. If he picked one up and intended to read something in it, sleep soon overcame him. He did not believe or take to heart anything that he did not hear. And he did not understand the meaning behind pictures or caricatures no matter how crude or elementary they might be. In order to receive any agreeable or lasting sensory impression, he had to hear it, its sound, its musicality.

Ever since he first became accustomed to it, music enchanted him; songs, even those from some trivial *modinha,* sent him into a state of rapture; he also enjoyed poetry when it was recited, a great deal; and even a great speech whose simplest terms he could not appreciate until he read them later filled him with enthusiasm no matter what the topic as long as the speaker was a great orator. He had a limited vision and its perceptiveness was limited to the rudimentary necessities of life.

Even though he was regularly employed, he always had time for music. He did not play in bands or orchestras but he did perform on an instrument at times and he also composed and made a little money from it. Every afternoon after work; he met other dedicated musicians to have a few drinks and chat. They talked about their Art, cinematic orchestras, the music for one production or another, and they remembered their deceased colleagues. At six o'clock or there abouts, he set off for home with a role of music under his arm.

After eating, he worked on the compositions people had hired him to do. He dressed in slacks and a short sleeved shirt on hot days and in an old jacket on cold days, and immersed himself in bars, sharps and harmonies until quite late at night.

He had taught his daughter the rudiments of music, and their respective calligraphy, but he had not taught her how to play just any instrument because he wanted her to know the piano. The flute was not appropriate for a young girl; the violin gave off an ominous sense of foreboding and the Spanish guitar was corrupt and demoralizing. There were others who did play it, either with or without music, but his daughter would not. He allowed her to play only the piano but he did not have the resources to buy one. He could rent one but then he would still have to pay for the girl's music teacher and these were two expenses with which he could not cope. The income derived from his music was not a sure thing and his regular income was already being used up for clothing himself, his wife and daughter, for supplies from the general store, etc., etc.

This is why he never advanced his daughter's study of music. Because he lacked the necessary time and wherewithal, her studies never passed beyond the little that he had been able to teach her. But then, she had no real enthusiasm for music, either for following, reproducing, and certainly not for creating. She liked to listen, though, and that was sufficient for her simple nature. Not even the relative independence that the study of music and piano had given her was able to furnish the girl with the enthusiasm she needed to perfect her studies. Her ideal in life was not to acquire an authentic personality, not to discover and become herself either under her father's protection or as somebody's future wife. It was, rather, to serve her father while she was single, and her husband when she got married. She could not imagine any of the unforeseen catastrophies of life that sometimes force us off the track — to places where we never expected to go. She did not see that by acquiring some small, honest profession appropriate to her sex, she would be a help to her parents and to her husband when she got married. Quite close at hand she had the example of Dona Margarida Pestana who, left a penniless widow, had, even so, acquired a house, made herself respectable, and was now raising and educating her son, making steady progress and doing everything necessary so that he would ultimately graduate from high school or some similar institution.

After a lot of trouble and thanks to Dona Margarida's insistence, the girl consented to help the older lady with the embroidery that she took in and from which she managed to make a little money. It was not that the girl was lazy. To the contrary, but she had some foolish reservations about making money by means of her own effort. To her, it seemed unseemly for a girl or a woman to be doing such a thing.

Clara's personality was soft and viscous and needed strong hands to mold and shape it, but her parents were not capable of doing this. Her mother, in the good sense of the word, did not have the character to do what was necessary about Clara's development and limited herself to doggedly keeping the girl under constant vigil. Her father, because of his other chores, spent most of his time away from her. Clara lived in a world of her own, completely enveloped in the languid and dreamy realm of *modinhas* and similar music intoned by sinister singers like Cassi and the other exploiters of the Spanish guitar's morbidity. The world revealed itself to Clara as being full of uncertainty and misgiving, the wailing of guitars and the sighings of love. It never entered her head that our lives hold much that is serious and that requires a sense of responsibility no matter what our class or sex might be. No matter how humble we may be, each of us has to meditate about the anguishing mystery of Death in order to be able to respond fully — if we are able to do anything at all — to the question of how we wish to spend our existence. In Clara, there was no show, either exact or approximate, of her social individuality. Concomitantly, there was no desire to elevate herself from her condition or to react against that condition. Without being frivolous, the postman's daughter had a limited capacity to reason about her situation and this made it impossible for her to meditate even for an instant about her destiny or to observe the facts as they existed, draw inferences from them, and arrive at definite conclusions. Her age, sex and the specious education she had received were all partially responsible for her situation but her lack of any individuality certainly did nothing to correct or even improve her rather oblique vision of life. For her, the opposition to Cassi present in her home was without basis. Oh, he had done this and that but, she would ask herself, who could say that he would do the same thing in her father's house?

Her father, she thought, had a good job, good connections and was generally well respected. Cassi, therefore, would not be so foolish as to attempt to dishonor such an honest family, especially one which had a man like her father for its head. As for the rest, well . . . those boys are not altogether responsible for what they do; the girls are quite willing. . . .

Through this kind of reasoning, Clara, because of the ingenuousness of her age, and because of the misconceptions her lack of contact with the real world caused, and because of her lack of any mental capacity for observation and comparison, concluded that Cassi was a worthy young man and one who was fully able to love her sincerely.

Her godfather, Marramaque, seemed to be her enemy. Whenever he had the opportunity, Marramaque told about another of Cassi's infamous deeds or about one of his deceits. He never tired of the subject.

At times, Clara had the desire to say to her godfather, "Godfather, this Cassi fellow must be very rich indeed if he's already bought off all the police and judges so he won't be put in prison. Listen, if he were condemned for even half of the crimes you attribute to him, why he'd already have been in jail for more than thirty years!"

But she was deceiving herself because she knew nothing of life. In order to get away with Cassi's crimes, a little protection was enough and that the accused fellow be both exceedingly cynical and audacious.

This was the way she lived, anxious and yet eager, both wanting and not wanting to see the *modinha* player again; sometimes she was convinced by what people said about him, other times she did not believe it and, sometimes after Meneses came to work on her teeth after a particularly bad toothache that might send her to bed, she discovered certain doubts about the objections to him arising from her own spirit.

One particular day her father, upon leaving the house in the morning, left her some sheets of music to recopy so that they would be ready later that afternoon. It wasn't a long job but it required close attention. After lunch, along about eleven o'clock she began to recopy them but suddenly suffered a terrible toothache that made her groan with pain and even cry.

Engracia, her mother, ran in to help her daughter but as usual, she panicked and didn't know what to do, what palliative to give her. Though unable to speak clearly, Clara told her mother to call Dona Margarida.

Dona Margarida came, applied some home remedies and then directed the servant girl in the house to get some mallow leaves. She made Clara wash out her mouth with this solution and a bit later, returned home to continue to work on her sewing and embroidery.

Engracia, however, couldn't calm down and was pacing from one side of the room to the other impatiently awaiting her husband's arrival. She was convinced that her daughter was suffering from all the diseases occurring in nature plus all those that doctors, for their own amusement, invent.

There was not a bit of lucidity in her ratiocinations whenever some serious event touched her life and this condition became worse if the matter touched her daughter.

Her love for Clara was a mute, absorbing and unwholesome sentiment. She always wanted her daughter close by her side but she almost never chatted with her or talked about life's complications or her duties as a girl and woman. Except in Cassi's case, in which her mother's instinct spoke louder than did the voice of her natural inertia, she never put into practice any efficacious steps that would offer her help and direction to the girl. She thought about doing so but never reached the point of realization.

The two women spent the entire day, each one immersed in her own thoughts.

The mother washed clothes in the tank on the side of the house and the daughter attended to other domestic chores. Both women took care of kitchen duties although Clara would often work alone when her father didn't ask her to copy some musical score or when her mother had a lot of washing to do.

Joaquim, or Quincas as his wife called him, had gone out early that morning. He went to the general store where he made his orders, drank a little rum and chatted for a while with Seu Nascimento.

"I don't think he is going to come. . . ."

"That would be good for you. . . ," Nascimento was saying.

"Who? I don't even know him. . . . What? I don't have anything to do with him."

"But he's your fellow-countryman. . . ."

"So are you . . . so are other people. . . . We're all Brazilians . . . I, *Seu* Nascimento, only care about my wife and my daughter . . . and a little about music."

"Speaking of music, how's Cassi?"

"Do you want me to tell you something? As a musician, he's not worth a nickel. He makes some terrible blunders."

"Well, he's certainly famous. . . ."

"His fame comes from his over affected style, from the stickiness that he puts in his music. . . . It gets to be almost indecent. He sings as if he were in some cabaret, in the midst of women of questionable reputation. . . ."

"People like him a lot around here."

"The silly women around these parts don't have anybody who can really open their eyes for them . . . , *Seu* Nascimento, he's never going to set foot in my house again."

"Your *compadre,* Marramaque, told me the same thing not long ago."

"My *'compadre'* tends to exaggerate a lot. Being a poet, my *compadre* always sees a point of honor. . . . Did you know that he was once fairly famous, that he wrote for newspapers and magazines and was a member of, and was quite important in a literary circle? He can't tolerate seeing a virtual illiterate like Cassi gaining fame as an artist. . . . The fault isn't his as much as it is that of our environment . . . it doesn't offer anybody a chance for real instruction or preparation."

Seu Joaquim, have you seen the notebook somebody sent your *compadre* concerning Cassi?"

"I have."

"What did you think of its contents?"

"If it's the truth, then he ought to be hanged."

"Well, they say it is. . . . Do you know who Aunt Vicencia is, the woman who lives near here on Redencao street?"

"No."

"I do. She's the housekeeper at Cassi's parents' house and she says that everything in it is true. She's even got more details to tell."

"Who is distributing this notebook?"

"It's an Army officer, a well-educated man who is an engineer or something. His present wife is the girl Cassi disgraced, the one whose mother killed herself over the affair about five years ago."

"Who told you this?"

"Vincencia. She knows not only the guitarist's own family but also the families of many of his victims. She says that this girl's husband didn't finish the scoundrel off only because he didn't want a scandal; and that now, from the moment he learns of one of Cassi's escapades, this man always takes up the victim's cause, no matter who she might be."

Joaquim dos Anjos listened to all this, fell silent for a moment but then, without responding to what he had just heard, advised his friend:

"Don't forget to send our order, especially the firewood . . . we need that to make lunch. Well, it's time for me to go . . . I'll see you later."

He left thinking about Cassi. No matter how hard he tried to forget him, he was increasingly on Joaquim's mind and his name was always being brought up by other people as if he were important — a man of position and authority. What did people mean by everything they said about him? Were they trying to warn him about Cassi? The postman smiled to himself, "He wouldn't dare try anything with me," and thought of his double barreled muzzle-loader, the one he carried with him when he traveled around Minas and which had been a present from the Englishman, his very first boss.

A strong, loyal, and direct man, Joaquim had unlimited confidence in himself and in other people. He had never suspected or mistrusted anyone or even admitted to himself that he could, but this Cassi. . . .

This confidence was extended to his wife, and for good reason, but he should not have had any in his daughter. He should not have because, if he had considered the vulnerability of her age, the narrowness of her domestic education and the general atmosphere of corruption in which her social environment enveloped her, he would have had to admit at least tacitly that she was destined to fall victim to the same fate as all the other girls of her condition. But Joaquim dos Anjos did not have the intellectual capacity to consider so many things. . . .

He ceased thinking about Cassi and began to cogitate about his work, his good fortune, and his bonuses. He arrived at his office, checked his route for the day, greeted his colleagues and his superiors and at the appointed time, arranged the mail so he could later carry it around to the various offices and business concerns distributing letters and packages.

His mail always came with strange, tongue-twisting names in French, English, German, Italian, etc. but since they were nearly always the same, he ended up by memorizing them and being able to pronounce them more or less correctly. He liked dealing with those blond, robust, and rubicund people with eyes the color of the sea and among whom he could never distinguish the bosses from the subordinates. But when these people had Brazilian working among them, he could quickly see that his countrymen were never the bosses. Joaquim ate a very frugal lunch and worked at his job until five o'clock — that is, he delivered mail to various places all afternoon.

When his working day was finished, he sought out his artistically inclined friends and about five o'clock or five-thirty, got aboard the train to go home.

On that particular day, he did everything according to his usual routine without any variation or discrepancy as if he were obeying some prearranged program. When he arrived home, it was already getting dark and the public street lamps were lit and were replacing the light of the sun as best they could. That sun was dying in a slow, changing sunset behind the mountains which stood out from the horizon where it was beginning to hide against a backdrop of silver, gold and purple hues.

His wife ran to open the door for him and before anything else could happen, she told him:

"Oh, Quincas! You don't know what a terrible time I've had here today. . . . If it hadn't been for Dona Margarida. . . ."

"What happened, Engracia?"

"Clara suddenly got sick and started moaning and I — there wasn't anybody else around — I didn't know what to do. Fortunately, though, I shouted for Dona Margarida and she came right over."

"What happened to Clara, woman?"

"It was her teeth, Quincas; they were causing her terrible pain."

"Well, now . . . you're really something . . . what a simpleton! How can anyone be so frightened by a toothache?"

"You don't realize how serious it was."

"Well, I'm going to see how she is."

He went to Clara's room and found her there with her jaw bound up with a doubled-up handkerchief. He said to her:

"What happened, Clara?"

"Oh, nothing. I've just got a cavity that hurts from time to time. Today it ached more than usual and made me cry and I had to lie down. Fortunately, the remedy Dona Margarida gave me made the pain go away but I still have a swollen jaw."

"Is it better now?"

"I think so," said Clara, adding: "Papa, I'm sorry but I wasn't able to make a clean copy of your music."

"Don't worry about it; I'll do it myself."

Moments later, he returned to his wife and said:

"We've got to take our girl to the dentist, Engracia, before this thing gets any worse."

"A dentist! God forbid!"

"Why, in God's name?"

"Because a dentist's office is always a den of iniquity, Quincas!"

"Oh, den of iniquity nothing! Only somebody who wants to be iniquitous is . . . or somebody who's already a lost soul."

"Well, you'll have to take her, then, Quincas. I can't go out all day . . . you know I can't walk much. . . ."

"Well, I can't either because I've got to go to work."

He began to think about the problem, looking at the girl there with her meek, dark eyes silently interrogating her father and suddenly a thought came to him:

"I'm going to get Meneses. He doesn't have a degree but he's had a lot of experience in dentistry and he could certainly do whatever needs to be done here. What do you think, Engracia?"

"I think it's good . . . if he can come here."

"He'll come . . . tomorrow morning. He'll eat lunch with you and I'll arrange to pay him a little something."

"Do you want to do it, Clara?" asked her father.

"Yes, and I think it's a good idea. I won't have to leave the house and mamma won't be put out at all."

Thus it was that Meneses came to treat Clara's dental problem, a fact Cassi had so opportunely learned about from *Doutor* Praxedes at the Meier train station. For old *doutor* Meneses, the job was truly a salvation. In spite of all the work he did, he was either not paid or if he was, it amounted to very little money and did not come in regular installments. When dealing with the postman, such matters were always somewhat different than for other people. However, aside from this, he had the opportunity to eat lunch there every day and this was an advantage he could not disregard.

Knowing that Meneses was with Clara every day, Cassi resolved to make contact with the girl, and decided to try and take advantage of the state of misery and moral destitution in which the old dentist found himself in order to realize his unspeakable intentions. He had arranged for the verses to be written by Flores with old Meneses and then gave him some money for them, already calculating that Meneses would spend it all and not get the poetry. And this is exactly what happened except that Meneses, when on the following day he remembered Flores' rejection of the proposition and recalled that he had spent all of the money he was to use to pay for the verses, saw no other alternative but to write the poetry himself. He spent an entire day hammering away at the job, scratching out a few words and then revising them, line after line. By Sunday night, he had actually created a few quatrains that more or less made sense. It should be noted that he had never before written any poetry but, having led such a varied and interesting life, he had some dealings with men who were poets, and he did have an educated ear. He selected the popular meter, the seven syllable quatrain, and worked so hard on it that by early afternoon, his lines of verse were nearly finished. The poor old man was very pleased with himself; it was as if he had created some truly significant work of art. He drank for a while and then had a satisfying sleep. He had kept his word in spite of everything. If the poetry wasn't actually written by Leonardo Flores, it was, at least, authentic. It would not be as good as Flores' but it would excuse him for spending his friend's money, an act that had been bothering his conscience.

On Monday evening, after having walked all around with his old suitcase full of metal dental tools, Meneses finally stationed himself in the Fagundes bar. He sat down as was his habit at the last table in the back, up against the wall; he had a journal under his eyes and a glass of rum in front of him. He was drinking down his rum in great gulps in full view of everybody but was causing no trouble at all. Such activity was bad for him, as it is bad for anybody, but he was driven to drink in order to benumb himself so that he would not have to remember or be left alone thinking of his wasted past. He wished to escape the terror which life, enveloping him in misery, inspired in the poor man. It had abandoned him in a state of virtual destitution. An old man, over seventy, he was broken, sick, friendless, without relatives who could help him and had no income at all.

Cassi found him engrossed in reading his newspapers.

"I thought," he said, sitting down, "that you had forgotten about me."

Laying down his modest *pince-nez* on the table where he had already dropped his journal, Meneses responded:

"Oh, come now! I am a man of my word. . . . Besides, you gave me some money as a retainer and that made it a binding agreement."

Cassi was having great difficulty in being agreeable, in getting the proper intonation in his voice, in looking Meneses in the eye and in maintaining his deliberately pleasant countenance.

Cassi wasn't capable of doing so when he was sincere and one can well imagine what it was like when he was acting! Everything about him was rude, hard, gross and coarse. Finally, he did what he could to appear civil and said:

"That wasn't it at all, *doutor!* I don't remember any such thing! The money I gave you was just for a few drinks . . . did you get things arranged?"

"I did, but not with Leonardo."

"He didn't want to, or. . . ?"

"No, he didn't . . . but it's all right now. As I told you before, Flores is a bit too proud when it comes to his poetry. When I told him about our deal, he gave me a long lecture, saying that he was this and that, that he had done such and such things and, finally, that he would not sell any of his poems."

"How about giving them away?"

"I didn't propose anything like that but I'm certain that he wouldn't. From what he said, I gather that the poems that leave his spirit are his and his alone."

"Then who did you arrange it with?"

"I did it myself. They won't be. . . ."

"We'll see, *doutor.*"

Meneses reached inside his ash-grey cutaway to his vest pocket and pulled out a voluminous pile of soiled papers. Then he sorted through them for the ones on which the verses were written, and putting on his *pince-nez* said:

"I'll read some to you so you'll understand them better; my handwriting is really very bad."

"Read on, *'Doutor.'*"

Meneses adjusted his glasses, moved to a position with somewhat better light and began to read:

"My beloved grieves / behind prison bars / but Love enjoins / that her heart be calm."

The old itinerant dentist finally ceased and looked questioningly at the minstrel. Cassi had assumed a grotesque air of one who understands such things but was merely staring vaguely into space pretending that he was sorting out his thoughts. After Meneses had asked him what he thought of the poems, the cunning guitar player said:

"They're not quite what I had in mind but even so, they're not bad . . . some are even good. They'll do for the *modinhas* at least. . . . You wouldn't happen to know anyone who writes *modinha* music, would you?"

"I know of Joaquim dos Anjos."

"Ah . . . that's right! How is he?" asked Cassi, pretending to be embarrassed.

"Don't you get along with him?"

"I do but I don't know him well at all. But perhaps I could get to know him better if I got acquainted with his daughter . . . why don't you ask her about it for me?"

"I could ask her, but there's her godfather . . . I don't know why but he doesn't like you. If he were to find out. . . ."

Meneses immediately regretted having offered so much information but his will-power was far weaker than he knew and he was unable to find any means of escaping the ultimate consequences of his rash confidences. Cassi had already taken advantage of the old man's opening and said:

"I know but I'll write a letter to Dona Clara so she'll be able to avoid her god-father's ill will and everybody will be able to see that my interest is only in the *modinha.* . . ."

Meneses couldn't restrain a show of fright.

"Don't worry, *doutor.* There's absolutely no malice in what I'm going to do. You will read the letter."

Meneses felt better upon hearing this and continued to drink resolutely while Cassi told him about his extraordinary winnings at *Cangueiro,* a game of chance played in the suburbs.

"Look, *doutor,* Cassi concluded, "whenever you need a little loan you only have to ask."

The dentist was already well along in his drunkenness and upon hearing this, looked eagerly and in a beggarly way at the guitar player who was preparing to leave for an appointment.

"How much do you need, *doutor?*"

"Oh, two *mil-reis* maybe, that's all. . . ."

"No," said Cassi pulling a wad of bills out from his wallet, "take five . . . but don't forget to be here tomorrow at seven o'clock. I need the music in a hurry."

Meneses went home without thinking about what he had promised. Guided as if by instinct, he climbed up and down the hills, took all the right shortcuts and finally ended up as he did every night on his miserable couch. He had no desire to eat — drunkenness had overwhelmed him completely. He woke up the following day not knowing what he had done during the last few hours he had been out the night before. He remembered vaguely that he had stopped in at his usual bar. He went outside to wash his face and to satisfy his bodily urges and when he came back in, his sister said to him as she did every morning:

"We don't have a thing to eat in the whole house, Juca."

Meneses didn't know if he had any money left or not. But to ease his conscience he began to go through his coat pockets. He found about forty cents and thought: "Well! We've got enough for sugar and coffee at least!" He continued to search and suddenly found a five *mil-reis* note crumpled up and stuck in the bottom of a pocket. He was disturbed; who could have given it to him? He pondered the problem and struggled with his memory while his sister continued to grumble:

"Juca, didn't you hear what I said?"

"I heard. Wait just a minute . . . I'm looking for money now."

He forced his memory and thus pieced together his vague recollections and after a few moments, he was able to recall the entirety of his conversation with Cassi. He had an urge to tear up the note, not to do what he had promised, but at this juncture, he no longer had any moral strength at all; he was afraid of everything, the slightest breeze, the most innocent rustling of a tree. . . . All creation was against him . . . it had conspired to do him in — what could he do against everything and everybody? And his misery, his hunger? If he tried to resist, what would become of him with no job, no future, no friends, or relatives and sick? His fate was truly pathetic. . . . Where was his aptitude for mechanical things, for engineering? He had accumulated a puerile mountain of books and papers but had done nothing else. For nearly fifty years, that is, ever since he had left his parents' house, he had led a gypsy's vagabond life without ever having entered seriously into any profession, trying one thing today, another tomorrow. And what had all this gotten him? Nothing. There he was at the end of his life, obliged to lend himself to certain roles, that he would not have subjected himself to when he was sixteen or so in order to beg disguisedly for something to eat with his relatives. He felt like crying but his sister shouted at him from the backyard:

"Did you find any money?"

"Yes."

That was his response — a single word — and he poured himself half a glass of rum and drank it down in a single gulp.

Meneses was still thinking about his seventy-odd useless and sterile years, and he felt infinitely sorry for himself, for the misery of his end. What should he do about Cassi and the letter? He shrugged his shoulders and thought to himself: "What can I do? Life has brought me to where I am now, so. . . ."

Cassi came to the tavern bringing the letter for Meneses to read, just as he had promised. Full of sorrow and with a bitterly pained conscience, the old, wandering dentist had spent the entire day trying to drink as much as he could hold. He had arrived early at Joaquim dos Anjos's house and finding him still at home, asked him for his money. Then he ate lunch, left, and continued on his way for the rest of the day drinking at every bar he passed. By the time he arrived at the Fagundes street bar, he found there waiting for him a letter from one of his clients. He opened it. The person had sent him ten *mil-reis,* on an account of fifty that was owed him. Meneses gave five *mil-reis* to the barman and then went off to the city. There, he knew no moderation. Everybody settled accounts with him so that by the time he met Cassi, although he didn't show signs, he was oblivious of nearly everything.

The guitar player read what he wanted him to hear, then sealed the letter and gave it to the poor old man. His mind was made up; he would throw himself forcibly into the winds of fate, into the caprices of his torrential poverty, his pain, into the humiliation that was dragging him down. Fate had swept him to where he was now and it was useless to resist any further. He handed the letter over to Clara. On the following day, he received her reply which he handed to Cassi. Then, for more than a month, he acted as the intermediary between them. By that time, however, he no longer had any sense of revulsion about what he was doing. He had resigned himself to carrying out his ignoble role, the one the force of destiny had imposed upon him. Against this force, there was no resistance, he thought; the wisest thing to do was simply to give in to it. At first the guitar player satisfied his requests entirely; later, he satisfied only about half and finally, he began to say that he had no more money and wasn't going to give him any more.

Meneses, however, passively continued to carry out his shameful role. Although he knew that it was not a seemly thing to be doing, he had had to learn to compromise himself in the face of his atrocious and irremediable destitution. He could no longer even call himself a man. . . .

Clara was receiving these letters with the emotion of a recipient of divine messages. They were, however, so poorly written and so full of spelling errors that at times, they were virtually unintelligible. The postman's daughter saw none of this since she blocked out any defects they might suggest in her lover. For her, Cassi was the perfect model of gallantry and faithfulness. She was constantly dreaming about him . . . about Cassi and the Spanish guitar. She would be moved from happiness to tears and her mother began to notice these abrupt changes in mood and would question her about them. Clara responded to them in a rude and insolent manner. She began to do less work or she did nothing at all. Almost consistently, she began to forget all sorts of things. Engracia finally told Joaquim about this and he said:

"It's true, Engracia. Something's wrong with the girl. . . . Before, her copies of music were sharp and clear. Now, they're not . . . they're full of mistakes, erasures and ink blotches. . . . What's wrong with her? I'm going to take her to a doctor. . . . What do you think?"

"Maybe that would be the best thing."

A few days later, Joaquim took a day off from work and took his daughter to the doctor. The doctor examined her and then said to her father:

"Your daughter isn't ill. Whatever is wrong with her has to do with her age and sex. . . . She needs pleasant diversions, walks in the country, companionship. . . . But in any case, I'm going to prescribe. . . ."

Joaquim passed on this information to his wife who then arranged with Dona Margarida to accompany the girl every time she went out, to go shopping, etc., etc. On the following Sunday, Joaquim himself took her for a stroll through Niteroi.

But the seaside was not good for the girl. If previously her soul had been full of the vague and the intangible, she became absorbed with a sense of infinity and with the limitlessness of the Universe when she saw the ocean.

Upon returning, she cried all night long without knowing why. Morning found her with dark purple circles under her eyes, lackadaisical in spirit and angry at everything and everybody. She believed that life was a bitter thing, and she saw no way of sweetening it. But at the same time, she remembered Cassi and was filled with hope. . . . She went out with Dona Margarida. Much more perceptive than Clara's parents, the German woman immediately guessed what was wrong with her and cleverly induced the girl to confess. After a while, Clara told her frankly what the origin of her unhappiness was.

"But this fellow is a despicable sort."

"Not for me, he isn't. I believe that. . . ."

"People say so many bad things about him. . . ."

"It's just that he lets himself take a beating while everybody else around here. . . . He's confessed to me that he's sorry for what he's done and says that now he wants to get a job and marry me."

Dona Margarida looked squarely at Clara, drilling her probing eyes deep into the girl's. Then she thought to herself:

"Can this be possible?"

She hurried to tell Clara's mother about the confession. Engracia hated Cassi. If she had ever had any kind of strong sentiment about anything, it was her hatred for the guitar player. She didn't know just how to explain it but he inspired a great rage within her, a desire to kill. When Dona Margarida told her about her daughter's confidence, she suffered an attack of muted fury. But it was not directed against him; rather, it was directed against the girl whom she had reared with such great care and affection only to see her madly in love with that good-for-nothing Cassi, a degenerate cursed by everybody, even his own father. Then she calmed down and decided to tell Joaquim before the perverse *modinha* player could ensnare them in some escapade.

Joaquim received the news without distress. He didn't like Cassi, either. For Joaquim, however, an upright and hardworking man, Cassi was a bit of a rogue, a social outcast and often in trouble with the police; he was also talked about a lot for being a bad sort. But, even so . . . if he wanted to marry their girl — in spite of all the precedents — he would not oppose it. Should he call him up? Or should he have Cassi come to *his* house? Or would it be better to wait?

He thought about it for a while and then decided to seek the opinion of his *compadre*, Marramaque. The old doorman held a great moral and intellectual superiority over his friend, the postman, who obeyed his will blindly. He decided, therefore, to ask his advice in the matter.

That Sunday, their card game had gone on well into the evening. It must have been eleven o'clock when they decided to have done with it. They were playing in the dining room where, along with Joaquim, Marramaque, Lafoes and Dona Engracia were also gathered. Clara had already retired to her room. Thinking that his daughter was asleep, Joaquim decided to present the problem. He began by explaining the girl's nervous condition, the measures he had taken to treat her, and finally, he reached the crucial point of the matter. By that time, however, Marramaque stood up, furious:

"Well, there you are. . . . *Compadre,* do you intend to bring some pustule like that into your house? Don't you know who this Cassi is? If his own father doesn't want anything to do with him it's because he's no good! He not only dishonors his victims' families but he even brings shame down upon his own! His sisters, quite unusual young women, ought to be married by now but nobody wants to be Cassi's brother-in-law. He always says the same thing . . . that he wants to get married. After he gets what he wants and is satisfied, then he slides through the police and the nets of justice and just laughs at the poor little girls he's pulled down into shame and disgrace. Don't you see that if he really wanted to get married, he wouldn't pick Clara, a poor, mulatto girl, the daughter of a simple postman? Joaquim, I'm your friend and. . . ."

"That's what I think, too," said Dona Engracia. "He could get somebody whose social and financial situation was a lot better."

Sobbing in her room Clara heard this and wanted to protest, to cite examples she knew to the contrary, but she contained herself.

Joaquim, who had listened silently to his *compadre's* impassioned speech, finally observed:

"I think you're right . . . but what shall we do?"

"Let it go ahead as it is for a while. . . . How does my goddaughter receive her messages from him, *compadre?*"

"She says that it's some friend that brings them to her," responded the postman's wife.

"Some friend indeed!" commented Marramaque, laughing bitterly. "The thing to do, Joaquim, is to let things go on the way they have been but to make it known to him that you do not approve of his insistence in contacting the girl."

"And if he persists. . . ?" Engracia asked.

"Then publish that pamphlet I received in the newspapers . . . go to the police and denounce him for what he is once and for all. And then let him do whatever he wants."

Everybody grew silent. But Lafoes didn't because he had kept quiet from the beginning. The postman turned to him suddenly and asked:

"What do you have to say to this, Lafoes?"

"This . . . this is a very delicate matter. I'm not a member of the family and I don't think I have the right to. . . ."

"Neither am I," interjected Marramaque. "I am merely giving my frank opinion, which was requested. But I am certain, Joaquim, that if you permit this no-good scoundrel to come here, in spite of everything I owe you, I shall never set foot again in your house."

He got up, took his walking stick and left, plunging into the darkness of the night. It was already quite dark, an almost starless night, and he walked slowly with his lame step until he finally got to his modest house where he arrived with no sense of trepidation and with a calm conscience.

Clara could not get to sleep. The most absurd ideas kept passing through her mind. She thought about fleeing, about running off with Cassi, about killing herself. . . . She was filled with anger for her godfather and finally, she resolved to relate in a letter to her lover everything that had transpired that evening.

The next morning, she left her room just as soon as she was sure that her father had left for work. She was greeted by her mother naturally, washed-up and had breakfast. Since the delivery man had not yet come by, she told her mother she was going to copy some music while she waited for him. But this was a pretext. What she really wrote was a long letter narrating what she had heard the night before about herself and Cassi. Later, even before Meneses could begin to work on her teeth, she gave him the missive which the poor old man bitterly put into his vest pocket. "Why do I go on living?" he thought to himself as he cleaned his iron tools on a spotless white towel.

When Cassi learned what had happened, and seeing his plans perhaps failing because of that miserable old so-and-so and, even worse, under the threat of publication in the papers of all his scandalous life, he was filled with an evil fury. At the height of that fury, he firmly resolved to get rid of that stumbling old cripple who was always meddling in his plans that by then, he believed had already cost him quite a sum of money — in truth, his expenses had not exceeded fifty *mil-reis.*

Cassi's rage was towering, so much that, as he read the letter in a low voice at the bar with Meneses at his side, the old man actually noticed the profound alteration of his physiognomy. Cassi's eyes were blazing, his teeth gnashed and his entire countenance, vile, ferocious, and crude, revealed itself in a hideous grimace.

He paid for Meneses' drinks and then said good-bye without saying anything else.

Meneses continued to sip his consoling shots of rum and asked himself:

"What's happening . . . what's going to happen . . . what might happen?"

What happened was quite simple: Cassi — simply, coldly, cruelly, and in premeditated fashion — laid the plans for Marramaque's murder. But when he spoke to Arnaldo about this, Cassi limited himself to saying. "We're going to give him a real beating."

"Why?" the other asked.

Cassi responded:

"Because this old man is abusing his condition as a cripple and insults me. He deserves a whipping." But the two sadistic thugs really understood that they weren't just going to beat him up; they were going to kill him. . . .

It was Saturday, the day when Marramaque usually stayed a little longer than ordinarily in *Seu* Nascimento's store. It was raining as the night closed in quickly — dark, and thick with black clouds hung low over the landscape. Flickering in the strong wind, the gas street lamps only poorly lighted those appalling suburban streets surrounded on all sides by trees and dense, tangled thickets of shrubs and bushes. On the way home from work, Marramaque allowed himself to stay in the store until almost eight o'clock. Along about that time, he said good-bye to everyone and left for home. To get there from the store, he, like others, preferred to take a street that was almost completely constructed but ended up on a deserted hillside. One one side, the left, it was a wasteland full of tall thickets, and on the right side, there were huge trees located in the backyard of an old country house that fronted onto the street parallel to this one. In addition to being deserted and lonely, this particular stretch of road was naturally grim and melancholy, especially on nights such as that one.

Under a relentless drizzle and wrapped-up in a rain cape, Marramaque climbed up the hillside so he could descend on the other side into the gully and eventually arrive at home. Just as he reached the highest point of the little elevation, two figures suddenly jumped out in front of him and said: "Now, cripple; you've got to learn that you shouldn't poke your nose in where it doesn't belong." He didn't have time to utter a single word. The two men fell upon him and began beating him with clubs about his head and all over his body. With the first blows of the cudgels, poor Marramaque tumbled over the side of the road gasping for breath but unable to speak. Enraged, the two assailants continued to smash away at him with all their strength and with no thought of mercy or pity. When it seemed to be the right moment, they fled into the night.

By the following day, as the first travellers were passing by, he was found dead. Such were the circumstances surrounding the death of poor, courageous Antonio da Silva Marramaque, a man who, at age eighteen in the back room of a country general store, first dreamed about the glories of Casimiro de Abreu and who ended up a doorman, murdered because of the greatness of his character and because of his moral courage. He never wrote poetry or if he did, it was not good; but in his own way, he was a poet and a hero. . . . May God reward him!

IX

Any crime surrounded by such mysterious and atrocious circumstances as was Marramaque's murder is bound to excite the imagination of an entire city. Any common homicide whose cause, author — whether captured or not — and certain other details are known by all fails to inspire any interest in people because it is just another banal, albeit fatal, everyday event in the life of the suburbs, like births, natural disasters and burials. But the cruel cudgeling to death of a poor, pathetic, crippled, and inoffensive old man makes it clear that, free and circulating with other people on the streets, the public squares, streetcars, in stores and trains, there were murderers around, men who killed merely for pleasure, without reason or rhyme or motive for their acts. When such an incident occurs, the innumerable and insidious enemies in our lives increase with the addition of the threat of men who murder for pleasure, for amusement, for sport. . . .

One such murder or many, whatever the number, is always a threat hovering over each and every one of us, jeering at the most obvious poverty and never making an exception of the most pusillanimous or tranquil lives.

Marramaque was not rich; he didn't wear jewelry and he certainly never carried much money on his person. The motive of the crime, therefore, could not have been robbery. Quite to the contrary, a scrupulous examination of the pockets of the garments on the corpse did not suggest any attempt at robbery. The little money he was carrying, three *mil-reis* notes and some small change, was found intact, and a billfold, found in one of the interior pockets of his jacket, contained only papers. At the time he was murdered, he was wearing his doorman's uniform: a Navy blue jacket and matching trousers. Underneath the jacket he was wearing a common black vest. In one of its pockets he carried an old silver watch. It was held in place with an old gold chain made of numerous strands of braid tied together with ferrules of the same material and formed in the shape of a stirrup and had a pendant consisting of a black stone. Not even this piece of jewelry which did have a certain value was stolen. Laying aside the robbery theory, what could have been the motive of the crime. Love affairs or some other amorous intrigues? His state of health and his semi-invalid physical condition would immediately preclude such theories. Politics, family problem. . . ? These couldn't explain the crime either. Only in the perversity, in the desire of some extremely evil or bloodthirsty creature to kill would the cause be found. Was this really what had happened, everyone was asking?

News of the crime spread all through the suburbs. Although the crime was discovered on Sunday, Marramaque's mutilation made it even more sensational and made the news spread even faster so that people everywhere were talking about his murder. The police carried out their customary procedures but they only began their investigations on the following day. Statements were taken from everybody in the store but those people had little or nothing to add to what the police already knew. Neither was there anything they could do. When Marramaque arrived there, the rain had stopped. It was Saturday and all the habitues of *Seu* Nascimento's general store were there, including Meneses who was revealing himself to be quite a chatterer and a generally jovial fellow. They were all talking light heartedly and even Meneses had been able to interject some hilarity into the discussion when he explained his rather transcendent theory about "Columbus' egg." In the course of the conversation somebody said:

"Say, that's like Columbus' egg."

Marramaque had spoken and Alipio took advantage of that moment to inquire:

"What the devil does this reference to 'Columbus' egg' mean? Everybody talks about it but I don't get it."

Among those who were listening was Senhor Moncao Mindela, a buyer and seller for the huge grain company of Belmiro, Bernardes and Cia. He was a knowledgeable fellow and liked to chat with people as a way of taking a break from the tiresome drudgery of his job as a hawker for the retailers. He sold them beans, rice and corn at a good price.

He was a Portuguese, likeable, good looking and rather well-educated. He enjoyed great liberty in that circle of friends and there was never any surprise when he took part in their discussions:

"Why, Alipio! You mean to say that you don't know what 'Columbus' egg' is?"

"No, *Seu* Mindela, I don't."

"It's simple. In the midst of the learned Spanish, just after his first voyage to America, Columbus, seeing that his efforts were criticized and described as simple by the Castillian know-it-alls, decided to challenge them to set an egg on its end."

"And did they set one on its end?" asked Alipio.

Then Meneses hastened to add:

"They couldn't but Columbus could!"

"How?" inquired Alipio.

Taking over the floor from Mindela, Meneses began to explain, and speaking like a man of real learning, said:

"By giving the necessary rotary motion and proper tilt to the egg, Columbus dissolved its yolk. This then sank down to the egg's base, down to its lowest part, and thereby lowered its center of gravity so that it would stand up on its end."

Everybody looked at everybody else and saw the absurdity of Meneses' explanation. Nobody challenged him but suddenly, Marramaque, again taking the floor from Mindela who was about to speak, interjected with a jestful tone to his voice:

"Oh, come now, *Seu* Meneses! This story of tilting . . . of rotation . . . of centers of gravity . . . why, it's all nonsense! What really happened is. . . ."

"Nonsense, Marramaque? It's a transcendent matter of mechanics just like the cat always landing on its four feet no matter how it's tossed, even when it's tossed any way from high up."

Marramaque met the challenge without batting an eye:

"This doesn't have anything to do with cats! An egg has as much to do with a cat as it does with a roasting spit! Nonsense, *Seu* Meneses."

Everybody broke out laughing, everybody, that is, except Meneses who began to stroke his long and abundant white beard, silently contemplating his defeat in the argument about mechanics and related topics. Suddenly, though, he recovered his courage and challenged the doorman:

"Marramaque, I'd like to see you explain how Columbus made the egg stand on its end."

"Very simple, Meneses. I'm going to tell you the story just as I read it. At a banquet once, some Spanish noblemen were trying to discredit the value of Columbus' discovery and one said:

'The Indies were already there and if you hadn't discovered them, somebody else would have.'

Without answering him, Columbus asked for an egg. They brought him one and he then challenged anybody to set the egg on end. 'Impossible,' they all exclaimed. The navigator took the egg, knocked it against the table so that he just barely crushed the tip of it, the bluntest end, and set it down on the crushed end.

'Oh . . . that's what I would have done, too,' they all responded.

'Yes, . . . after you saw me do it. It's simple, but one has to study the situation first and then find the way to do it.'

That's how the deed was accomplished. It didn't have anything to do with gravity, rotations, translations, constellations or repulsions . . . it didn't have anything to do with any of these big words at all, Meneses!"

And once again the guffaws were general and prolonged. Very abashed, Meneses limited himself to saying:

"That isn't scientific; it's just a playful explanation of some almanac anecdote. I could demonstrate my interpretation with the aid of some computations but it's not convenient to do it here. I'll leave it for another time."

And so, with no more pressing concerns during that stormy afternoon, the men continued their chatting while Marramaque was present and after he had left. It is clear that none of the persons present could have guessed what would befall him on the road. It had been raining steadily but it was not a torrential downpour at the time the poor doorman finally said good-bye to his friends. It is true that the night was dreadfully black and threatening clouds hung low above the ground making the atmosphere even darker and dimming the light of the street lamps whose flames were flickering because of a lashing, cutting, and constant wind. One could not, as people say, see one's hand in front of one's nose. As far as the police were concerned, it seemed that the mysterious murder, apparently without motive, had been inspired by some secret that only he, Marramaque, or perhaps his intimate papers, could reveal. The authorities decided to investigate his personal papers in search of some clue.

Marramaque had been living with a maternal aunt who was a bit younger than he and who had two nearly grown sons, one ten and the other twelve. As a widow living in the country, and having been able to save some money, she decided to buy the house she now lived in and to invite her nephew to live there to keep her company, initiate the education of her children and help them get started in life.

Her house was quite different from Meneses'. It was always clean, its furniture was in repair and neatly arranged, and its little garden was carefully kept up. Helena, Marramaque's aunt, was very methodical and frugal and because of these qualities, her nephew's domestic life was regular and placid. She was a seamstress for the government arsenal and by adding what she made to Marramaque's meagre income, their lives went along with few financial problems. They did not have any trouble getting to the Central train station because they could travel via the Inhauma streetcar which stopped on a corner near them. If, on the fateful night of his murder, the doorman had taken the shortcuts and climbed up the hills, which he frequently did when he was walking to Nascimento's store or when he was going to Joaquim's house — he would have gotten on the other, shorter road and avoided the ambush. Helena lived for her children; she rarely went out. When she did, it was only to arrange for her sewing or to visit the postman's house once in a while. When she visited them, she became upset and distressed at Engracia's taciturn manner. Helena helped in unearthing her poor nephew's papers from his trunks and chests.

The police authorities were polite in requesting authorization and the Chief went personally to examine the poor doorman's personal remains. But he found nothing of any value. In his archives, there were letters from members of his family, notes from friends, a collection of some rough drafts of poems among which was one by Raul Braga, a poet friend of Marramaque, and also the celebrated folder on Cassi, of which the police already had a copy. Along with these rather unimportant papers, they also found a notebook of poems all ready to be printed authored by Marramaque himself. They were entitled "English Daisies and Tender Thoughts" and were the efforts of a good and honest man who was not a poet. The police also came across a picture of a woman in a popular pose with her left arm resting on a column and holding an enormous fan in her right hand. The fan was hanging down the entire length of her body. She was an attractive woman about thirty, strong, and healthy looking. On the back of the picture there was this dedication: "To my Antonio; Eponina 25/12/92." Below this, in Marramaque's own handwriting, was this observation: "It is said that Love conquers all; but it is unable to conquer the obligations of loyalty that ought always to exist within perfect friendships. Good-bye."

Who was she? The police asked but Dona Helena was unable to explain. At the time of the date on the letter, she was still unmarried and her nephew had already gone to Rio. Who could the woman be. . . ?

The police found nothing, and the crime began to be forgotten. Only two people could have set the authorities on the right track: Clara and Meneses.

As soon as she heard of her godfather's murder, Clara was beside herself. She remembered all the veiled threats that Cassi had made toward her godfather in the letters he wrote her and she also recalled the letter in which she had told her lover about Marramaque's attitude toward him when her father spoke to his *compadre* about the necessity of arriving at some frank and clear understanding with the guitar player. Because of this and certain other incidents and circumstances, she believed her godfather's murderer was Cassi and that she was an accomplice! She was overcome by a sudden fear of the affected and saccharine singer. In spite of his evil, tin-plated mien, she saw clearly in a flash just how deceitful and false his tender letters were, letters full of protestations of good intentions and sincere, honest love.

Immediately, however, she explained away his criminal and insane action as being merely a sporadic act of madness, a momentary delirium brought about by the power of his love for her. It was a thorny problem . . . and it was distressing for Clara to ponder the issue any further. . . . It wouldn't be long before it would be explained to her in person because she had finally consented to seeing and talking to Cassi beneath the grill work of the house. But this was a meeting that would take place only after her parents had retired for the evening, of course. On that occasion, she would be able to judge for certain how true her suspicions were. Meneses had carried one of her letters referring to this matter. Flustered because she sensed that her mother was close by, Clara was unable to seal the missive properly. With the letter still open, the girl, in order not to be caught with it on her person, hastily passed it to the old man who received and guarded it jubilantly. Later when the opportune moment arose, he read it.

Like many women of scant formal education, Clara took to the pen and didn't want to let go of it. She related details, she also insisted that she and Cassi exchange vows as well as demanding that they swear to oaths of fidelity. One of these was that he respect her always. If he didn't, she would break off relations with him. She was prepared to wait for him at the grill of the window at ten o'clock at night within a week. She decided to do this because Meneses had already completed his work on her teeth.

Truly disgusted with the exchange of letters, with Cassi's disdainful treatment, and with the ignoble farse in which he was taking part, Meneses had resolved to put an end to the affair. The reading of the letter didn't cause him any surprises; he had been expecting this result. Meneses was inured by the indifference of a beaten man and he felt that his hands and feet were bound. He was denied any chance of censuring or giving council. But news of Marramaque's brutal murder had not yet reached his ears. However, when he finally learned of it, he felt a deep sense of shame for his part in the sordid affair and for his cowardice. He understood that those allusions of Cassi's about Marramaque and the horrible smile he had seen on one other occasion when they had been talking about the doorman, and which had so disfigured his countenance, were the premonotory symptoms of the murder of the kindly old man that the guitar player had been planning. Wretched, Meneses spent the entire day and night wrapped up in his own thoughts. He no longer knew how to cry but his remorse was intense; he also judged himself to be an accomplice in the cold-blooded murder. Why was he silent about what he knew? Why had he allowed himself to be intimidated to the point of serving as a go-between? Dear God . . . he was no longer a man . . . he had no more dignity. . . .

Cassi, on the other hand, showed not the slightest distress about what he had done. He read the newspaper stories which were bitter objurgations against the murder he had committed and which were numerous and he overheard people's condemnations about the crime and its agent everywhere in cafe conversations, in streetcars, everywhere. . . . But he felt no remorse for what he had done. In fact, for his inhumanity and his abject, innate calm to be complete, he lacked only a sense of deep-seated pride at having effected such an uncommon deed. He felt no pride at what he had done but he did feel a sense of relief on seeing himself free of the evil eye, of the phantom, which lived only to persecute him.

Arnaldo did not feel the same. After the deed was done — while he was reading the papers and observing the bitter censure bursting forth from people's mouths, even from members of Cassi's own gang, characters quite accustomed to criminal acts, Arnaldo began to feel afraid if he did not actually feel remorse. But he was unable to resist the compulsion that forced him to look at the cadaver. Marramaque's remains were still just as they had been when he was found; the doctors had not yet performed the autopsy. His skull was split open, his eyes had popped from their sockets, his entire face was covered with a bloody mire, his semi-paralyzed arm was broken, his clothing soaked in a bloody muck . . . it was horrible! At the morgue, a group of people had crowded together to gaze at the corpse and everybody, speaking in low voices, was hurling oaths, abuse and curses on the heads of the cruel thugs who had carried out such a bizarre and unthinkable crime. A black man, very dark of skin and powerful looking with bulging pectoral muscles said in a loud voice for everyone to hear:

"I'm no saint . . . I've done a few things myself . . . I know what the insides of a jail look like, but may God punish me — may He strike me dead with a lightning bolt and let me rot forever — if I ever did such a filthy thing as this. Why would anybody want to kill a poor, old crippled man like this anyway? I say skinning them alive isn't a good enough punishment. . . ."

Arnaldo returned home from the funeral proceedings apprehensive. Strictly speaking, he had no real regret for his actions; although what he felt was fear of being discovered, of being stuck in chains and then left to rot in prison for thirty, long, uninterrupted years. He knew he couldn't last through that! He returned to the suburbs very frightened and when he bumped into Cassi he said with a wild look in his eye:

"My God, Cassi! The old man looked awful!"

The guitar player turned and gave Arnaldo a hard look with his lackluster gaze. Then he snapped at him with fire in his eyes:

"Shut up! Do you want to blow everything?"

Even though Arnaldo was afraid of the fury of his comrade and accomplice, he couldn't escape his own terror and the fear of being discovered by the police. He took to drinking and Cassi had to watch him carefully, fearing that Arnaldo would get loaded and spill the beans. Cassi never left him alone, not even when the gang was out drinking together.

Whenever they were in some bar, no stranger ever came in whom Arnaldo didn't look over from head to foot, meticulously and carefully. At times, he wasn't able to restrain himself and blurted out:

"Cassi . . . that guy's an agent for the Eighteenth precinct!"

"You're crazy! What do you want to do, get us tossed in jail for the rest of our lives?"

At the beginning, Cassi was afraid that Arnaldo's drunkenness would cause him to give them away but very soon he saw that his binges only gave him a whining, blubbering disposition and that they made him effusive so that he wanted to embrace everybody present. Also, from time to time he went around repeating these words in a deep-seated and sorrowful voice, without ever really knowing what he was saying to the people around him:

"I'm not bad . . . I'm good . . . I've never hurt anyone. . . ," etc., etc.

Then Zeze Mateus, usually very drunk as well as often prostrate in his chair with his eyes unfocused and glazed looking, drooling and stammering, would answer him back:

"My dear Ar . . . Arn . . . Arnaldo! You're . . . you're a prince of a fellow."

Then, after wiping away his slobber with a handkerchief, he would add:

Who was it who . . . who said that . . . that you're . . . you're bad?" Then he would add, "Just bring . . . bring . . . bring this guy here and . . . and I'll bust his head open!"

About this time, Arnaldo was deeply moved and got up on his feet to embrace Zeze Mateus who, barely able to stay in his chair, struggled to raise up his arms so he could hug his comrade.

This scene repeated itself from time to time with very little variation and Cassi even attempted to crack some awkward jokes about it. Such spectacles, however, never failed to anger Cassi although his other companions always had a good laugh, suspecting nothing.

Even so, the guitar player was not very confident that Arnaldo could continue to keep his mouth shut about what they had done. Drunkenness, Cassi knew, is capricious and no matter what Arnaldo did about it, it was quite possible that he might let something slip out, something about their crime. It was necessary, therefore, for Cassi to take appropriate precautions. His rendezvous with Clara was scheduled for the end of the week. He had to go, he had to see through to the end of this affair that had caused and was continuing to cause him so much trouble. However, before anything else was done, it was necessary to be prepared for any and all unforeseen complications that might arise. He couldn't count on his political protection any longer; Barcelos wasn't worth anything to him any more and only required Cassi's services for some minor jobs on the eve of election day. When the elections were far in the future, Barcelos scowled and put his faith in a jug of whisky, not in Cassi and his gang. Cassi had to get everything arranged so that he could run away from Rio de Janeiro at the first sign of trouble. Such preparations were all the more urgent because he now knew, thanks to certain of Meneses' indiscretions that he overheard in *Seu* Nascimento's store, that Nair's husband — Nair was the girl he had seduced and whose mother, because of her daughter's fall, committed suicide — was prepared to prosecute him much as he had already been persecuted by the famous notebooks, but now more efficiently since her husband was said really to have something that would stick on Cassi. He saw clearly that things would soon be more difficult for him and that even now, the stones that lay scattered in the street, seemed to rear up and try to trip and tear at him.

Cassi made a rather extreme decision: he would sell his fighting cocks! He would deposit whatever money he made from the deal in a savings bank so that it would always be at hand if and when it became necessary to run away. His mother, seeing the wagons pull up in front of their door and watching them as they were loaded with the coops and cages, steadily passing through the door and placed in the wagons, went to her son and asked him what was going on:

"Oh, nothing, mother. I'm just going off to work. . . ."

"Going where, Cassi?"

"I'm going to Mato Grosso to get a job with the railroad construction company."

"As a pickax worker, my son?"

"Oh, no mamma! I'm going to be a crew chief first but then I'll practice with the tools until I become a section boss."

Even with this explanation, Dona Salustiana was not content. She was well aware of her son's ignorance, of his mental inferiority, and of his inability to apply himself to anything that might require even the slightest mental exertion. She saw clearly that, because of all this, on any railroad construction crew her son could only be a simple manual laborer, someone who could pick up a scythe and clear land or pick up an ax and chop down trees or grab a pick and dig holes in the earth . . . he was incapable of doing anything more. She went back in the house crying, and encountered her two daughters:

"Catarina . . . Irene! Do you want to know something? Oh, my . . . dear God!"

"Mamma, what is it?" asked Catarina.

"What's wrong, mamma?" Irene wanted to know.

"Oh, children . . . you don't know what a disgrace our family . . . our family . . . Cassi. . . ."

"What's happened?" demanded Catarina, becoming alarmed.

"Cassi's lost his mind . . . he wants to shame all of us, even my grandfather, the English ambassador. Oh, my God. . . ! If he were only here today to see what a terrible shame we're undergoing. . . ."

"What is it that Cassi's done?" muttered Irene, calmly.

"He's going to be a pick and shovel worker on a railroad construction crew in Mato Grosso."

Irene, who was rather severe and who never pardoned her brother for causing all the malicious questions her schoolmates asked her whenever Cassi's name appeared in the papers since her brother was constantly mixed up in some shady, amorous escapade, was deeply vexed by his behavior. And so she commented:

"So what, mamma? He's healthy . . . besides, rather than his staying around here doing the things he does, shaming all of us everywhere he goes, it'd be better if he would go off somewhere and go to work."

Dona Salustiana gave the girl a horrified look and said in a voice full of sorrow and heartbreak:

"The problem is that you're not a mother . . . well, you will be before long and then you'll see."

But Catarina sided with Irene:

"Mamma, I don't see any reason to feel bad. What's really reproachable here is the type of life he leads. The best thing would be for him to try something else . . . somewhere else. . . !"

Their father had not yet learned what his son, whom he had not laid eyes on in nearly two years, had decided to do. But when he found out, he could not restrain his joy exclaiming:

"Let him go! Let him got to the devil for all I care! It's about time!"

Later, he added:

"You'll soon see that he's pulled off another of his stunts and that now he's just going to run off and leave us here, ashamed and sorrowed if not actually taking the blame for him. But it's all in God's hands now. May he just go away and leave us in peace!"

Once the roosters, hens, and chicks were sold, he received 500 *mil-reis* that he wanted to deposit in the bank the day after.

On that morning, Cassi woke up early, bathed carefully, took pains to put on his best underwear, checked carefully to make sure his stockings weren't worn through, brushed his belted, three piece suit and he began to dress himself for his trip down to the city with the utmost care. He rarely went downtown; he usually went only so far as the Campo de Sant'Ana area. He didn't like the downtown area at all because it meant mingling with all the chic and modish young men who congregated there on the street corners and sidewalks. He thought they were ridiculous, showing off their expensive walking sticks, rings and wrist watches. It's true, he thought to himself, that he also used such things but he was more modest. He didn't make such a spectacle of himself. . . . Cassi also was aware that he wasn't able to strike such dapper poses but he thought if he were able and willing to do so, he certainly wouldn't appear as ridiculous as they did. . . . He also applied this attitude to his philosophy of elegant dress, one reflecting the vanity of the suburban fop, to young women. How vain they were! He questioned their studied gaits and their affected ways of bidding good-bye. . . .

Cassi thought all of this ridiculous, exaggerated and copied but he didn't recognize the model. What he did in fact feel was not the attitude exhibited to his friends or to the suburban beauties whom he wooed if he was lucky. What he really sensed about all this — their manners and gestures — and about all the conversations he did not understand, was his own ignorance, his own natural crudeness and lack of education and good taste. His hatred, therefore, was intense toward the poets and newspapermen, especially the latter. Cassi could never forgive them for the insults and jeers heaped upon him whenever they found it necessary to denounce him for one of his infamous misdeeds. "They're just a bunch of perverts," he said, "a bunch of bums who'd like to dictate morals to everybody!" His first impulse when he read their articles about him was always to assault physically one of the writers, naturally, the one who seemed weakest, and beat his brains out. He had to restrain himself, however, because he knew that if he were to do so he would surely be lost. A real row would result, one without respite for him, and the full extent of his bad actions, including those unknown before, would surely be brought out into the open. Inwardly, Cassi had a certain respect for the city and its inhabitants; it was the respect of a true suburbanite, a man poorly educated, stupid and illiterate.

As soon as Cassi drank his morning coffee, he fixed his tie and went down the street. It was early but he was worried about the money he carried in his vest pocket.

He didn't want anyone to know he was carrying such a large amount of money on his person or even less, that he was planning to slip away. He got on the first train that came along. Later, jumping off the car at the Central station, he took care to avoid meeting anybody he knew who might ask him indiscreet questions about what he was doing there.

Suffering no setbacks to his plan, Cassi Jones set out across the middle of the Campo de Sant'Ana area, in the midst of the multitude gushing out of the doors of the Central station. It was a crowd full of people who were going to work in honest haste and Cassi's immediate sensation was that he was in some strange city. In the suburbs, he had his loves and hates; in the suburbs he had his cohorts, and his reputation as a guitarist was widespread. No matter where he went there, he was always well-known. In the suburbs, of course, he had a personality . . . he was Cassi Jones de Azevedo. But, in the city, especially in the Campo de Sant'Ana area, what was he? He was nothing. His fame and his prestige ended where the tracks ended at the Central station. In the city, his braggadocio evaporated into nothingness and he saw himself squelched by all those strange faces there, faces that didn't even bother to look at him. Whether in Riachuelo, Piedade or Rio das Pedras, Cassi always met somebody he knew by sight at least. But in the midst of the city, if he were to run into one of these faces in one of the groups of young men on Ouvidor street or out on one of the avenues, he was nothing more than one more suburbanite who didn't deserve any notice at all. How is it, he asked himself, that such types as they, dressed in such poor taste, are celebrated and hailed while he, Cassi Jones, passed unnoticed? He had a clue to the answer but he didn't wish to face up to reality. As soon as he formulated it, he quickly thought about something else.

In the city, as we have said, Cassi became acutely aware of his inferior intelligence and education. He also sensed his rusticity compared to those young men who were discussing issues and telling jokes and talking about things he couldn't understand. Noting the avidity with which they read the headlines of the journals, on subjects whose importance he could not comprehend, Cassi became angry because of his inability to learn how to read. Observing the ease with which the customers ordered varied and strange drinks, he realized that he didn't even know how to pronounce their names. And looking at the ladies and young girls who seemed to him to be queens and princesses (just like the barbarian who could see only kings in the Roman Senate), Cassi felt humble and insignificant. In short, the entire spectrum of fine things, of refined attitudes, polished and urbane habits, and of free spending habits tended to reduce Cassi's personality to that of a mediocre suburbanite, a domestic vagabond, almost nothing. . . .

After getting off the Central railroad, Cassi did not try to get into a streetcar. Instead, he plunged into a part of the crowd heading in the direction of the City Hall and marched along toward the downtown area. From Largo do Rossio on, he kept stopping in front of all the store windows. He stopped to look at all the jewelry through the thick, strong glass that protected it from people's greed. He looked at rings and watches, at bracelets and earrrings (more at the former than the latter) although no sentiment for presenting any of these objects as gifts to his lovers beat in his heart. So expensive, he thought, it's just not worth the trouble. . . ! A rush wood walking stick, angular and gold capped, tempted him, however, but the five hundred *mil-reis* he had in his pocket began to whisper something in his ear and he soon refused to give in to the temptation. He had to play it safe. . . .

He turned on to Rua de Sete de Setembro and walked along its length admiring the ready-made clothes in the shops. Continuing his stroll along the entire lengthy front of the Parc Royal, he stopped in front of the showcases behind which were clothes and other pieces of men's wardrobe. He saw cutaway coats, suspenders, garters, shirts and shirt collars. . . . How lovely they all were!

Then he took Ouvidor street and began to move downhill, still stopping in front of each store that carried men's apparel. For amusement, he decided to try something different and stopped to look through the showcases of a bookstore. Then he looked inside: books from top to bottom. Why would anybody want so many books? Books were only good for driving people crazy. Cassi possessed a few books . . . but they were books about Love. And dear God, what books they were. . . ! Then he felt like having a cup of coffee . . . but he hesitated for a moment. A second later, however, he made the plunge and bought himself one.

Now, however, it was almost time for the bank to open; it surely would not be late in opening. But walking up to the bank, he still had to bide his time for a few more minutes until the doors were finally opened. There were already some other people waiting there, too, and Cassi watched them. They were of different sizes, dressed differently and were of differing skin colors; there were old women with their mantillas, girls with sunken chests, bearded Portuguese men who seemed to be laborers, store clerks, streetcar conductors, and hotel and tavern waiters, cooks whose hands show the innumerable burns of stoves, and the wrinkled fingers of humble washerwomen. In short, that group of people represented an entire world of poor people, men and women who went to the bank to deposit the money it had cost them so much travail and hardship to earn or who went there to withdraw it so they could undertake some drama in their impoverished lives. Cassi hated to be in contact with such people. . . .

Moving into the lobby of the bank, Cassi tried to read the signs on the billboards where the legal provisos were posted that would be of interest to the public. Damn! Luck just wasn't with him. . . . In order to confirm what he thought he had been able to make out, Cassi moved over to an employee in a cage who had this sign above him: "Information." But he had no luck at all; in order to withdraw more than two hundred *mil-reis* at a time one had to give prior notice. No, no he wouldn't deposit anything; the money had to stay within his reach . . . . He left, and, not seeing anyone who knew him, decided to move through the São Francisco plaza for a while, crossing the filthy old side streets that begin with Rua Misericordia and end with Rua Dom Manuel and the Moura plaza. He moved into this area, the ancient part of the city, today dotted with dark and gloomy boarding houses but once, in its own era, enjoying a certain dignity and brilliance. The bars and cheap saloons were peopled with the most sordid elements of our population. The dark streets were lined on both sides with two-story buildings from whose windows poorly washed clothes were hanging. They were infrequently travelled streets and together formed a strange section of the city, a district set apart from the main section of the metropolis. In it, the men and women who had fallen into the basest kinds of misery and degradation, and were buried there on the lowest rung of the economic and social ladder, found refuge. Here, among the shadows of the narrow, colonial streets, in the lightless alcoves of the buildings and in the dark, dank and misty interiors of the sordid dives of that section of the city, the misery, the shame and the infinite unhappiness of the disinherited, forgotten people of all this earth are hidden. Among the men, however, there were still some with definite occupations; sailors, stevedores, soldiers.... But the women who ended up there fell unfailingly into the ultimate degradation. Dirty, hair uncombed, some barefooted, some wearing thin house slippers and others in open toed wooden clogs, all of these women aroused in men more a sense of pity and pain than desire. And, as in any and all categories of our society, this group of miserable, pathetic people was a good index of the larger social structure. There were black women, white women, mulattoes, and *caboclas* [person of mixed Portuguese and Indian ancestry], all made equal here thanks to poverty, civic neglect and their common, pitiable condition.

Cassi Jones was crossing through that freakish, shadowy part of town when suddenly, from out of the depths of a cheap saloon, someone shouted at him:

"Hey! Hey! *Seu* Cassi . . . hey, *Seu* Cassi!"

Impassively, Cassi stopped to see who it was calling to him. From inside the bar and with a hurried step, a black woman came running to him. She was dirty, frowzy looking, had kinky hair that had a piece of broken comb sticking in it right on the top of her head, and she was pulling on a pair of patched-up house slippers. She was also half drunk. Cassi felt uneasy about meeting her. Assuming the airs of someone who is annoyed, Cassi asked her, sullenly:

"What do you want?"

Putting her hands on her hips and swaggering a bit, the black woman looked challengingly at Cassi and said:

"So . . . you don't know me anymore, eh, *Seu* scum? So you don't remember Ines anymore, the little black girl your mother raised and who you. . . ."

Then, suddenly, Cassi remembered who he was confronting. She had been his first victim, the girl his mother had thrown out of the house in an advanced state of pregnancy without a second thought. Recognizing her now and recalling this, Cassi had an urge to flee but the woman grabbed him by the arm:

"Don't run off . . . oh, no . . . you bastard! You're going to have to hear some more about all this!"

By this time, the habitual frequenters of the area saloons and boarding houses had come outside to see what was going on and were forming a circle around Cassi and Ines. There were men and women and they were all asking:

"What's going on here, Ines?"

"What'd this guy do to you?"

Cassi was bewildered in the midst of all these hostile faces, especially since these were people who were quite accustomed to brawling and murder. But he struggled to speak:

"I don't know this woman . . . I swear. . . ."

"Not much you don't!" answered Ines, swaying a bit from side to side. "When you were busy hustling me . . . all that kissing and hugging and sweet talk . . . I wasn't unknown to you then . . . I was something else then, wasn't I . . . you filthy pig!"

Just then, a tall, lanky black man with a fearless appearance and the decided manner of a *capoeira* [originally, an acrobatic form of self defense] fighter, intervened:

"Come on, Ines. Once and for all, who is this guy?"

"He's the one who did me in, the one who ruined me, the one who got me in the mess I'm in now."

"Me?" exclaimed Cassi.

"Yes, you . . . and nobody else, you shameless coward! I remember it very well . . . you even did it in your mother's own bedroom! I was just tidying up the house and. . . ."

Then another woman, a white woman with brown hair in which one could see lice, commented:

"That's always the way it is. These spoiled sons go around disgracing innocent girls, get them knocked up and then run off . . . it's always the girls who suffer. . . . You animal!"

Cassi was listening to all this not knowing what to do. He was totally yellow and was aware only of the glaring eyes of everybody there. He was praying that the police would come, that he could get some help from anywhere. Then the black woman continued:

"Do you know where your child is? He's in jail, that's where. He's an ornery child . . . got himself mixed up with some thief and they hauled him off to prison. And it's all your doing, you bastard, you good-for-nothing! And even worse than you is your whore of a mother, you shameless devil!"

Cassi flashed a sign of repulsion and the woman didn't miss it.

"There," she said to everybody who was listening, "he says he doesn't have anything to do with all this but he just now accused himself when I called that big rat of a mamma of his a whore. . . . He's a devil but that mamma of his . . . she's really something . . . thinks she's got English in her blood. English, my foot. . . !"

At this point, Ines directed an unbecoming sound at Cassi, a sound accompanied by an obscene gesture, and this provoked general hilarity among those present. But Cassi remained silent, numb with fear while the pathetic, social outcast continued:

"You are evil but your mamma is even worse! When she found out that I was carrying a child in my belly, why she tossed me right out. She didn't care . . . didn't have mercy or pity on me because I didn't have any place to go to. And the child was her own grandchild and she had raised me. . . ! I'd just come here from out of the backlands . . . oh, dear God, dear God! If it hadn't been for a friend of mine who helped me, I'd have had to put the child out in the street. . . . God forgive your mamma for what she did to me and to my child . . . the child of the man standing right here, too. God forgive him."

Then the poor black woman bent over to grab the hem of her filthy skirt so she could dry the tears she was shedding over her sad destiny. Perhaps, though, even more than crying over her own fate, she was sobbing about the miserable existence of her child, a boy who had already come to know the House of Detention before he had reached ten years of age.

Thanks to the intervention of the owner of the local saloon who, along with the police, had the responsibility of maintaining order there in that forsaken, poverty ridden stronghold, the gathering of people began to disperse and Cassi was able to continue on his way down the road. As a good-bye, however, the women yelled after him using coarse, vulgar language while Ines continued to curse him:

"You scum . . . you miserable cur! Don't you feel any shame for what you did to me? You'll pay for it some day . . . you son of a bitch. . . !"

As soon as he saw that he was free from danger, Cassi breathed a great sigh of relief, regained control of himself, felt the money still in his vest pocket and said to himself:

"It happens every time! Why did I have to bump into that black woman. . . ? Fortunately, it was in a part of town where nobody knows me. If it'd been anywhere else . . . what a scandal! The papers would have been sure to get hold of it and then. . . . Well, I'm never coming around here again and as far as she's concerned, well . . . she can go to hell for all I care! I'm going to stay home with my money."

Although his child — his first child — already knew the inside of the police station, no thoughts about him or his future were running through Cassi's head. . . .

X

Clara dos Anjos, leaning halfway out of her bedroom window, was looking out at the motionless trees submerged in the shadows of night and contemplating the abundantly starred skies. She was waiting.

The evening was lovely and moonless; it was silent and august. The trees were standing straight and their outlines were traced against the sky. Not a breath of wind was stirring but it was still cool. Not even the slightest of sounds came from the natural world, neither the chirping of crickets or the hooting of owls. The quiet and mysterious night seemed to be awaiting an interrogator who, deep within its realm of peace and tranquility, would seek out his own heart.

Clara was contemplating the dark heavens above dotted with twinkling stars. The darkness was not total, however, thanks to the luminescent dust that sifted down from the limitless skies. Leaning out of the window that looked out upon the back-yard of their house, Clara was able to take in nearly all of the celestial dome above her. She didn't know the names of any of those heavenly jewels and she could recognize only the Southern Cross but her eyes, along with her errant thoughts, strayed all across the night sky taking in everything she could glimpse. Then her eyes returned to the Cross. For the first time she noticed that there was a black spot very close to it, a splotch of sky as black as charcoal. And she asked herself:

"Are there blemishes in Heaven, too?"

She related this discovery to her ordeal. Tears would not be long in coming now, and sighing, she thought to herself:

"Dear God . . . what's to become of me?"

If he had abandoned her, she would be completely broken, lost, with no hope of remission, salvation or redemption. . . . A girl in the flower of youth and full of life, she was like that lovely evening sky, alluringly illuminated by starlight, but along with such beauty, heavenly light, and indescribable poetry, was that black, charcoal-like blemish. Could Cassi have really abandoned her? She couldn't bring herself to believe it, although it had been nearly ten days since he last came to see her. If he had abandoned her, what would happen to her? A need came over her to ask how, if indeed it was true that she had been betrayed, how it had happened? How could she have allowed herself to be so hopelessly lost?

Clara wasn't able to grasp the various aspects of her downfall; she could remember only a few of the different phases and she was unable to see them with any real clarity. For her, everything seemed to be headed at a full gallop toward disgrace. . . .

In the beginning, Clara's first impression of Cassi had been positive; she remembered the mournful wail and twang of his guitar followed by the rolling of his eyes, a movement he exaggerated and into which he poured a strangely sweet, but at the same time, blazing hot flame. Fully prepared for the effects of his playing, the girl was deeply impressed by all this. Later, there was the general opposition to him; the continuous talking about him, evil things said about him. Clara's godfather did this as well as her mother and Dona Margarida. This insistence upon denigrating Cassi made Clara picture him in her own mind, as an exceptional young man who inspired envy in others because of his boldness, his prowess with the Spanish guitar and his singing. She never believed any of the things they said about him. . . . In fact, the very first time she ever saw him he seemed so modest, so reserved in manner and so refined in demeanor that she knew he couldn't possibly be any of those awful things people said he was . . . months later when she talked to him alone for the first time through the grill work of their house, this conception of him was even more reinforced. His conversation was so innocent and honest. . . . He spoke of getting a job and marrying her. . . . Cassi seemed to sweep away all the objections and doubts she brought up about the viability of their marriage and he could do this with frankness and endless assurances. Moreover, to show off better his legitimacy as a suitor aside from the great passion that he said, fired him, he compared his own poverty to the opposition of her parents and his lack of status and learning to the liability of her skin color. The conclusion of this comparison of their relative positions was, he argued, that he could not aspire to a greater, more prestigious union with any woman more educated, more learned than he.

His ideal, therefore, was Clara; poor, affectionate, simple, modest, a good homemaker and a woman who would be careful with the meagre amount of money he was able to bring home. . . .

And day by day, he increasingly won the girl's confidence. She began to convince herself of his worth and dreamed constantly about the little white house in the mountains where she and her love for Cassi would nestle. Each time she saw him, Clara inquired about the steps he had taken to secure employment. But with blandishments and caresses, Cassi said to her in sugar-coated words:

"Be still, my dearest love! Rome wasn't built in a day. . . . We've got to be patient. . . . I spoke to doctor Brotero the other day and he gave me a recommendation for Senator Carvalhais. I looked this fellow up and he told me that as far as work on the docks was concerned, he couldn't arrange anything for me just now. . . . He said that he'd already asked those people to do a lot of things for him and that now, he owed them some favors. . . ."

Hearing all this, Clara felt herself being undone by the warmth, the sweetness and the dizzying amorousness of his voice. Her Cassi was truly good, sincere and a sweetheart . . . a real lover. . . .

"Why don't you ask daddy for my hand?" Clara asked him one day.

Cassi, without hesitating, and with the most convincing and frank tone, answered:

"I can't just yet, my love. Your parents don't. . . . Even though your godfather isn't with us any more. . . ."

On hearing these words, Clara became frightened and looked at him, terrified. Cassi, however, didn't notice the girl's shock nor was he aware of the suspicions that, from time to time, arose in her mind about any part he might have played in her godfather's murder. In the beginning, Clara had been virtually certain that Cassi was somehow involved in the crime but days later when she spoke to him whether it was because of the emotional impact of their first rendezvous or because of the tenderness that exuded from his entire being and with which he soon engulfed Clara, she brushed aside her suspicions and lost that sense of terror that Cassi had begun to inspire in her. Her feeble intelligence and her lack of experience in and understanding of life, in addition to the strong inclination she had, all acted upon Clara's mind in such a way that, in her eyes, Cassi appeared to be innocent of anything to do with her godfather's death. Even so, certain doubts still came over her . . . but he was such an amiable man. . . !

Without hesitation Cassi responded to her question in his most persuasive and frank tone of voice.

"I can't just yet, my love. Your parents don't. . . . It's true that your godfather isn't with us any more but Dona Engracia can't stand me. Besides, Dona Margarida doesn't seem to like me either. . . . By the way, wasn't it strange what happened between her and Timbo?"

"Why do you run around with him, Cassi?"

"What should I do? He's not good or bad as far as I'm concerned. He looks me up and I can't just chase him away, can I? That's all there is to it."

"But is all this really the only reason you don't ask me to marry you right now? Is it just because there are people around who don't like you? No, that can't be the only reason, . . . no."

"No, you're right. It's not the only reason. It's really because I'm unemployed. If I had a job, it would be all right with everybody. But, and you can be sure of this, just as soon as I get a job, I'm going to ask you to marry me."

Thinking of this, Clara once again contemplated the profusely star-studded sky, but she came upon the black blemish and was sad.

Remembering other such words and incidents, Clara directed all her strength toward trying to analyze what she had been feeling for Cassi. She could not understand why she had allowed Cassi, whose pretext was a need for shelter from the torrential downpour he said was about to begin, to get into her bedroom very late one night. Clara did not know how to break it down. She could not understand what had happened. Trying to remember, it seemed to her that at the critical moment, she suffered a lapse of willpower or resolution and ceased being the person she really was and became something else, merely a puppet in Cassi's hands. Her eyes were blinded to what was happening as if she were lost in some sort of cloud, and a wave of heedlessness swept over her. Grouping together all of her memories and recollections of what had happened that evening, Clara seemed to recall that she felt as if she were transcending herself . . . she felt light and airy, soaring. . . . Then, with cold-blooded design but without brutality or violence of any sort, Cassi took her, stealing the only treasure Clara possessed and damning her for the rest of her life, shaming her from that night forth in the eyes of all, and leaving her bereft of any hope for redemption or salvation.

Clara began to weep silently. Deep in the night a locomotive whistle echoed through the still air like a mournful wail and even the trees trembled. Above a neighboring meadow a firefly was emitting its bluish-silver light and above the house, bats silently darted about. In the distance the mountains took on a sinister aspect like black shrouded giants standing sentry duty. Everything was silent and Clara strained her ears and eyes hoping to receive some sign from the mysterious darkness which would inform her of her destiny . . . or a sign which might show her the path to salvation. But she waited in vain.

Clara looked up again at the heavens, at a sky embellished with stars that never seemed to tire of sparkling brightly. Then she found the Southern Cross once more and offered a prayer to God for forgiveness and salvation. Still watching the heavens, Clara moved her line of vision a bit to the side . . . the indelible black spot was still there.

Cassi never came. The roosters were beginning to crow and Clara, sobbing, closed the window. Still crying, she lay down on her bed. But sleep did not come. Instead, the menacing spectre of discovery by her parents who might well have noticed her absence passed in front of her eyes and filled her with terror like a vision of some ghost or goblin might.

But neither inside or outside their house did anybody suspect her. The indications of pregnancy were, for the time being at least, not apparent, although she often felt sick and nauseous without reason. Clara was able to disguise her sickness so well that her mother didn't notice anything.

Dona Engracia was her normal self, perceiving very little but completely confident in the vigilance she exercised over her daughter. During the weekdays, Joaquim rarely saw the girl except in the mornings as he was leaving the house and in the evenings just as he arrived home from work.

The miserable death of Marramaque, his *compadre,* had left Joaquim truly sad and deeply grieved. Their friendship had been an old one and Joaquim owed many unforgotten favors to the poor, old doorman. Marramaque had increased and put the finishing touches on the scant knowledge that he, Joaquim, possessed so that he could become a postman. Clara's father still felt that he was indebted to Marramaque for this unsolicited service. More than once Marramaque had attained recommendations for Joaquim so that he received promotions and the result was that, to some extent, Joaquim owed everything that he was to Marramaque. The card games on Sunday afternoons would never again take place. Even Lafoes had been transferred elsewhere to tend to some fountains. This wise old guard had finally realized that Cassi would bring disgrace and misery to somebody. He was unable to prevent this but he did not wish to witness it any further, especially since he was feeling sorry about having brought the *modinha* player into the postman's house in the first place. That good-for-nothing scoundrel Cassi had deceived him! He, Lafoes, had acted in good faith, but. . . .

The only person who still dropped by at Joaquim's house was Meneses. He, however, was quite insane by this time, a total monomaniac. He fled from any type of normal conversation and insisted upon presenting his plans for a motor car that was to have no wheels. "It's a great invention," he would end up saying.

"The wheel, my dear Joaquim, is a retrogression in our world of machines. In its actuation, because of the friction of the shaft on the bearings and the friction on its other means of transmitting force, all of which result from the laws of passive resistance, it loses a lot of its effective energy. If, in order to move about, we or horses or elephants — any or all the animals — were to make use of wheels to move from one point to another, the force we expended would be many times greater than that we really should be using. I eliminate the wheels on my 'Walker' (this is what his apparatus was called) and I imitate the locomotion of land animals. I hesitated between reptiles and mammals, but finally I decided to use the mammals as models. By coupling feet together in a set connected by chains that can expand and contract like our spring chairs, I shall create a machine which, with the same amount of force and fuel that any regular locomotive uses, will produce double the usable energy return of the locomotive."

Hearing all of this, Joaquim began to yawn, but Meneses, entirely immersed in his private mechanical dream, did not notice that he was boring his friend. He kept right on talking, babbling about his crazy dream, the "Walker," and drinking his rum.

Sometimes he would still eat with the postman and his family but whenever he did so, he directed very little of his conversation to Clara, at least as long as they were at the table. He was afraid that in talking to her, the secret that existed between them would get out.

The old dentist, however, had stopped seeing Cassi. Cassi, in his turn, avoided Meneses fearing that the old man would discover his plans to run away and tell everybody, thereby arousing Clara's suspicions.

Other times, in search of some conversation and a meal, the old dentist looked up Leonardo Flores. Strictly speaking, Flores was not going through hard times. With his pension and the financial assistance his children provided, the family always had enough to eat and never had to go hungry.

Thanks to his wife's dedication and care, his household ran along smoothly. He never interfered with the economic operations of their home. He surrendered each entire monthly pension check to his wife and she bought everything for him — clothes, newspapers, tobacco, liquor, everything. . . . In the beginning, the good Dona Castorina wanted to see if he could do without alcohol but she soon saw that it was worse if he did; he fell into a deep depression, and suffered from an apathy and listlessness that made him seem more dead than alive. She resolved to make one more sacrifice to their sad marriage — she would allow her husband to have his liquor, and when he wanted to go out, she gave him a few coins for the purchase of his favorite drink.

Meneses' visits were particularly pleasing to Flores' wife because not only did her husband enjoy them but they tended to reduce his desire to go out.

There were times during which Flores did not move from the house unless it was for some very important reason such as going to the Treasury Building to pick up his pension check, but there were also times when he was completely taken by the delirious urge to get out and roam about. Although she understood that her husband was unable to stay home all the time, Dona Castorina always tried to prevent him from ever going out because of the insane things that he did. A certain day would always come, however, and then. . . .

On Sundays when Meneses came visiting, Flores received him with a grandiloquent, heraldic and aristocratic wordiness. But then, with great melancholy and heartbreak he knew would not be remedied, he said:

"Only you seek me out now, Meneses! The others have abandoned me. . . . Ah, well. . . . But poetry! Poetry has given me so many great moments but it estranges me ever more in my dedicated service to it. . . ."

They began drinking and, when they were properly warmed up, each man lost himself in his personal mania. Meneses explained the subtle mechanics of his "Walker" and Leonardo recited his most recent sonnet, usually a poem which, although somewhat disconnected, still retained a certain music, the imponderable nostalgia of things encountered in a dream, and was permeated with perfume, all characteristics of his poetry.

Suddenly, Meneses began snoring on the sofa and Leonardo, leaving his sonorous world of rime and verse and standing up to contemplate better his prostrate comrade, arms folded, declared:

"Imbecile! Sleep, you imbecile! You Philistine . . . you bourgeois. . . !"

And then he returned to the creation of verse, which he continued with a vengeance until it was supper time. Then, he shouted at Meneses to wake up, upbrading him with poetic invective and insults.

According to the usual practices of our poor families, Sunday's supper was set on the table before the usual hour. This meal was known as the *ajantarado* and it was so in Flores' house on Sundays. On the other days of the week, however, it was served later, almost at the usual dining hour. Their meal that Sunday was not a pleasant one. Meneses was lost in his mania and Flores in his. During the entire meal, both men, having given themselves over completely to their respective obsessions, kept babbling about things that nobody else could understand. Meneses, at least, was calm; his friend however, was making faces while he ate, roaring noises, and agitatedly stroking his still black beard which terminated in a sharply pointed *cavaignac*.

From time to time, Dona Castorina, Flores' wife, reprimanded him as if she were speaking to a small child:

"Flores, show some manners when you eat! You're acting like a child!"

It was a rare occasion when one of the children was present at the table. They were usually out playing soccer and their mother would hold supper for them. If it happened that they were present, the poet's offspring looked at their father with expressionless faces, with no desire to admonish him for his behavior but without the heartlessness to laugh at him. Flores' madness was a curious thing; it manifested itself now and then, often with much time in between attacks, but it could also occur frequently within the brief space of a single day. Alcohol had certainly contributed to his mental degeneration but, even without it, his mental estrangement would have taken place. Everybody who had known him since he was a small boy knew that he had always possessed an excess of insanity's symptoms. His tics, his whims, his deliriums and his other confusedly understood traits had caused his close friends to fear continually for his mental stability. Moreover, and in spite of all these characteristics, he himself added the destructive force of the strong alcoholic drinks he consumed. In order to understand the true nature of Flores' insanity, one must take into account all the whisky, gin, rum and cane liquor he drank.

On this evening, after eating supper and while drinking coffee in the little garden behind the house, a garden that Flores himself cultivated with a rarely seen devotion, much to the astonishment of all who knew his condition, Leonardo, suddenly looked up to the heavens and shouted at Meneses. Flores quickly set down his cup and said:

"Meneses! Come see how lovely this afternoon sky is! It's not just the gold and purple of the twilight you're seeing, it's not the dark blue of the hills which, with the approach of nightfall, is going to grow increasingly black. . . . No, there's more, my dear old Meneses! There's a greenish hue to the heavens, an immaterial green, not the green of the sea, not the green of the trees, not the green of emeralds and it's not the green of Minerva's eyes . . . it's a celestial green distinct from all the other greens we're accustomed to seeing. . . . Let's get out, let's rejoice in Nature!"

"Let it be, Flores. We can see it from right here, from where we are."

"You're an idiot . . . you're certainly no artist. . . ! Well, if you're not coming with me, I'm going alone!"

Dona Castorina intervened, saying in a natural voice:

"Why do you want to go out, Leonardo? You're just fine right here with your friend, Seu Meneses. Anyway, you need rest and relaxation. . . ."

"Woman! Do you know who I am?" asked Flores, with his habitual habit of crossing his arms and burying his chin in his chest when he intended to speak of something with great solemnity:

"I know very well who you are. You're Leonardo Flores, my husband," responded his wife smiling.

"That's not all I am. I'm more than that!" Flores insisted, glowering.

"What are you, then?" Dona Castorina asked him.

"I am a poet!"

Saying this, Flores strode first into the living room and then into the bedroom.

"Where are you going?" his wife asked him.

"I'm going to get dressed. I want to see this jeweled twilight, this sunset of precious metals, of dreams and chimeras. I am a poet, woman!"

Dona Castorina knew that when he was so excited about going out, it was bad to oppose him. She said nothing further to her husband but went to where Meneses was sitting and asked him to go along with Leonardo. The old dentist was not feeling well and his only real wish was to rest. But since Dona Castorina had asked him to, he had no other choice except to accompany his comrade. They set out on foot, together, walking all over and drinking heavily whenever they found an appropriate place. Meneses was dragging himself along with Flores, dilating his nostrils and forcing his face into horrible contractions, was smoothing out his "beard" and saying:

"What beauty! What beauty! I want to breath it all in, to fill myself with it . . . I want to absorb all the perfume of this divine twilight! Were it not for Nature, for the heavens, the birds, the murmuring waters, how could we survive. . . ?''

But after a pause, he added disconsolately:

"Life is so banal, so tiresome . . . we're part of Nature too, but what are we worth to it? The bourgeoisie and all their rules and regulations choke us off. . . .''

Night had already fallen but Leonardo Flores showed no signs of wanting to return home. Meneses, however, was having a great deal of difficulty in keeping up. They were crossing a stretch of deserted street when the old dentist said to his friend:

"Leonardo, my legs have had it. Let's rest a while."

"Where?"

"Let's sit down over there on the grass. There's a little thicket just off the roadway . . . I just can't go any further, old friend."

So they abandoned the public thoroughfare and sought out the thicket. Meneses had a lot of trouble in just sitting down but Leonardo stretched out immediately. They had been drinking quite a lot and drunkenness was overtaking them. Leonardo, still able to speak was looking up at the stars which were beginning to twinkle and shine:

"How lovely the sky is! Up there in heaven, I'm certain one would never find any ministers, congressmen or presidents. . . . How fine that must be!''

The dentist didn't sit up very long; he quickly lay down. Just as soon as he had uttered those final words, Leonardo also fell into a deep sleep. They slept on the grass with their eyes raised toward the star-filled heavens. . . .

* * * * *

At daybreak, Leonardo woke up in the meadow, muddled and dizzy. Noticing Meneses who still lay at his side, he tried to get him up. But his efforts were in vain. The old man had died. A cardiac arrest had carried him away. Realizing that his friend was dead, Leonardo quickly stood up, picked up the cap that was lying near his head, and placed it over his old friend's face. That face still displayed Meneses' venerable white beard and Leonardo began to exclaim:

"Oh, Sun! Glorious Sun of dawnings and resurrections! Divine Sun, you who hold the spirit of life for all of us . . . men and plants, beasts and geniuses, insects and vampires, snails and all things beautiful! Come, O Sun, come and kiss this august Emperor's head (pointing to Meneses' stiff body), one who for evermore has plunged into the eternal darkness and who will see You again only when he returns as a tree, as a bush, as a bird or finally, when he returns again as a man! Oh, kiss him yet one more time! Kiss him because he loved You and because so many times he soared through the sidereal spaces hoping only to glimpse Your brilliance and then to die, having gazed upon Your face!''

Leonardo did not realize it but several passers-by had stopped to listen to his words and to watch his strange facial expressions. The most curious ones drew nearer to observe this curious and bizarre scene, a man who appeared to be either drunk or crazy, babbling incomprehensible things and gesticulating wildly in front of some poor, old, dead man. They called the police, and Leonardo, still jabbering away and gesturing, was taken off to the station; after his picture was taken and after the other police officialities, Meneses was taken off to the morgue.

The first official police action when they received him at the station was to have Leonardo removed *immediately* to the asylum. In truth, the poet was speaking incoherently; he couldn't even tell them who he was. Many people recognized his face but for these people, he was simply ''the poet.'' With the arrival of Praxedes, however, things changed. Praxedes was in the habit of going down to the police station every morning to see if he could pick up some business. When he came by that morning, he happened to meet Leonardo and learned that an old man who had been drinking a great deal and who had often been seen with Leonardo was discovered dead, lying next to Flores, and that the deceased was carried off to the morgue. Praxedes realized immediately that they were talking about Meneses. Making himself useful — (being an accommodating fellow by nature) — Praxedes, from whom the police held no secrets, informed the Commissioner about the identity of both Leonardo and Meneses. The authorities then gave him the responsibility of informing the relatives and friends of both men about what had happened. Praxedes ran to Joaquim dos Anjos's house to fulfill his mission but he was greeted by only Joaquim's wife and daughter:

''Quincas isn't here right now,'' said Dona Engracia, ''He went out earlier.''

''But you could telephone him at the Post Office,'' Clara suggested.

''I thought about that but I can't remember his section number.''

The girl gave it to him and doctor Praxedes stood up to go, very diplomatically. After bidding the ladies good-bye, he begged their pardon:

''You dear ladies must forgive me, but I couldn't avoid coming here. I knew of two close friends of doctor Meneses: one was Joaquim and the other was Senhor Cassi, but he's not around any more. . . .''

Clara suffered a terrible shock:

''He's not around any more! ! ! ?''

''Goodness, Clara!'' said Dona Engracia, ''Are you so alarmed about it?''

''Oh, no; it's only that a couple of days ago Seu Meneses said that papa had seen him,'' said Clara, disguising her true feelings.

''It must have been some time ago, my dear lady,'' ventured Praxedes, putting it as delicately as he could, ''because it's been more than two weeks since he left for Sao Paulo. I know because I even said good-bye to him.''

Praxedes left and as soon as she could Clara ran to her bedroom to cry. She was hopelessly lost; he had in fact abandoned her. What was she to do now? How could she hide her pregnancy, a condition that little by little, was beginning to make itself apparent? What would her parents do to her? Her fate would be atrocious! ! ! She could formulate all these questions but she could not supply any answers to them. . . . Cassi had run away, he had fled. . . . Now, she saw clearly just what Cassi was really like! Everything that the others said about him was the truth! Her innocence, her lack of experience in her life, her good faith and her juvenile ardor had completely blinded her to the truth. It was all as they said. . . . But why had he chosen her? Because she was poor and, in addition to being poor, she was a mulatto. Her unfortunate godfather had been right. . . . And Cassi *was* the one who murdered him.

He had actually told her so, not acknowledging that there hadn't been any real reason to do so, but showing the same indifference everybody shows about the fate of a poor girl like Clara. Things always worked out that way; it was the rule. . . . It was from this state of societal indifference to such things, and from the sure knowledge that no one in such a morally degenerate environment would pursue him and see that he received his proper punishment that Cassi was able to acquire the necessary courage to do the things he did. For above all else, Cassi was a coward. He never succumbed to his desires or whims for just any girl; he always sought out carefully his victims from among the girls of poor economic and social standing, girls who could do him little or no harm, thinking not only of anything the authorities might possibly do but also of what the girl's parents and friends might try to do to him.

That was where his strength lay; the rest of it, all the paraphernalia of the *modinha,* the guitar performances, the letters, the sighs and longing glances — a complete arsenal of make-believe love — Cassi, bereft of character and an utter cynic besides, knew how to use better than anyone else.

What would become of Clara now, dishonored, shamed in the eyes of everybody and indelibly stained for life?

She felt lost, isolated, and alone in life. Her parents would never look upon her as they had once looked upon her; she knew that as soon as they found out about what had happened, people would scorn her; and there wasn't a single libertine in the area who wouldn't be after her, believing that anybody who's done it once will do it a hundred times. With her condition nearly exposed and her imminent ostracism, rejected by everyone, Clara felt like running away and hiding somewhere. But where? Inexperienced, poor and young, she would only fall prey to the sexual voraciousness of a large number of Cassis or people even worse than he. She would end up like that other poor girl, the one they call Mme. Bacamarte — filthy, alcoholic, and contaminated by all manner of shameful diseases.

Clara thought about dying, about killing herself, but finally, she simply broke down and cried. Sobbing, she prayed to Our Lady for courage. Suddenly, a thought came to her! Could she eliminate her condition? Could she undo what had already been done? To do so would be a crime and it would involve a danger to her life . . . but it was worth the risk to try! Who could show her the remedy? She ran through her brief list of friends and found only one who might be able to help her out, Dona Margarida!

At this moment, however, Clara's mother shouted at her from the back of the house:

"Clara! Are you asleep? Go see who's knocking at the door."

"I'm going, momma."

It was a messenger bringing them a telegram from her father saying that because he had to take care of Meneses' burial arrangements, he would arrive home late that evening, but he would have dinner there.

Clara and her mother, however, didn't wait for him. They ate supper earlier. Clara was deeply preoccupied, thinking about the remedy that she was going to see Dona Margarida about arranging for her but Dona Engracia, disturbed about Meneses' death said:

"Poor Meneses! To die like that way out in the boondocks. . . . Why didn't he go home? He was really quite old, wasn't he Clara?"

"He must have been over seventy."

"Oh, that doesn't mean anything. Why, there are some who last longer than. . . . Clara, has it crossed your mind that for some time now, there've been a lot of bad things happening to us?"

"Not so many. Only two really; my godfather's death and. . . ."

"And that's not many? Especially the *way* they've been happening. . . . God help us! You know, I've even got a feeling that something else bad's going to happen to us. . . ."

"Oh, momma! I know that all this has been painful for you but you've just got to face the facts. . . ."

"Well, I'm happy that Cassi has gone away. He was a bad apple . . . let him go to the devil!"

Clara felt like crying but she held back. Her mind was made up; tomorrow she would ask Dona Margarida to help her get an abortion.

Joaquim dos Anjos finally arrived home and told Clara and Dona Engracia about everything that had happened to Meneses and Leonardo. Since Meneses didn't have anyone to tend to things for him, Joaquim had taken care of the burial details. As soon as he was cleared of having anything to do with the death and as soon as he was in his right mind again, Leonardo was brought to his wife by the police. Just as soon as he got home again and in the company and care of Dona Castorina, Flores seemed to recover his senses and to have a perfect understanding of what had happened to his friend. He was lucid and rational; it was the true Leonardo who, showing not the slightest delirium, wept over his comrade's passing, sensing perhaps, that in it there was some indication of his own end.

Engracia heard "Quincas' " narration and then asked him, ingenuously:

"This Leonardo . . . is he an intelligent man, 'Quincas'?"

"He is Engracia. Why?"

"Then why does he drink so much?"

"Who knows? Just his vice, maybe . . . a habit, some quirk of his nature, unhappiness . . . nobody knows," observed her husband.

"But I see a lot of learned men around these parts who don't drink."

"Engracia, do you think that all learned men are also intelligent men?"

"Well, I thought so."

Clara was surprised that her mother's opinion was not correct; she, too, narrow-minded and believing in popular notions, thought that any kind of a *doutor* had to be a wise and intelligent man.

Announcing that he was tired, Joaquim went off to lie down. His wife and daughter followed.

Soon, everything was silent in the house and on the street outside but Clara no longer waited in the half open window for a visit from her seducer. She had worn herself out standing vigil for so many nights in a row and now, after what she had learned from Praxedes, she had lost all hope. Cassi had fled and she, facing society's condemnation and her parent's shame and anguish, was left alone with a child growing in her womb. Immediately, her thoughts again were of the remedy she hoped would remove the stain before her mistake was noticed. She was afraid and full of remorse; she was also afraid of dying and she deeply regretted having to plan coldly the murder of an unborn and innocent being. But it had to be done. . . . Clara began to consider carefully just how Dona Margarida might answer her; she weighed the pros and cons and realized, there in the calm of her room, that Dona Margarida would neither take part in or even suggest any such criminal remedy. She was a respectable woman with a rigorously strong will, profoundly honest and courageous. There was no amount of tears and supplications that could make her take part in any criminal act whatsoever. What, then, could Clara do? She again examined her list of acquaintances hoping to discover on it someone who might be able to perform this service for her. But she found no one . . . and there were very few acquaintances indeed for her to choose from. But if she had the money and with Mme. Bacamarte's help, maybe. . . . And yet another idea came to her. Clara was helping Dona Margarida with her sewing and embroidery and was able to earn a little money. She had never had much to do with the woman but she believed she might be able to ask her for a loan of twenty or thirty *mil-reis* and pay her back later. But what would the pretext be? Clara thought about it and tried out several different lies and finally thought of one which might do: she would say that she had to buy a present for her mother whose birthday was soon. Clara smiled contentedly when she had finally organized her elaborate web of lies and thought she was saved; but there was one thing with which the girl had not reckoned: the sagacity of the old German woman.

Dona Margarida was a tall, robust, muscular woman with a large head and energetic features. She had blue eyes and brownish blond hair. Her entire life had been marked by heroism and goodness. Although she had been born in another land and surrounded by different people, her unconscious and humanitarian mysticism, inherited from her maternal grandparents, had kept her constantly ensnarled with the Czar's police and made her identify immediately with the strange people she discovered here. She learned their language with all its quirks and idiomatic expressions, picked up their habits, and came to appreciate their food, but she never lost a bit of the tenacity, of the stick-to-itiveness or of the forthright courage of her origins. She liked the postman's family a great deal but, deep down, she also believed that they were too docile, too passive, poorly equipped for the struggle against the evil and insidious forces of life.

When Clara spoke to her about the loan, the advance, she became concerned. The postman's daughter had never asked for anything like this before. . . . What did it mean? Dona Margarida did not respond immediately to her solicitation but looked her squarely in the eye with her piercing and, at the moment, hard gaze. After a moment she asked:

"Clara, dear . . . what do you want this money for?"

Unable to bear up under the German woman's gaze, the girl lowered her eyes and almost in a whisper, explained the purpose of the money she was asking. But Dona Margarida didn't believe her and, with her eyes peering in an inquisitorial way into Clara's, she observed with maternal energy:

"Clara, you aren't telling the truth . . . you're hiding something."

The girl tried to deny it but Dona Margarida, sensing that she was hiding something of grave importance, bombarded her with questions and, finally, Clara had no other choice except to confess everything. She began to cry but Dona Margarida, not allowing herself to be shaken visibly by what she heard during Clara's confession even though she was deeply shaken by her story, was already thinking about what they should do next. Dona Margarida was suddenly filled with an infinite sorrow for the disgraced girl and for her parents, but the sorrow grew even keener when she thought about Clara's horrible future. Even so, she gave no indication of what she was feeling deep in her soul.

Without giving any explanation, Dona Margarida stood up a moment later and turning to Clara, ordered imperiously:

"We're going to speak to your mother."

Not making the slightest objection, the postman's daughter obeyed her. When they got to Joaquim's house they found Dona Engracia inside innocently going about her domestic chores. Dona Margarida took Clara's mother to one side and began to tell her about what had happened to her daughter. Dona Engracia couldn't control herself; as soon as she comprehended the gravity of the situation, she began to cry profusely, to whine, sob and pity herself. Between one torrent of tears and another, she was finally able to say:

"But Clara. . . ! Clara, my child. . . ! Oh, my God, my God. . . !''

Her daughter, also crying, went to her, knelt down at her mother's feet holding her hands in the manner of one who is praying, and still sobbing, uttered these words:

"Forgive me mamma! For the love of God, forgive me. . . .''

Standing up, Dona Margarida said nothing but watched this dismal scene — the disgracing of a poor but honest home — with profound and unlimited sadness. Her pain, however, would not have been noted by anyone because of her apparent calm and because of the steadiness of her gaze.

Finally, when both women seemed to have become calmer, she interjected:

"Clara, do you know where the family of this fellow lives?"

Clara, still sobbing, replied:

"Yes,"

Dona Engracia then asked:

"Why?"

Dona Margarida explained that before they did anything else, even before they told *Seu* Joaquim about what had happened, they had to come to some kind of understanding with Cassi's family. She, Dona Margarida, accompanied by Clara, would go to his house immediately. Mother and daughter agreed; and Clara got dressed.

The residence in which Cassi's parents lived was in one of the suburban districts which was still thought to be elegant by the people who lived there, people who still bothered to make such distinctions. Certain parts of the area are considered to be chic and specific parts of certain districts also enjoy such consideration, although they may or may not truly merit it. Meier, for example, is not thought to be very chic but

Boca do Mato is or at least, was. Cascadura, however, doesn't enjoy any reputation for fashionability or for any other vain-glorious distinction. But Jacarepagua, the station which the former serves, basks in the highest esteem.

The house of the famous Spanish guitar player's parents wasn't located on the street that bordered on the Central railroad but on one of the clean, well-cared-for cobblestone streets that cuts across the area. This often happens in the suburbs; alongside some street nearly hidden in the dense underbrush, one unexpectedly finds an elegant little avenue, one with a distinctly urbane air about it. One asks why such a little used thoroughfare should deserve such care and attention; the local historians explain that the reason is that years ago some deputy or minister or some city councilman must have lived there. . . .

The house of Senhor Azevedo looked good from the outside but anyone who looked at it carefully would have to conclude that the most imposing part of the house — the coping and the outcropping and grated balconies built-up high on the house — was all new. In fact, when Cassi's father bought it, the house was a simple and modest chalet but with time and with his sluggish though secure prosperity, he was able to continue slowly to improve the residence, finally giving it the aspect of a solid, middle class family dwelling. It was not high in front; the land, however, fell away rapidly as one moved toward the rear so that in the back of the house, there was a basement, in which Cassi had lived lately. The new wing, also behind the house, had a basement containing very unpleasant rooms occupied by the boy's chickens and by old or useless things that the family kept, not wishing to throw them away.

Dona Margarida rang the bell decisively and climbed up the short staircase leading to the front door of the house. She told the maid that she wanted to speak to the lady of the house. Dona Salustiana, ready for anything except that particular visitor and the message she bore, did not hesitate in asking the two women to come in. Both were nicely dressed and nothing gave any indication about what had brought them there. Clara's eyes were red from crying but this passed by unnoticed. Dona Salustiana, greeting the two women exaggeratedly, made a great show of welcoming them. Without hesitating Dona Margarida told her what had happened. After hearing her story, Cassi's mother thought for a moment and in an ironic tone of voice, said:

"What do you want *me* to do about it?"

Until then, Clara hadn't said a single word but even before she knew that the girl was just another victim of her son's libertinage, Dona Salustiana didn't bother to look at her or, if she did, it was with evident disdain. Clara noticed all this and was filled with anger and rancor at what she had to go through not to mention all that she had already suffered and all that she had yet to suffer.

When she heard Dona Salustiana's question, Clara couldn't control herself; frantic, she blurted out:

"I want him to marry me!"

Dona Salustiana turned livid; the little mulatto girl's intervention had exasperated her. She glared at Clara full of malevolence and indignation, intentionally allowing her gaze to linger on for a moment. Finally, however, she spit out her response:

''What did you say, you little nigger?''

Dona Margarida, not giving Clara a chance to respond to the insult and immediately raising her voice, spoke with a commanding force:

''Clara's right. What she's asking for is the only proper thing . . . and you'd better know that we're here seeking justice, not to listen to any of your abuse!''

Dona Salustiana then turned to Dona Margarida and asked, speaking slowly as if that would give her words greater significance:

''And just who do you think you are . . . raising your voice like that in my house?''

But Dona Margarida was not intimidated:

''I know very well who I am, madam! When I decide to do what's right, I am not scared off by anything or anybody! ! !''

Dona Margarida spoke in a calm voice and Dona Salustiana, taking note of this attitude, decided to change her tactics; she screamed at her daughters:

''Catarina! Irene! Come here this instant and see how this woman is insulting me!''

The girls came immediately and seeing the aroused countenance of the Teutonic/-Slavic woman and the pitiful figure of Clara, understood at once that Cassi was somehow mixed up in and at the bottom of it all. Dona Margarida explained it to them but just as she spoke of Cassi's marrying Clara, Dona Salustiana broke in again:

''There! Do you see. . . ? That's it. . . ! Can you imagine such a thing? Just think of it . . . my son married to this . . . this. . . .''

The girls intervened:

''What do you mean, mamma?''

Their mother went on:

''Married to somebody like this . . . indeed! Why, what would my grandfather, Lord Jones, the British Consul in Santa Catarina, say about this? What do you think he would say if he could see such a shameful thing befalling us? What would he think of such a thing?''

She stopped talking for a moment but an instant later, added:

''These people are ridiculous! They're complaining about being abused, really! It's always the same, old, song. . . . Did my boy bind and gag them . . . did he threaten them with a knife or a gun. . . ? No, of course not. The fault is theirs and theirs alone. . . .''

Dona Margarida was about to ask, ''What's your decision, then?'' when she heard footsteps on the stairs. It was the master of the house. Coming through the door, Senhor Azevedo came unexpectedly upon the scene. He walked no further but stood very still in the middle of the room looking at everyone. Then he asked:

''What's going on here?''

''Oh, papa,'' said one of the girls, but Clara, realizing who the man was, suddenly ran over to him, kneeled down at his feet and implored him:

''Have pity on me, *Seu* Azevedo! Take pity on a poor, wronged girl! Your son disgraced me!''

Old Azevedo put down his packages, lifted the girl up and sat her down in a chair. Then, pained and sorrowful, he also sat down in a chair alongside Clara and began to gaze into the girl's anguished face. Everybody's eyes were fixed upon him; nobody breathed. Finally, Azevedo spoke:

"My child, I can't do anything for you. I don't have any authority over him any more . . . I've already cursed him and thrown him out. I've disowned him. . . . Besides, he's already run off. I thought that his flight was just so he could try to hide another one of his ignoble acts. You, dear girl, you kneel in front of me now but I should get down on my knees in front of you to ask for your forgiveness for having given life to such an outlaw, a brigand who is my own son! As his father, I am unable to pardon him but I pray to God that He will forgive *me* for having fathered such a horrible man. My dear girl, you must have pity on me, this old man you see before you, this embittered father who, for more than ten long years, has suffered for the infamies his son has spewn about. . . . Feel sorrow for me more than anybody else! I can't do anything. . . . Forgive me, my child! Have your baby and then come to me if you should need. . . ."

He did not finish the sentence; his voice faded away, his body slumped into the chair and his eyes were swollen with tears.

His daughters went to him, his wife too, and one of the girls, weeping, asked Clara and Dona Margarida:

"Please, as a favor to us . . . could you leave us alone, please. . .?"

Once again on the street, Clara thought about what had just transpired, about the painful scene she had just witnessed and about the shame she felt. Now she knew exactly what her place in society was. During the vulnerability of her maidenhood, it had been necessary for Clara to suffer an irrevocable outrage to hear the insults of her tormentor's own mother in order to be convinced that she was not "just a girl" like all the others. According to her society's generally accepted beliefs, Clara was something much less; Her godfather had seen all of this clearly. . . . The poor, old man.

The upbringing she had received, an upbringing excessively cautious, delicate and vigilant, had all been wrong. Clara should have learned from her parent's own mouths about the enemies of a girl's or woman's purity and virtue in this life and she should have been shown real examples of them.

The streetcar came by fully loaded, and Clara got aboard, looking at the faces of all the men and women. There was not a single one among them, probably, who was not utterly indifferent to her trouble. After all, she was just a little colored girl, the daughter of a mere postman! What was really necessary for Clara and for all the other girls like her was to be properly educated to give them some character and endow their spirits with the same qualities of the virile Dona Margarida, qualities with which girls like Clara could defend themselves against the likes of Cassi and with which they could battle against those who would oppress them in one way or another, and against those who stood in opposition to their social and moral advancement. Nothing made Clara inferior to any other girl except the generally held prejudices, and the cowardice shown by the girls who allowed this kind of thinking to continue.

They finally arrived home; Joaquim had not yet arrived. Between the sobbing and sighing of the mother and her daughter, Dona Margarida related to Clara's mother what had happened.

Suddenly, Clara jumped out of the chair in which she had been sitting, ran to her mother, hugged her tightly and said, her voice choked with desperation:

"Mother, Mother!"

"What is it, my child?"

"We're nothing in this life. . . ."

Todos os Santos (Rio de Janeiro)
December, 1921–January, 1922